R lasse
[0]
kj

xx + 312 pp.

ADMIRAL SATAN

Admiral Satan

THE LIFE AND CAMPAIGNS OF SUFFREN

RODERICK CAVALIERO

I.B. TAURIS PUBLISHERS
LONDON · NEW YORK

Published in 1994 by
I.B.Tauris & Co Ltd
45 Bloomsbury Square
London WC1A 2HY

175 Fifth Avenue
New York
NY 10010

In the United States of America
and Canada distributed by
St Martin's Press
175 Fifth Avenue
New York
NY 10010

A full CIP record for this book is available from the British Library

Library of Congress Catalog card number: 93–61254
A full CIP record for this book is available from the Library of
Congress

ISBN 1–85043–686–X

Typeset by The Midlands Book Typesetting Company,
Loughborough
Printed and bound in Great Britain by
WBC Ltd, Bridgend, Mid Glamorgan

Contents

Illustrations

Maps and Diagrams

Maps and Diagrams drawn by Russell Townsend

Maps

Diagrams

Preface

India was perhaps the greatest prize in the centuries-long conflict between England and France, and the phantom of a French Empire in the east was to tantalize Bourbons, Bonapartists and Republicans alike. This is the account of an astonishing man whose fame is based on the equally astonishing campaign he fought in the Bay of Bengal in 1782–3, during what was to prove the last challenge from France to Britain's overwhelming power in the sub-continent. It was a testing time for the East India Company, fighting for its life not only against the Maratha Confederacy but also against a new and deadly enemy in Mysore. Into what was later to be called the Second Anglo-Mysorean War the French sent a sea officer of eccentric and vital genius, whom sailors of all nations have never ceased to admire. He was a Knight of Malta, with the appetite of Gargantua and the energy of a daemon. He was the one indisputable hero of the *ancien régime*. Napoleon wondered whether he might have been his Nelson. Nelson studied his tactics on the eve of his last and greatest battle. The lascars aboard his ships called him Admiral Satan. To history he is known as Le Bailli de Suffren.

Fate matched him with another commander of heroic proportions, both physically and morally. Sir Edward Hughes, unlike many lesser admirals, has never given his name to a line-of-battle ship. He was outclassed by his furious opponent but never defeated. The five battles they fought off south India and Ceylon, between squadrons of seldom more than a dozen ships each, were marked by casualties of Trafalgar proportions. That both commanders were able to keep going over nearly 18 months was a tribute to the spirit of both navies. If these eighteenth-century Paladins resembled in girth the legendary Tweedledum and Tweedledee, the prize at stake was the survival of British power in south India. The spectre of another Franco-Mysorean alliance during Napoleon's time was to induce Richard Wellesley, Earl of Mornington and brother of the Iron Duke, to fight the first of his preventative wars with the Indian country powers which were, by the end of the Napoleonic wars, to colour nearly all India red.

There is a constant problem in a work of this kind over the use of proper names. I have not been consistent but have used forms immediately meaningful to British eyes (thus Trichinopoly, not Tirucharapali), or which appear constantly throughout the literature of the period (like Negapatam not Nogappattim). But when modern forms are in current use as well as being unmistakable, I have used them; thus Marathas, Trincomali, Haidar Ali and Tipu Sultan (rather than Hyder and Tippoo) because there is no virtue in ancient forms which are no longer in use.

In the eighteenth-century 50-gun ships were not considered ships of the line but were frequently pressed into line during engagements between small squadrons. Throughout the campaign in the Bay of Bengal 50s were used as line-of-battle ships and have been described as such in the text.

I acknowledge a deep debt to Mr John Munday, formerly Curator of Presentation at the National Maritime Museum, who read the typescript in an early form; to Professor Sheik Ali, then Head of the Department of History at Mysore University, who was good enough to lend me the typescript of his thesis, *British Relations with Haidar Ali*; to Mr Mohibbul Hasan, then Head of the Department of History at Jamia Millia Islamia, New Delhi, for the loan of his book, otherwise unobtainable, on Tipu Sultan and for the loan of microfilm in his possession; to Mlle Régine Pernoud for permission to translate extracts from her *La Campagne des Indes: Lettres Inédites du Bailli de Suffren*; to Mr Peter Moore who transcribed entries from the archives in Malta; to Dr Michael Duffy of Exeter University for advice on the text and bringing to my attention recent work in France; to Mme Nan Levanneur of the British Council in Paris who helped me to obtain material. I must also thank the staffs of the Royal Malta Library, the National Archives of India, the Bibliothèque Nationale, the India Office Library, the British Museum, the Public Records Office and the British Council India Collection in New Delhi now at the International Cultural Centre. Finally I am specially indebted to Helen Simpson, my editor at I.B. Tauris & Co, whose enthusiasm for the subject was infectious.

It is with particular pleasure and gratitude that I acknowledge the support of His Most Eminent Highness, the Prince and Grand Master of the Sovereign Order of St John of Jerusalem, Fra Andrew Bertie, and of the Order itself, whose generous assistance made the publication of this book possible.

Roderick Cavaliero
Malta-New Delhi-Tunbridge Wells, 1956–93

Prologue

On the eve of Trafalgar, Horatio Nelson took out the newly published edition of a naval treatise by an obscure Scottish laird and sat poring over the pages devoted to two sea battles fought when he was only 24 and captain of the *Albemarle* frigate off Quebec. The first combat had been a close draw between a British and a French squadron off the coast of India, in which the honours went to the French admiral. A few months later, in a second encounter off the coast of Ceylon, the French admiral repeated his success. Nelson studied the accounts with care. The tactic that the French had adopted on both occasions was the one he now proposed to employ against the combined Franco-Spanish fleet. He shared the Scotsman's belief that it was the right one and that if it had not been wholly successful, it was because the French admiral did not command the superbly trained and experienced battle squadron that was Nelson's. Tomorrow he would use the 27 ships at his disposal to effect a crushing superiority over one part of the larger forces of the enemy, after which he could polish off the remainder. In this way he was to win one of the most decisive naval battles of all time.

Scotland in 1782 was an unlikely place from which to expect a book on naval strategy, certainly one that was to help to change the history of Europe. But a large dinner table can make a good war-room, and John Clerk, a retired Edinburgh merchant who had purchased the small property of Eldin, about six miles from the city, had more than once demonstrated the theory he had developed from a close study of England's long naval duel with France. By the dextrous use of small model ships which he carried around in his pockets he would demonstrate that a squadron of line-of-battle ships, attacking an enemy from windward, would never achieve a decisive victory if it merely measured itself against the enemy line, ship for ship. This was the accepted way of fighting a battle at sea and, for the last 90 years, the English had been able to claim no victory in a battle between two close-hauled lines. In 1747 Edward Hawke at Finisterre and 12 years later Edward Boscawen at Lagos Bay had won crushing victories over enemy squadrons but on both occasions the enemy had been in flight. In most of those other contests in which the British and French met, the skill and stamina of the British seaman had failed to triumph over an intrepid and well-trained enemy.

So, asked John Clerk, when he printed at his own expense *An Essay on Naval Tactics* in 1782, had the French, by preserving a close line and firing high into the masts and rigging of their enemy while giving way before them in order, developed a tactic that would frustrate the Royal Navy and cheat them of the overwhelming victories the Admiralty and the public demanded? It looked very much as if they had. But Clerk suggested that the British could break the mould by taking a lesson from one of their opponents. By massing their strongest ships to break through the enemy line, and then by concentrating on one part of it, preferably the rear, by doubling on it from both sides, a decisive advantage could be obtained early in the battle, the French line would break up and in the subsequent conflict, fought as a general mêlée, the greater experience of the British could achieve total victory.

Even as the book was with the printers, Admiral Rodney had on 12 April retrieved honour from the disastrous war in the Americas by breaking through a gap in the line of de Grasse's squadron off the coast of Dominica in the West Indies and decisively defeating it at the Battle of the Saints. Clerk immediately claimed credit for the manoeuvre, which was in truth more accidental than contrived, because it transformed the marginal superiority of Rodney's squadron over de Grasses's into overwhelming superiority over the broken sections of the French line. The result was the surrender of de Grasse in his superb flagship and of four other major prizes. Clerk also noticed that on the other side of the world a French admiral had twice tried to achieve superiority over part of the opposing English line, on 17 February and 11 April, without the same overwhelming success. Had he been better supported by his captains, the result could have been bitter for the British India squadron.

When Clerk produced the second edition of his *Essay* in 1804, he claimed to be the author of the tactic of concentration on part of the enemy line, and, by the retrospective analysis of the three battles fought in 1782, the year in which he had first described it, he tried to prove his point. Though the future Admiral Thomas Graves, then a mere lieutenant, had thought of the tactic in pencilled notes on his *Admiral's Signals and Instructions* in 1779, the armchair Scottish strategist, Lord Rodney—after the event and at the prompting of Clerk himself—and the faraway Frenchman in the tropics had all claimed credit for its conception, quite independently.

Clerk could take the credit of being the first to write it down and illustrate it with diagrams. Lord Howe, who had greeted the *Essay* in 1782 with some scepticism, if he did not actually break the French line as Clerk recommended at The Glorious First of June (for he intended each ship in his line to break through the French line at whatever gap they found themselves individually to line up again on the windward side, still preferred by British admirals despite Clerk's advice), saw it broken by six of his ships in six different places, so that they shattered its cohesion and brought about the mêlée, and thus victory. On St Valentine's Day (14 February) 1797, Admiral Jervis cut off and isolated a whole division of the Spanish fleet at Cape St Vincent, and on 11 October of that same year Duncan cut the Dutch line in two off Camperdown and destroyed its centre and rear by overwhelming fire power. Clerk felt that he was vindicated, even though Earl St Vincent was sure that the treatise had had absolutely nothing to do with any of these victories. Clerk could later claim that his greatest pupil had already at the Nile shown how right he was when he attacked Brueys's fleet at anchor in Aboukir Bay from both sides. Trafalgar was to confirm the Scotsman's judgement. He had only just written his *Essay* in time.[1]

The two battles in the Indies which Clerk had described in admiring detail and in both of which the advantage had been with the French were Sadras, fought on 17 February just south of Madras, and Provedien on 12 April 1782, near a small coral island off the coast of Ceylon. The French commander whose strikingly original tactics seemed to prove Clerk's thesis was Pierre-André de Suffren, Knight Grand Cross and Bailli of the Order of Knights Hospitaller of St John of Jerusalem, Rhodes and Malta, captain-general of the Maltese galley fleet, *chef d'escadre* in the Grand

Corps de la Marine of France, and one of the stormiest petrels in pre-revolutionary France. And one of its few undisputed naval heroes.

The time now switches back a year from Clerk's first *Essay*, to Versailles, 1781. Through its crowded corridors a powdered flunkey threaded his way towards the king's apartments. Behind him stumped a sea officer, encased in a uniform that bulged at every seam and strained at every button, with ungloved hands as coarse as pig's hide, and porcine eyes goggling above fat and hectic cheeks. If he had not been wearing the eight-pointed Cross of Malta on his breast, no one could have guessed that he was the fruit of seven aristocratic marriages, every great-grandparent (except, in his case, one) being at the time of their birth a member of either the *noblesse d'épée* or the *noblesse de robe*. But, like so many Knights of Malta, he was a stranger to this great city of a palace, for his family came from the far south and lived on its estates and he had spent most of his life at sea. Those courtiers who were within earshot when this strange pair reached the royal presence heard the uncouth visitor thank his guide. 'Today, sir, I am in your debt. Next time I come, I shall know how to make my own way.'[2]

A royal audience for a sea officer usually meant a special mission. But if the courtiers at Versailles wondered what it might be, it was no secret to the British Lords of the Admiralty. Their spies had given them all the details. They knew who he was, where he was going and why. In the next six months the news trickled back to Paris: of a neutral port violated, an enemy squadron worsted, the Cape saved, Île de France (Mauritius) reinforced. Then as the months passed came news of three violent battles with the enemy in the Bay of Bengal, each one a victory, the startling capture of the enemy's base in Ceylon, a fourth battle, a fifth, the glorious relief of the Marquis de Bussy and the salvation of the French army at Cuddalore. Only the peace of 1783 brought an end to these marvels.

Then on a cold Lenten day, 3 March 1784, a coach from the south drove into Paris and halted at the steps of the Treasury of the Navy. The treasurer himself came down to greet his visitor and a few hours later the two men were bowling along the road to Versailles. This time, as he had predicted, the visitor had no need of a herald. The navy minister was there in person to announce him to the guard of honour drawn up in line all the way to the royal

presence. Louis XVI kept him for two hours, insatiable for details
of those bitter battles fought 6000 miles away under a tropical sun.
Marie-Antoinette drew the Dauphin forward from gazing tongue-
tied behind her skirts at the colossal figure standing, legs astride,
before them. 'This is M de Suffren. He has served His Majesty
well.' The little prince stumbled over the name. 'Learn quickly, my
son,' she reproved him gently, 'to pronounce the names of those
heroes who have defended their country.'[3]

The most studied welcome came from the Grand Prior of France,
one of the most honoured dignitaries of the Knights Hospitaller,
the infant Duc d'Angoulême, the son of Louis XVI's brother, the
future Charles X. 'Sir,' he fluted prettily, raising his eyes from the
Plutarch lying open on his knees, 'I am this moment reading the
lives of illustrious men, but I put them aside with pleasure because
I now behold one.'[4] The sheltered child did not really know what
he was saying. For the man before him, in court dress and smiling
with the favours of a beloved sovereign, was the pomaded version
of an original genius whose energy, resilience and disregard for
convention had carried him through a campaign of two and a half
savage years.

During that time he sailed half-way across the world, fought five
battles without a base in which to refit, and a sixth with only 15
ships against 18, and did not lose a ship in action. This alone was
unprecedented. So also was the terrible casualty list of French
captains—five relieved of their commands for incompetence, four
others resigning their commands before they were sacked and four
killed in battle. For over a year he kept France's most formidable
ally, Haidar Ali, Nawab of Mysore, in action against the East
India Company and put the relentless expansion of British power
in India at hazard.

To his Grand Prior, Suffren might have looked almost courtly.
To the young Calcutta lawyer who was his prisoner at Trincomali
in January 1783, he looked more 'like a fat English butcher than
a Frenchman of consequence'.[5] William Hickey, beginning his
career in India of amorous gluttony, liked the decorous externals
to healthy appetites and was surprised to find that this fifteen times
blue-blooded French sailor wore no wig to cover his bald pate while
his side and back hair was gathered into a three-inch queue tied with
a piece of old spun yarn. The straps of his shoes had been cut off
to make them into slippers. His blue cloth breeches—worn usually

by auxiliary officers only—were unbuttoned at the knee. A pair
of dirty stockings hung about his calves. He wore neither cravat
nor waistcoat and his shirt was open at the throat and dripping
with sweat. Sleeves rolled up to his elbows completed the picture
and Hickey thought he had disturbed him at his toilette. But, he
was surprised to learn, this was how the French admiral always
appeared before lunch![6]

The war in the east was really a side-show to the great issues
being fought in the west, a distraction to British power challenged
on the shores of Virginia and in the West Indies by an alliance
of American rebels, France and Spain. Suffren had fought it as if
the result of the war depended on his exertions and had brought
back the only comfort for the French monarchy from what had
proved a disastrous conflict. The uncouth admiral died on the eve
of the Revolution and his fifteen times noble bones were rooted
from their grave during the Terror and scattered in the streets.
The Directoire rehabilitated his memory and called a ship of the
line after him. Napoleon Bonaparte agreed to give a pension to
the impoverished ladies of the Suffren family because their uncle,
he was told, had been a warrior worthy of *le grand siècle*. But it
was only on St Helena that he had the leisure to find out more
about him.

A man of creative genius, burning ardour, mighty ambition and
iron character was how the fallen emperor's companion, Las Cases,
described Suffren, one of those, in short, whom nature had made
capable of everything. Very hard, very strange, extremely self-
centred, a bad sleeper, a worse comrade, loved by none but admired
by all, difficult to live with, above all difficult to command, a bad
subordinate, critical of everything, a constant decrier of tactics but,
when required, a supreme tactician, he was all his life tormented by
the restlessness and ill-humour of a genius never given opportunity
enough to show what it could do. Bonaparte's envious interest was
aroused.

In India, Las Cases went on, Suffren commanded his ships in a
way in which French ships had never been commanded before. He
took everything on himself, daring, planning, foreseeing everything,
breaking his craven and incompetent captains, promoting junior
officers into their places, equipping and fighting ships which should
have been condemned. 'Why,' sighed the exiled emperor, 'did he
not live until my time? Why could not I find someone of his kind?

I should have made him my Nelson and our affairs would have taken a very different turn. Instead I spent all my time looking for such a sailor and never found one.'[7]

Had Suffren lived beyond 1788 he would have either emigrated or perished on the scaffold and his services would probably not have been available to Napoleon. But the qualities he possessed the emperor would certainly have known how to use. Demonic energy, frenetic impatience, uncontrolled fury, contempt of caste and passion for battle—these were the five dominant characteristics of· the man who burst unexpectedly into the Bay of Bengal in January 1782, and which earned him the soubriquet from his admiring lascars of 'Admiral Satan'.[8] He is now remembered as the most distinguished seaman in France's history, but it is a fame that rests not on the handling of great battle squadrons in the Atlantic but on a campaign barely two years long, fought in a backwater of the Great Debate between England and France.

The passion of that campaign was to be so fierce that it burned on the imagination of his countrymen, traditionally unsympathetic to the avocation of the sea, a sense of grandeur which they had come to associate with their great marshals. At the Restoration Suffren took his place among the heroes of the *ancien régime*, with Henry of Navarre, Maurice de Saxe and Louis II, Prince de Condé. For over a year he was the thundercloud that hung off the Coromandel coast and threatened British power in India. He was also the darling of John Clerk of Eldin.

ADMIRAL SATAN

PART I

Apprenticeship to Failure

1. Beginnings, 1729–47

Until that day in January 1781 when he had to be led through the palace of Versailles, the career of Pierre-André de Suffren had been in no way remarkable. It had followed the almost predetermined course for any younger son of one of France's older aristocratic families. Four hundred years earlier, the Suffrens were political refugees from Lucca who settled very happily in Provence. There the Lucchese Suffredi suffered a sea-change into Suffren, pronounced with a nasal twang rendered better by the English spelling of Suffrein. By the end of the seventeenth century the family had become inextricably entwined in the thick shrubbery of Provençal gentry. For a hundred years Suffrens served as Conseillers du Roi in the Parlement of Aix, and their younger brothers were professed Knights of Malta.

The Knights of Malta, founded five centuries before to manage and protect the Christian pilgrim hostel in Jerusalem, had now declined into a useful club for aristocratic younger sons and brothers to join. They all had to do service before the mast as young men in the perpetual *guerre de course*, or privateering war, that the Knights fought against the Barbary pirates, and in due course were provided with an estate or commandery in the country of their origin on which they could live comfortably and at no expense to their families.

Those who wished to do so could stay in Malta and serve the Grand Master with a career for life. Others served their king. A few, usually the old or the lazy, lived on and cultivated their commanderies, sending a tenth of their revenues to Malta to

meet the expenses of that little theocratic state. To be a Knight
of Malta in one of the three French *Langues* (or Tongues) of
France, Auvergne and Provence, parents, grandparents and great-
grandparents had to have been born noble. The Pope might, if
asked, dispense with the need for one or more of these to satisfy that
requirement and in fact Pierre-André's paternal great-grandmother,
being of bourgeois stock, had to be so dispensed. Pope Clement XII
had obliged.[1]

There were two lines of the Suffren family but the junior
branch to which Pierre-André belonged had married better than
the senior so that by the end of the seventeenth century its head
was Paul de Suffren, chevalier, Seigneur de Saint-Torpes (which
was transmogrified during his lifetime into St Tropez), then a sleepy
fishing village with a small yard for building privateers and showing
no promise of being the sun-baked Mecca for topless starlets. He
was also Seigneur de Richebois, and of la Mole and in 1725 became
Marquis de Saint-Cannat. As *premier consul* and *procureur du pays*
(an officer of the Parlement of Aix), he was a man of substance and
entitlement. Two of his brothers were Knights of Malta serving in
the Royal Comtois Regiment. His wife was Marie-Hieronyme de
Bruni de la Tour d'Aigues, and her family was also a nursery
of sailors, producing, among others, Bruni d'Entrecasteaux who
should have sailed with Pierre-André to India and who was later
to perish in the search for the lost explorer, La Pérouse. There
were nine surviving children of that match, four boys and five
girls. Pierre-André was the third boy and eighth child.[2]

Marie-Hieronyme had hoped to have her tenth accouchement
(for two sons had died shortly after birth) in their comfortable
family house at Aix, but the coach broke down at Saint-Cannat,
a small market town on the road from Marseilles, and the Suffren
winter house was opened to receive her. It was a great barrack of
a building, several centuries old, to which successive Suffrens had
added such a variety of extensions that it was a maze of passages
and tiny courtyards (it is now the *mairie*). There, on 29 July 1729,
she was delivered of Pierre-André.

Another son followed a year later and Paul de Suffren, who
despite his string of *seigneuries* was not a rich man, decided that
his two youngest sons should follow their uncles into the Order
of St John. By an ancient convention a hundred young novices
could be entered during childhood—a device to provide the Grand

Master with a suite of pages and to help keep the old families still interested in the Order. Though they could not assume their duties as Knights until their formal profession at 18, they did acquire seniority from the moment of entry and this gave them a head start on the others in the race for comfortable and lucrative commanderies.

At their profession Knights of Malta took priestly vows of chastity, poverty and obedience to the head of their Order, but by Suffren's time very few Knights expected either that these vows would incommode them much or that they need spend much time in Malta beyond the statutory service in the fleet, an essential requirement if they were to acquire their commandery and thus their livelihood. But profession could provide an arrow of opportunity for younger sons who had little else in their quiver. Paul de Suffren applied accordingly to the Grand Prior of Aix in the Tongue of Provence, who in turn applied to the Pilier or head of the Tongue in Malta, who put the submission and the dispensing brief of Clement XII before the Sacred Council of the Order in Valletta. The Suffrens had been a good source of supply of Knights Hospitaller and the Aragonese Grand Master, Raimond Despuig, recognized this when, on 23 September 1737, he conceded the privilege of entry *de minorité* to two of Paul's sons, aged eight and seven.[3]

For the moment shades of distinction were not to disturb the boyhood of the young Knights. Provence had never been properly assimilated into France. A former imperial county, more Italian than French, it spoke a dialect rich in poetry, powerful in invective and lurid in obscenity. Its *maquis* was scorched during a cruel summer and dusted with the fall-out from the maddening mistral. The young Suffrens were fluent in the language and Pierre-André was at one with the scrubby countryside which he preferred to studied life in the great house at Aix. There his unbridled and obstreperous animal spirits had full reign as he roamed the *maquis* with boys of the town, birds-nesting, poaching and playing cruel jokes on his elder sisters.[4]

To his boyish contempt for women there was one exception, his cousin Marie-Thérèse de Perrot de Seillans, three years older, whose hoydenish high spirits endeared her to him. As the years passed so his affection may have grown into love, but his cousin was married shortly before he went to Malta to be professed as

a Knight dedicated to a life of celibacy, and became the Comtesse
d'Alès. Widowed after a year, she never remarried. She entertained
a life-long correspondence with Pierre-André, in which she shared
his hopes, felt his disappointments and rejoiced at his triumphs.
But her cousin was no great hand at letters and the land-locked
lady had to read despatches identical to those sent to the Ministry
of the Marine. She, more than John Clerk of Eldin, knew how
many broadsides he had fired, what tactics he had intended to
adopt, the extent of the despair and the carnage. But that was
all.[5] Suffren had no love-life that is known to us. The legend
is that he had an eye for a pretty lady and he was certainly
unusually obliging to William Hickey's companion, the hapless but
beautiful Charlotte Barry, in Ceylon. But if he had any outlet for
his sexual energies it is likely that he found it among the nervous
boys who beat the drum to quarters and the adolescent topmen
who scrambled up the rigging to attend the upper sails.[6]

Suffren's main public vice was gluttony. A passion for the red-hot
pilaus and bouillabaisses of his native Provence followed him round
the world and he could happily shovel into his mouth curries that
reduced his fellow mariners to tears. His appetite was gargantuan
and, like many meridionals, he ran quickly to fat. But it did not
diminish his energy. Indeed his sweating bulk was able to cope with
the torrid tropical summer better than thinner men from northern
ports. Food, not women, was Suffren's preferred means of dalliance,
and the vigour and coarseness with which he ate it was almost the
glutton's equivalent of rancid coupling with a whore or catamite.
When asked once why he did not use a spoon and fork like other
well-bred men, he replied that one did not caress a beautiful woman
with an implement.[7]

That intemperance had so far been perceived only by his
geometry tutors. At 14 Suffren began his apprenticeship to the sea.
He was delivered to the Society of Jesus which, rather improbably,
ran the College for the *gardes-marines* at Toulon. This was a
French Dartmouth founded by Louis XIV's minister, Colbert,
where future naval officers received formal instruction in their
faith and perfunctory training in ship-design, mathematics, hydro-
graphy, dancing, fencing, sword-drill, musketry and the science of
gunnery.

But the fathers had lost control over their young Cherubinos,
who were often the terror of the town and a cause of anxiety to

stale husbands. Many of them were sons of sea officers and a sprig of Le Grand Corps de la Marine could not be allowed to fail his examinations. Suffren was not impressed, then or later, by his training. In despair at the limited competence of his younger officers, he was to write from the heart of his Indian campaign that 'it is charlatanry of the worst kind to persuade the Ministry that a boy who knows his two books by heart at 14 years old is best suited to be either a sailor or a fighter ... At the moment, with a false certificate and three geometry teachers well-paid by the parents ... a boy of 12 can become a *garde-marine*. At 14 he has forgotten everything, is made an *enseigne*, knows nothing about how to command as that is not in his nature, and learns nothing more.'[8]

Suffren saw his first battle as a *garde-marine*, and it was to make a deep impression on him. If the Battle of Toulon was not one of the great combats of the century, it was certainly memorable, for after it the English court-martialled two admirals, ten captains and four lieutenants. And it was to prove very instructive to the young *garde*. On 11/22 February 1744 (the English and French followed different calendars until 1752) a Spanish squadron, blockaded in Toulon by the English, decided to sail out under escort of the neutral French under Admiral de Court. He was over 80 years old and he had not been in action for 40 years. The English squadron was commanded by two sailors between whom relations were as sour as insensitive pride and wounded feelings could make them. As the combined squadrons stood south in a long and straggling line, the English did not seem able to get themselves into line at all, while a gap began to yawn between van and rear.

Seeing the enemy (and the French, though neutral, were to all intents and purposes enemy) escaping towards Gibraltar and the Atlantic, Vice-Admiral Mathews determined on action and followed the combined squadrons through the night. Rear-Admiral Lestock, commanding the rear squadron, for complicated reasons in which pique played a large part, allowed the gap between him and his flag-admiral to yawn to between seven and eight miles. When Mathews decided to engage the Spanish ships in the centre it was impossible for the whole British line to come into action. In the event Mathews and his next astern were virtually unsupported. Admiral Rowley in the van, uncertain what to do, decided to attack the neutral French, and when de Court tacked to the north-west in order to assist the Spanish ships in the centre Rowley tacked too, and the day ended with both fleets lying to for the night. The following day the Spaniards sailed away to the west, Lestock started to chase but Mathews called him off.

From that moment the Spanish armies in Italy were able to resume the initiative so that the tide of the land war changed. But that did not infuriate the Lords of the Admiralty as much as the fact that a Spanish squadron of inferior size had escaped an English squadron. Such things in the eighteenth century could not be endured.

To the young Suffren Admiral Mathews in the *Namur* and Captain James Cornewall just behind him in the *Marlborough*, had done the only possible thing: to engage the Spaniards in the centre and beat their opponents out of line so that the following ships could break through and destroy the Spanish squadron. Amazingly, with one exception they had not. In the subsequent court-martial Admiral Mathews was found guilty of being the 'principal cause of the miscarriage off Toulon'![9] For he had left his line and so failed to bring it all into action simultaneously. The whole judicial force of the British navy rallied to the defence of the line.

Admiral Mathews was no brilliant original tactician. In fact he had spent too much of his career ashore and had joined the squadron so recently that he barely knew anyone in it except his rear-admiral, who cordially hated him. But his tactic, though unorthodox and opportunist, had not been wrong. Suffren never forgot the sight of the *Namur* sailing down to tackle a ship 20 guns heavier, nor of Captain Edward Hawke's *Berwick* running down the line to join the mêlée in the centre. That they had not achieved anything was because the rear squadron was too far away and the van was uncertain whom to attack, when ranged against nominally neutral French. In his very first taste of action Suffren saw the result of not attacking in force and with decision, and the defects of the doctrine of the line, professed by both sides and upheld as dogma by an English court-martial. It was a splendid lesson in the absurd. Clerk of Eldin believed that the court-martial of Mathews 'was the source of all the many naval miscarriages since'.[10]

France and Britain were soon to be properly at war again and Suffren spent more time in the next three years at sea than in the vaulted assembly room of the Collège. Three times he crossed the Atlantic, and then, on 14 October 1747, he received a shock that was to be both invigorating and depressive. He was captured in action.

The Battle of Cape Finisterre was not his baptism of fire but his first communion. The two Suffren brothers had just made their solemn profession as Knights of Malta in the Grand Priory of Aix. Haloed with that spiritual commitment Pierre-André boarded the 74-gun *Monarque* in the squadron of des Herbiers de l'Etenduère ordered to escort 250 transports to Canada. On the night of 4/15 October the squadron of eight ships of the line and one armed merchantman left Aix la Rochelle. At dawn on the 14/25th the hero of Suffren's first engagement, Edward Hawke, who had been keeping an eye open for them, came up swiftly over the horizon with 14 line-of-battle ships.

There was no escape. Ordering his convoy to fly before the wind, de l'Etenduère made signal for line of battle ahead and prepared to receive the enemy. To his consternation, as Hawke's ships came up they divided and doubled on the French. The young *chevalier garde-marine* in the third ship in the French line was now to experience the bitter misery of an engagement from both sides. For de l'Entenduère 'gave himself to be crushed', to save his convoy. Two hundred and fifty ships escaped while his eight ships endured the martyrdom of an attack from both sides by almost twice their number. No ship carried enough crew and gunners to work all decks of guns, so that a commanding officer aimed to engage with either his port or his starboard guns but not both together. An engagement from both sides was the equivalent in land terms of an attack from front and rear simultaneously.

In later years Suffren liked to expatiate on the misery of that day. The *Neptune*, *Fougueux*, *Severn* and *Monarque* were assailed by 11 ships to windward and four to leeward. Action was joined at 11.30; Hawke himself reduced the *Severn*; at 13.40 the *Fougueux* hauled down her colours. At 15.00 the *Monarque*, her captain dead, surrendered to the *Nottingham* and *Edinburgh*. Fifteen minutes later, the *Neptune*, her captain also killed, struck to the *Yarmouth*. The French rear no longer existed. Before another two hours were up Hawke had received the surrender of the *Trident* and *Terrible*, but the *Tonnant* fought until nightfall when, with the *Intrépide*, topmasts down and sails cut to ribbons, she bore away. As the grey Atlantic night was lit by cannon flash and tongues of flame, the two ships struggled round the Cape to safety. Suffren, destined for Canada, sailed instead to eat the bitter bread of a prisoner of war.[11]

L'Etenduère's last stand against insuperable odds made an indelible impression on Suffren, who was proud to have been associated with an action of such evocative heroism. During the stirring months of his campaign in the Bay of Bengal he would rehearse the epic tale to his officers. He never forgot how vulnerable a squadron was, taken from the rear on both sides. He admired the vigour and precision with which the English squadron divided as if by plan. Thirty-five years later off the coast of India he was to try to use the same tactic against the English.

Suffren was slightly wounded in the action but Hawke's triumphal entry into the Thames, towing his prizes, followed by three months of captivity were to wound his pride more. He found the arrogance of the English in victory insupportable and their language incomprehensible. England and all she stood for became a subject of persistent rancour which drove him in his prime to fight her ships with unmatched ferocity so as to re-enact 'one of the most glorious actions ever to have been fought at sea'. Suffren learned some English from this and a second spell of captivity in 1759 but to William Hickey, his prisoner off Ceylon, it was 'abominable, indeed unintelligible'.[12] Hatred of the English was almost a requirement for French sea officers during the eighteenth century and anglophobia was a persistent characteristic of the French navy even into the nineteenth and twentieth centuries, as the English were to discover as late as 1940 at Oran. Revenge for Cape Finisterre and for other humiliations to follow, coupled with that venom, were the forces which drove Suffren to fight the English to a standstill six times between 1781 and 1783.

2. Malta, Minorca and Lagos Bay, 1747–60

At the peace Suffren was promoted to the rank of *enseigne* and went to Malta, for if he wanted to get on in the Order and be given a commandery, a young Knight had to complete his caravans. In the Holy Land, the Knights Hospitaller had been charged with escorting caravans of pilgrims from Acre to Jerusalem. In their island strongholds caravans were obligatory cruises in the ships of the Order. On a galley the caravan lasted six months, on a sailing ship twelve. Much of this was routine escort duty, with an occasional sweep to keep the *Canale* or the waters between Malta and Italy free of Muslim privateers. Sometimes there was action, but more often a caravan was little more than a gentle patrol in the more anarchic waters of North Africa.[1]

Malta at this date was virtually a French dependency and, though the Grand Master was a hard-headed Portuguese, he knew that what little power and independence he had derived from the tithes he levied on the income from the Knights' commanderies, many of the richest of which were in France. The main constituent of that power was a fleet of seven galleys commanded by a captain-general. But by the time Suffren was completing his caravans the Maltese navy was a spent force. Its principal activity was showing the flag in the ports of the western Mediterranean where the revenues of the Order had been gathered for shipment to Valletta. A small squadron of sailing ships had been built from the personal fortune of an immensely rich Spanish Grand Master but it was a crippling burden to the Treasury. France and Venice had both made their peace with the Turk so that the waters of the eastern Mediterranean were effectively closed to Maltese privateers whether flying the flag of the Order or the personal standard of the Grand Master, with a licence to cruise *en course*. The Order's 'perpetual war' (*course* or *corso*) against Islam could be carried out only against the small states of North Africa who lived off piracy and whom no great power could ever find time to extinguish once and for all. Against these the Knights practised the tactic of pursue and board, and for this the oar-powered *galliot* was the best instrument since it could navigate calm, shallow and sheltered waters, and was not dependent upon wind.

The year after Suffren's arrival in Malta, the Grand Prior of France, Jean-Philippe d'Orléans, died. He had, like Suffren, entered the Order, *de minorité*, at the age of five and throughout his life had resisted any attempt to integrate the independent galley corps, based on Toulon, into the French navy. He had as a Bourbon bastard been assigned the sinecure command of general of the galleys, and for largely sentimental reasons believed completely in the superiority of Mediterranean sailors, the greatest of whom was Louis XIV's admiral the Chevalier de Tourville, who had served 11 years in the Malta galleys against the Barbary pirates. This superiority had for the past 50 years been challenged by the sailors of the ocean seas.

The wars against Holland and England forced France to become an Atlantic as well as a Mediterranean sea power and Mediterranean experience was coming to be considered insufficient for an Atlantic sailor. The Bretons and Gascons, baptized in the green waters of the northern and western oceans and by the fire of two- and three-deckers, despised the intricate skills of blue-water seamanship and its infrequent, unspectacular encounters with the clumsy ships of North Africa and Turkey. The Provençals, known as *mocos* because of their incomprehensible dialect and swarthy skins, were not held to be their equals by the resourceful northerners, battered and shaped by mountainous seas and formidable enemies. The 'irreligious' Bretons found the 'religious' Maltese an easy target for mockery.

With Orléans' death the unification of the French navy, desired since the days of Richelieu, was achieved. Most of the galley officers retired and only 28 transferred to service under sail. But as most of these were Knights of Malta, and among the most aristocratic officers in the service, the close link between the French navy and the Knights was not severed. Despite the disappearance of the old galley fleet, the Knights, with their court connections and rich commanderies still enrolled in the service. In 1755, there were 50 Knights of Malta in active service; in 1759 there were 73. Despite the recognition that, in an age of sail seamanship mattered more than quarterings, the French navy did not relax the rule that its officers must be nobly born. And as Knights still professed a dual loyalty to their aristocratic order and to the sea, service in Malta was still regarded as an essential feature of their training.[2]

The Mediterranean was never an easy sea to sail and an apprenticeship in such difficult waters, given at no cost to the government of France, remained a valuable asset to young officers of La Grande Marine. As Malta was never at peace with Islamic nations, training was never broken off so that young French sailors could get practice in action in all years and in all seasons. France's dependence on it was reflected in the fact that command of a ship in the Order's navy was automatic qualification for the rank of captain in the French navy. Just how useful it was to Suffren can probably be gauged by his command of a xebec on anti-privateering duty in the Mediterranean and Atlantic North Africa in 1760. Knights of Malta were still prized sailors, and as late as the American War of Independence two *mocos*, Suffren and the Comte de Grasse, were able to vindicate the reputation of the south and of their Order. De Grasse, slightly Suffren's senior, had also entered as a minor. But he did not stay and had himself dispensed from his vows in 1746 to get married.

Little or nothing is known of this first period of Suffren's life in Malta, but he completed his caravans in July 1752 and returned to France for more Atlantic service.[3] It was ill-fated; the expedition of Dubois de la Motte to assist the beleaguered French in Canada ended in rout and the *Dauphin Royal* with Suffren aboard escaped to France. From her decks the disillusioned *enseigne* wrote to a cousin in Marseilles, merchant and *armateur* Georges Roux, suggesting that he purchase a vessel for him to ply a privateering voyage off the coast of America. Privateers were not looked for off those shores and there could be useful damage he could inflict on the enemy. But duly promoted to the rank of lieutenant in 1756, he was posted to the *Orphée* in the squadron of La Galissonnière at Toulon.

The French had decided to open what was to be known as the Seven Years War with a surprise attack on Minorca and on 10 April La Galissonnière sailed with the Duc de Richelieu and Suffren's elder brother, Joseph Jean-Baptiste, Marquis de Suffren, for Port Mahon, which was invested on 17 April. On 20 May the British and French squadrons met and from the gun-deck of the *Orphée*, leading the French rear division, Pierre-André was to have a grandstand view of the infamous action that cost Admiral Byng his life.

La Galissonnière's sole objective was to protect the Duc de Richelieu's expeditionary force on the island so that he took his position on the lee berth. Byng, as Suffren's already practised eye could see, thus had a perfect opportunity to run down on selected targets and do irreparable damage to individual French ships before the next astern could come to their assistance. But with Mathews's ghost at his elbow the English admiral refused to 'run down as if I were going to engage a single ship'.[4] Instead he held on in line to fight a classic parallel action. But as his rear division was too far behind for his whole line to come into action at once, his van was badly cut about by the French tactic of firing while their ships were on the upward roll and immobilizing the enemy by cutting his rigging to shreds. Only La Galissonnière's own deficiencies of generalship saved the English admiral from worse, for he did not tack to windward of Byng's badly mauled van and crush it. Byng broke off the action, retired, lost Port Mahon and his life. La Galissonnière returned to Toulon and just had time to commend seven officers, of whom Suffren was one, for 'having some knowledge and disposition for their calling', before he died.[5]

The French had the right to claim a victory since Minorca was captured, but Suffren, and not he alone, could have wished to see English colours struck afloat. If not all England's captains were eagles, at least some were Hawkes and if the French persisted in being mesmerized by the beauty of parallel and always indecisive action, then decisive victory at sea would continue to elude them. La Galissonnière had acted with perfect correctness by the book: his fleet was there to escort the expedition to Minorca and protect it while it was there. This could be served by keeping Byng at a distance, not by destroying him; and before Suffren was to sail for India in March 1781, the destruction of the enemy's ships was never the principal objective of a French commander at sea. According to the book, a French admiral could say, without fear of reproach, that if 'despite every care and precaution I am attacked by the enemy, I shall fight with all glory possible. But I shall do better to avoid action.'[6] This philosophy led to the action that was to be the next cauterizing experience of Suffren's life.

January 1758 found Suffren in the 80-gun *Océan*, flagship of de la Clue's squadron in Toulon. The admiral's orders were to sail to Brest and pick up a convoy to Canada, but the English blockade was so tight that he could not move for 18 months. Then at the end of July 1759, when Boscawen had to withdraw to Gibraltar to refit, his destination was changed. His squadron was, instead, to form part of an ambitious invasion of England so that he must sail at the first opportunity to join Admiral Conflans at Brest. By August he was at sea, hoping to slip through the Straits of Gibraltar at night and unseen. It was not to be. In the evening of 17 August he was sighted by a British frigate stationed in the Gut. Boscawen was summoned from dinner with the Spanish governor at San Roque and within three hours the English were in pursuit. During the night, as the French sailed without lights, five ships lost touch and made for Cadiz. By 08.00 hours the unhappy French admiral knew that his remaining seven ships were being chased by 14.

Boscawen, seeing them crowd away from him under press of sail, ordered his captains to engage as they caught up with their victims. At 14.30 action was joined between the leading British ships and the *Centaure*, of 74 guns, but only after four hours of fighting with all glory possible, with half her crew dead, her topmasts gone, her timbers riddled with shot and her captain wounded in 11 places, did she strike. The *Océan* was locked with the *Namur*, and Suffren working the guns of the upper battery saw first her mizzenmast then both topsail yards shot away so that de la Clue had to shift his flag. The uneven match could not be long sustained. When the *Centaure* struck, the battle was virtually over, though her gallant action had saved the squadron for that day. De la Clue, with one of his legs sawn off during the night, struggled with four ships into Lagos Bay. Here in the lee of a neutral shore the *Océan* ran through the breakers with all her sails set, and as she touched shore every mast went by the board and fell over the bows. Boscawen, believing correctly that it would be easier for the British government to apologize to the Portuguese for a breach of neutrality than for France to replace four ships of the line, sailed in after them and, in a few hours, two of them were captured and the other two, one of which was the *Océan*, were burning pyres. For a second time Suffren passed into captivity.[7]

It was not to be for long, as he was soon exchanged, but Lagos Bay marked the watershed of his career. He had taken part in four actions: two of them had been defeats which no commander could have avoided, two of them statuesque and limited combats. France could boast no trophies from any of them. The ships that had survived Minorca had chased de la Clue into the breakers off Lagos. A battle which did not achieve the destruction of the enemy's ships could not properly be classed as a victory. It was not a conviction widely held, even in the Royal Navy. But it was Suffren's. The Grand Corps de la Marine stood by the general rubric that ships had a secondary function in war, being primarily responsible for escorting and protecting military expeditions, disrupting trade and invading England. If it believed that the duty of a sea officer was to avoid any action that might render him less able to fulfil these functions, the English for their part had no monopoly of wisdom on what ships were for.

The *Fighting Instructions*, composed in the seventeenth century, had so carefully laid down the tactic of the line that commanders would spend the opening hours of an engagement like a football team, ship marking ship so exactly that on occasions they would order those without an opponent to fall out. If any ship beat her opponent out of line, it was not her duty to pursue her. Mathews was cashiered for not keeping his line, Byng lost his life for not bringing it into action all at the same time. Yet the *Fighting Instructions* did allow a captain to use his own judgement once battle was joined, and they did allow for the chase. Hawke was not reprimanded for his action at Toulon and Boscawen had authority for what he did at Lagos Bay. They showed that under certain conditions ships at sea were engines of destruction. It was knowledge Suffren had learnt the hard way.

The disasters of the Seven Years War prompted the French to examine the causes of their repeated reverses. Even before the end of the war young officers were resigning their commissions out of despair at the atrophy and lack of leadership at the top and the lack of promotion prospects within the officer corps. The fruits of their researches were to be seen in the 1765 *Ordonnances* promulgated by Choiseul. Their principal task was to lay down the order of battle so clearly that it would have satisfied the most exacting British devotee of the line.

They envisaged an unbreakable chain of magnificent ships, manned by superbly trained sailors, so that battles would be like heavyweight boxing contests in which the champions expected to win on points but not by a knock-out. A captain who without his general officer's signal left the line to chase, to double or to retire unless disabled could only expect to be court-martialled. The absolute discretion of the general officer (in the Grand Corps usually a lieutenant-general, roughly corresponding to the British vice-admiral, or a *chef d'escadre*, somewhat equivalent to a rear-admiral) reflected the absolutism that pervaded all French institutions. John Clerk of Eldin clearly agreed with Admiral John Jervis, the victor of Cape St Vincent in February 1797, when he said that two fleets of equal strength can never produce decisive events unless they are equally determined to fight it out or the commander-in-chief of one of them 'bitches it so as to spoil his line'.[8] And with the French tactician, Bigot de Morogues, who affirmed that 'there are no longer decisive battles at sea, that is to say battles on which the end of the war absolutely depends'. Of 15 engagements between the French and the English from Barfleur in 1692 to the Saints in 1782, only six could be called decisive and three of these were chases not battles between two lines.[9]

Choiseul had also embarked on a massive ship-building programme so that the French navy was rehabilitated with unexpected efficiency before war was renewed in 1779. When the English withdrew their ambassador from Paris there were 80 ships of the line ready for sea and nearly 78,000 mariners to man them.

Training for the *gardes-marines* at new naval schools and at the celebrated Académie de la Marine at Brest was of a professional order higher than a young officer could expect across the Channel, but, because it was essentially theoretical, Suffren remained suspicious of it. The new line-of-battle ships were more powerful than those built in British yards and the new signals were a great improvement on the old-fashioned system of the traditional enemy. Yet France's senior sea commander, the Comte d'Estaing, could still say in 1777 that 'if every captain knows how to manoeuvre his ship correctly we shall know that he will carry out his instructions.

Instead of there being any sudden decisions to make, in a combined order prescribed by a particular manoeuvre there is no call for foresight or guesswork. The route of every ship is pre-arranged, the choreography set and if there is no change of wind or other purely nautical phenomenon, the action will be completed passably well.'[10]

Suffren did not share this gallic confidence in order. He shared the conviction of men like Hawke and Boscawen that all naval action was futile unless it destroyed the enemy's ships. He chafed during the naval dress-rehearsals of the *escadres d'évolution* sent to sea to test the new ships and the newly trained sailors. No one actually fought a mock battle except once, in honour of the king's brother, the Comte de Provence, and the stately cruises during which the new signals were tried and the ships put through their paces, were only to ensure that the French line when it met its foe would give a good account of itself.

But Suffren had already decided that parallel broadsides were useless. Decisive results were achieved only by overwhelming odds. If a commander did not have them at the beginning he must create them by intelligent action, by concentrating his force against a selected point in the enemy's line. By shattering this in the early stages of the battle he would have the superiority of numbers to complete its destruction. In four of his five Indian battles he tried to put this strategy into action. But he only succeeded in dumbfounding his captains, who did not understand his intentions. Otherwise the English would have suffered a humiliation such as no squadron had received since the days of the Dutch admiral Michael de Ruyter.

The Anglo–Dutch wars of the late seventeenth century had been marked by naval battles of great size and complexity in which fleets 60 to 90 ships strong, equally matched in guns and skill, had evolved the theory of the line to bring order into chaos. The indisputable hero of this epoch was Michael de Ruyter, and in the months following his capture at Lagos Bay Suffren pored over the journals and narratives of those campaigns. He learned how Ruyter had defied the combined squadrons of his enemies, defeated them with inferior forces, broken the blockade of the Netherlands and destroyed any hope of a sea-borne invasion. Between the battles at which he achieved parity by concentration, his fleet, though its crews had gone ashore to fight invasion from the Low

Countries and it had surrendered its arms and ammunition to beat off attack by land, remained in being behind the sandbanks of the Rhine delta. From these unassailable reaches, Ruyter showed his claws in brilliantly improvised raids and convinced both the French and the English that his country could never be invaded by sea until his fleet had been destroyed.[11]

Ruyter's first 'pupils' were the Devonian George Monk and the Dieppois Abraham Duquesne, and soon the English were manoeuvring their ships like cavalry, sweeping down in attack together. It was the 'Maltese' Chevalier Anne de Tourville who locked his ships into line of battle in order to withstand them and only the 'Maltese' Chevalier de Suffren who, during the next 100 years, was to be a heretic about the doctrine of the line. For the faithful found the line a splendidly aristocratic thing. The authority of the flag was complete and there were good reasons in both navies why it should be so. For the English it helped the admiral impose his authority on wilful and quarrelsome subordinates. British officers were often divided by their partisanship of political rivals on whose patronage promotion depended, so that their admirals, uncertain of their loyalty or affection, were free with accusations of incompetence or cowardice. Battles were seldom won without recrimination or lost without court-martial.

In the French navy the problem was of a different kind, and the *Ordonnances* had scarcely addressed it. Among the grandees of France the senior service was the army. Even the navy employed military terminology and a squadron was usually commanded by a lieutenant-general. Though in both services age was never considered a reason for resignation and nobility substituted for competence, the army had managed to create an esprit de corps partly because of its tradition of victory, partly because royal interest in military achievement made it more ready to reward merit. In the navy, wrote one observer, 'they all hate each other'.[12] Though the families of Languedoc and Provence sent their cadets to Toulon and those of Brittany to Brest (there were surprisingly few Normans in the service and few from any of the provinces of central or eastern France), this did not produce cohesion or group loyalty.

The *Ordonnances* of 1765 did little or nothing to change the tradition that pedigree determined seniority and seniority determined promotion. The ban on marriage without licence from the king transformed Le Grand Corps de la Marine into something like a religious order. And because the caste was so small and inter-related, the awe of a British lieutenant for the captain of a man of war was wholly missing among the various ranks of the Grand Corps, who thee'd and thou'd each other freely and messed together. Yet no one could forget that promotion depended on connections, and birth counted more than rank, so that the service was characterized by insubordination, faction and jealousy. It was not rare for a naval officer to spend nearly 30 years as a junior officer, and another 15 or 16 as a *capitaine de vaisseau*. He might be nearly 60 when he secured the most junior grade of general officer, *chef d'escadre*. Royal favour, alone, could break this progression. Knights of Malta who could expedite their promotion by service in a foreign navy were not universally loved, and Suffren was to meet the hostility of one exclusive caste for the member of one yet more exclusive as soon as he was given his first independent command.[13]

Like all exclusive orders the Grand Corps ganged up on anyone who did not belong or who broke the rules of the caste. Particular venom was reserved for an unpopular general officer or for an *intrus*, usually an officer transferring from the army often on promotion (like d'Estaing) or originating from a province nowhere near the sea. The Grand Corps was no more welcoming to the *officiers-bleus* who were sons of the *petite noblesse* or roturier class and who were as a result seldom promoted above the rank of sub-lieutenant. They were called *officiers-bleus* from their blue breeches. The Grand Corps wore red and so could easily be distinguished even in the smoke of battle. Any attempt to break this rigid exclusiveness was doomed to failure before the Revolution. No matter what skills and experience the *bleus* might have, the Grand Corps did not look 'among the merchants of Bordeaux or Bayonne for the Counts they would need to fight its ships.'[14]

There was no questioning the courage and devotion of members of the Grand Corps but discipline was more a camaraderie of arms, a democracy of talent, and for them all to subordinate their personalities and desire for glory to the pursuit of one objective, they needed rules which had the force of a royal command. The line of battle had that royal imprimatur. Though the *Ordonnances* of 1765 demanded the most minute obedience of captains to the commands of their general officer, it was not always easy to obtain it. Every officer had the right of direct access to the minister and most had friends at court. General officers by and large found it easier to conduct their ships by the book and not to impose their will too heavily on their subordinates. But that was exactly what Suffren had learned was wrong with the French navy. And it was something he was resolved to correct when at last he was given command. By the time he had fought four battles in the Bay of Bengal, rendered inconclusive by the incompetence, disobedience, even malice of his captains, he had sent seven of those captains back to base. This was something that no general officer (which he was not, having only the rank of *chef d'escadre*), had ever dared to do. Like Napoleon Bonaparte, he was to leave no one in any doubt that he was determined to command.

3. War in the Mediterranean, 1760–78

Suffren when exchanged was out of the war. In October 1760, the Christian slaves on board a Turkish battleship mutinied, overpowered the officers and crew and sailed her to Malta. The Portuguese Grand Master Pinto welcomed her with delight, and added her to his fleet, re-baptized as the *Santissimo Salvatore*. The Grand Signor was not amused. He swore to recover her by force. Pinto prepared for war. One hundred and fifty knights were summoned under obedience to Malta for the defence of the island. Suffren's name was on the list, for Maltese embassies abroad knew about exchanged prisoners of war, and he obeyed with all speed. But the French did not want Turkish activity in the western Mediterranean. The *Santissimo Salvatore* was purchased from the Order by the king and returned to Constantinople with his compliments. In August 1761 Suffren was back in Toulon.[1]

Barred from fighting the English, he was given anti-pirate duties, especially against the Saletine corsairs who (according to Defoe) had once captured Robinson Crusoe. Unlike the pirate states of Algiers and Tunis the Moorish rovers of Salli, just north of Rabat on the Atlantic coast, were not bound by any treaty with France so there was an open season for hunting them. Unfortunately it was not always easy to be precise about the identity of shipping off the coast of North Africa and when Suffren in the *Pléiade* frigate sank a vessel that refused to have its papers verified it turned out to be Algerian which enjoyed immunity from attack. At once the French consul and vicar-general in Algiers were thrown into the *bagno* and the bey of Algiers tore up all his treaties. Before this little fracas could be papered over, Suffren had completed his cruise and written a paper on ridding the seas of Barbary pirates once and for all. The great Dutch admiral, Michael de Ruyter, had warned that it would be too risky to go into all the small anchorages to destroy the shipping there, but strict convoying of all Christian ships would in two years drive the Barbary regencies into bankruptcy and self-destruction.[2]

Apologies patched up relations with Algiers and Suffren was sent on another cruise, in command of the *Caméléon* xebec. During it he was nearly drowned on 14 September, when his launch was swamped; he was given up for lost until he came ashore in Minorca astride one of the oars.[3] The Saletines continuing both impenitent and impertinent, Suffren commanded another xebec, the *Singe*. Xebecs were three-masted lateen-rigged vessels much used by corsairs and anti-corsairs alike. Now he was part of a squadron of 13 small men-of-war detailed to find the Moroccan fleet and destroy it. Practical experience of sailing a xebec was just what made Mediterranean experience still valuable in the navy. Lightly armed, with oars so that it could be rowed like a galley, it was a perfect vessel for inshore work along the treacherous Mediterranean coasts, for it was manoeuvrable in all weathers and deadly in action. A simple error of judgement could, however, split its hull on a reef or capsize it in a gale, so that to sail it with confidence required command of every nuance of sailing skill, every faculty of instinct and science. Discipline on board was easy, comradely, based on mutual trust. The clean salt of the sea winds never lost the taste of sudden death.

On this occasion de Ruyter's advice was ignored; El Arraich was reduced to rubble by bombardment but the expedition sent in to cut out and destroy ships in hiding went astray. It was overpowered in an ambush and, for the loss of one frigate burned at anchor, the *bagnos* of Morocco received a welcome detachment of young able-bodied slaves. Among those captured was a young officer, Bidé de Maurville; among the wounded, Suffren's own cousin, Forbin—both of whom he was later to break in India. But the Moroccans were too wise to have a hot war with France and shortly afterwards requested an armistice. For their part in the expedition, the two 'Maltese', de Grasse and Suffren, were rewarded, de Grasse with a pension and Suffren with a gratification of 800 *livres*. The king would have liked to promote him but there were just too many officers senior to him in the lists. Instead he allowed him to accompany the Comte de Breugnon on his peace mission to Fez. He was even permitted to wear the Maltese Cross prominently in the heart of this fiercely Muslim country as Choiseul 'did not anticipate that it will give rise to the least inconvenience'.[4]

It did give rise to an anecdote. De Breugnon's entourage contained two other Knights of Malta, the young dandy François Joseph de Pérusse, the future Duc des Cars, and Montluc de la Bourdonnaye. During the presentation the Moroccan emperor noticed the eight-pointed cross of Malta on Pérusse's chest. 'El muchacho es un cavaliero de San Juan de Malta, demonios en la guerra, buenos hombres en la paz.' Breugnon then presented Suffren but, Pérusse added cattily, 'the Emperor could not have called him "un muchacho" for he is already grossly overweight, and the Moors don't like that in "muchachos".'[5]

Suffren certainly bore no resemblance to that romantic image of a Knight of Malta epitomized in the green and swooning Chevalier des Grieux of *Manon Lescaut* and personified in the impeccable figure of Pérusse. Intemperate eating and wilful non-conformity had already contrived to produce William Hickey's English butcher. Even in his own lifetime Suffren's gluttony was famous. In a footnote to his epic poem, *La Gastronomie ou l'Homme des Champs à Table*, Joseph Berchoux (1765–1839) at the line

> Rien ne doit déranger l'honnête homme qui dine
> (Let nothing disturb the honest man at dinner)

tells the story of the deputation from the Sumatran headmen of Achin who boarded Suffren's ship just as he was beginning his meal. Not wishing to be disturbed, he had them told that the Christian faith expressly instructed a Christian at table to concentrate on his food. The deputation retired respectfully, full of wonder at his exemplary devotion.[6] The Comte d'Estaing, while refitting at Boston in 1778, was astonished to see the quantities of food being taken on board Suffren's ship. 'Why so many birds?' he asked. 'Why not more powder and shot?' 'Mon General, I am very fond of fighting, but I also like my food.'[7]

He preferred to eat with his fingers and he was pretty indiscriminate about what he ate, as long as it was very highly spiced and very hot. He was to be in his element in south India and Ceylon. He was also seldom without a cigar in his mouth. Cheroots were primarily chewed to help salivation in hot climates and like Churchill and Fidel Castro he preferred the strong weed of Havana or Sumatra. In the Revolutionary fleet, it was smart to chew cigars and spit like Suffren.

He had no time for elegance. In full dress, he told William Hickey, he felt like a hog in armour.[8] When water was short, which it often was on long cruises, he would waste none on washing or shaving. He had seen the sailors of Turkey, Barbary and America in his time, dressed in motley and yet with no loss of efficiency. In the Bay of Bengal he exchanged his tricorne for a manila straw hat, laid off his cravat and wore his shirt open at the neck. Straw slippers were preferable to shoes and stockings, and the man whom Hickey thought he had disturbed at his toilette had already convinced his young men that it was more efficient to sail and fight unencumbered by clothing that made both more difficult. But it was not until 30 years after his retirement that officers were issued with open unlaced breeches instead of the tight leggings which Suffren refused to wear.

Suffren, too, used to sport a bishop's beaver hat in battle, a gift from his elder brother, the Bishop of Sisteron, in Provence. He very sensibly believed that in the smoke of battle his men were more likely to discern a bishop on the quarter-deck than an officer in a tricorne. During the battle of Trincomali it was only the triumphant appearance of this hat that convinced his men he was still alive. It soon became a talisman: once, before combat, when he was walking along the gun-deck encouraging the men, he heard one of them say: 'It's all right for him. He's perfectly safe in his hat.' Suffren at once threw it into the sea, shouting: 'Tron de goi, l'ou vaqui a la baio moun capèu fado.' ('Thunder of God, into the sea with my enchanted hat!') Two men instantly jumped overboard to rescue it.[9]

This eccentricity did not earn him friends, especially as he insisted that his junior officers appear before him properly dressed. For it was, first, a *trahison de caste*. Then, as his contempt for incompetence became unpitying, it seemed like pungent misanthropy. His opinions on folly were crisp and explosive and sounded more violent when expressed, as they frequently were, in Provençal. The lash of his tongue stung the regulars most, for in his distrust of mere rank he had learned to appreciate the often greater competence of the *bleus*. But if he was intolerant and critical of his

colleagues he himself was not amenable to criticism. In the fleet
of his enemies such an authoritarian temper would have secured
a grudging respect. In the generous camaraderie of blood that
was the French navy, Suffren's casual manners, coarse tongue and
intemperate rages, more than the hitherto un-naval traditions of
his family, made him as hated as any *intrus*.

The common seamen, particularly the Provençals, who savoured
his mighty oaths and vernacular blasphemies venerated him this
side idolatry. In 1781 the crew which he had commanded for two
years demanded to be allowed to serve with him in his new ship
bound for India. It was not because Suffren had a private devil
who came to talk to him during his siesta, or because he had a
magic hat, that the superstitious *mocos* were prepared to commit
themselves into his hands. They responded to leadership, to his
lust for battle, to his generous recognition of those who fought
well, to his appetites and his temper. No French captain since *le
grand siècle*, since Duguay-Trouin, since Jean Bart, so successfully
captured the imagination of his men.

But Suffren was 38 when in 1767 he commanded the *Union*
frigate at Brest in which he sailed with de Breugnon to Toulon.
He had reached a critical point in his career and when he looked
at that of his younger brother, his fellow Knight of Malta, Paul-
Julien, he did not seem to have done so well. On 11 October 1768,
Paul-Julien had been appointed second officer of a Maltese galley.
Within a few years—in Paul-Julien's, case five and a half—he
could expect to command her, and a captaincy in Malta was
traditionally a qualification in the French fleet for the same rank.[10]
Considering that he might pursue his career as well in Valletta as
in Toulon, he asked his brother to make discreet enquiries, and in
the new year of 1768 Pierre-André went to Malta as captain of
the galley *San Nicola*, commonly known as *La Vittoria*.[11] In June
she was cruising off Bizerta in a joint Franco-Maltese blockade
of the port until the 64-gun *Provence* arrived to bombard the
town in a bout of periodic punishment for the normally quiescent
Tunisian pirates, who had either wittingly or unwittingly attacked
a French ship.[12]

But Suffren was not seeking a career in Malta. The captain of a
galley co-operating with a French squadron in hostile action must
merit something better than command of a frigate; but though the
king promised him promotion, he did not say when and in fact

it did not come for four more years. In the meantime he had his commandery of Saint-Christol, worth 12,000 *livres* a year in rents, barely sufficient for anyone hoping to command a line-of-battle ship in the French navy. If His Majesty could not give him a pension, could he persuade the Prince Grand Master to give him a richer commandery?[13] His Majesty could not. So he applied for command of the Collège de Gardes-Marines at Toulon, a post which, besides giving him a chance to knock some sense into the young hopes of the Grand Corps, also carried full allowances.[14] But he did not get it and in October, perhaps with some relief as he was not really suited to a shore job, he was fitting out the *Mignonne* frigate for a cruise in the Levant.

The eastern Mediterranean was turbid with war. The Russian fleet which had defeated the Turks at Tchesma was still at Patmos and the smell of blood had drawn every pirate into the Aegean; to protect the trade from their importunities, Suffren's *Mignonne* and three other frigates were to winter there. The cruise was uneventful and Suffren had a chance to see if he could improve his claims on a richer commandery, by calling on the 90-year-old Grand Master, Manoel de Pinto, in Malta. But the old man was dying and the intrigues over his succession absorbed the attention of every senior dignitary of the Order in the island, so his appeal was lost. When it was clear that the new Grand Master was going to do nothing for him, he asked the French minister of marine to put his name forward to be captain-general of the Maltese galley fleet.[15]

This grand post was now largely a sinecure. The captain-general served for only two years, a left-over from the times when the perpetual war with Islam made longer service ruinous to the captain-general's health and pocket. But the appointment carried with it very strong claims to a rich commandery and promotion to the rank of Knight Grand Cross. The minister obliged, for Maltese commanderies were useful substitutes for royal pensions, but it was almost the last thing he did: on 24 August he was removed from office and the new minister, Gabriel de Sartine, former lieutenant-general of police, sent Suffren off on another cruise of the Levant. Suffren was glad to be at sea. 'Only long cruises,' he told the minister, 'can make good crews. The English keep their ships on regular service for years at a time and are way ahead of us in this respect.'[16] But there was no action.

Suffren experimented with various ways of keeping his crews healthy, being a great believer in the virtues of fresh air and soap, which, liberally applied to everyone but himself, helped to keep sickness at bay: in four cruises he had lost only four men through illness. He also found that the Greeks in the Sporades archipelago used a chalk-like substance which, when added to salt water, softened it sufficiently for soap to lather; as constant washing destroyed lice, he thought the Academy of Sciences should test its properties. While the Ministry were about it they might also be interested in the acorn which the Greeks used in softening and tanning leather and which might be grown in the south of France. 'A man of spirit,' he told Sartine, 'neglects no detail for he knows that in war great things are achieved by an accumulation of little details . . . But I should not like you to think that I occupy myself solely with natural history. I study it only as it affects my métier, for I regard time spent ashore as one more resource against the enemy. Such is the interconnection of all human knowledge that one thing can lead on to another.' Sartine rapidly passed the samples on to the War Ministry. The Chevalier d'Oisy acknowledged receipt with double-edged enthusiasm. M. de Sartine 'clearly thinks that projects like yours are purgative pills for his assistants so he has to give them to us soldiers to digest as we have stronger stomachs'. But he did at least send to Le Havre for sea water to see if the properties of the Greek chalk were so remarkable. The acorns he passed to the comptroller-general, Turgot.[17]

From 3 June 1775 to the spring of 1776, Suffren lived at his commandery of Saint-Christol and then commanded the frigate *Alcmène* in the first of the celebrated *escadres d'évolution* which put the revivified navy of France through its paces. He still wanted to be captain-general of the Maltese galleys and, with a new and French Grand Master on the throne in Malta, he applied for leave to go to the island for another try. Though he had commanded nothing larger than a frigate, few aspirants for the post were better qualified, but rank and privilege pulled harder and the command went to frigate captain the Chevalier de Brillane, who had sailed the *Sultan* frigate with Suffren to the Levant in 1774 and was to be governor of Île de France in the years before Suffren's arrival there.

At last, in his 48th year, the disappointed sailor was rewarded with the command he desired. In April 1777, he was ordered to fit out the *Fantasque*, 64, in the *escadre d'évolution* of the Comte de Barras, with orders to cruise in the Mediterranean and stage that mock battle for the king's younger brother, the future Louis XVIII. She was a better ship than he had expected and he was pleased with her performance. And events in the great Atlantic world were moving inexorably towards a renewal of war, in which he might find the opportunity to show her paces. In June, when the cruise had begun, Barras commanded two 74s, three 64s and two frigates. When he returned to Toulon in the new year of 1778 the squadron under his command grew to 12 ships of the line. Nothing of this size had been seen in Toulon since de la Clue had sailed to destruction in the roads of Lagos Bay.

4. Rhode Island and St Lucia, 1778

War with France's ancient rival could not be far off when, in February 1778, Louis XVI recognized the newly independent United States of America by signing a commercial treaty with Congress. And the news that the king had appointed one of the three vice-admirals of France, Charles Henri Théodat, Comte d'Estaing, to command the Mediterranean squadron was electrifying. The white hope and favourite of the court, as brave as Bayard, as proud as Condé, as bold as Saxe, with the royal quarters on his arms commemorating the ancestor who in 1214 had saved the life of Philip Augustus at Bouvines, d'Estaing could only have been appointed for some great project. In 1756 France had opened the war with a coup against Minorca. Would it be Minorca again (returned to England at the peace of 1763) or Jamaica or Ireland, or even England herself?

Speculation became intense when two strangers arrived in Toulon, travelling incognito, one clearly a foreigner. Who could the other be? Though British intelligence tried unsuccessfully to break his disguise, George III had already guessed who he was. His ministers, Lords North and Sandwich, however, remained convinced that d'Estaing was bound for Brest, where, united with the squadron of Louis d'Orvilliers, he would have a crushing naval superiority in home waters. To prevent this they were even prepared to leave Gibraltar undefended. But the squadron that left Toulon on 13 April 1778 was intended neither for Gibraltar nor for Brest. On 20 May, after an agonizing crawl through the Straits, at a point 50 leagues west of Cape St Vincent of unhappy memory, d'Estaing summoned his officers on board the *Languedoc*.

The mysterious strangers stood revealed as Silas Deane, the American envoy to Paris, and his companion Gérard de Rayneval, French minister plenipotentiary to the American Congress. Not Brest but the Delaware was their objective, their mission, 'to assist our very dear and great friends and allies' in war against the common enemy. Just as George III had feared, they were to chase Admiral Howe from the American coast, blockade Sir Henry Clinton in New York and, if events permitted, reap a rich harvest of sugar islands in the Caribbean. The glory of France was to be achieved in the independence of America and the humbling of proud and contumelious Britain. At a more practical level, the French hoped that a quick and decisive victory would mean it was no longer necessary to bribe Spain to enter the war on their side. It was a stirring occasion.

D'Estaing's squadron mounted 846 guns in line, a far more powerful concentration than Richard Howe commanded as he covered Clinton's withdrawal to New York. But as long as the British were unsure of d'Estaing's destination, the Admiralty would send no reinforcements to America and it was only on 9 June that George III was able to convince his ministers that the French were bound for the Delaware River. Vice-Admiral John Byron, grandfather to the poet, was ordered to sail at once but, a few days out of Plymouth, Foul-Weather Jack ran into the weather his tars expected him to meet and his ships were scattered in a storm. For weeks he was to know nothing of their fate, and Howe was left without news of reinforcements.

In the meantime the great French squadron pursued its stately course westward. For one who was the author of an apothegm almost worthy of Napoleon ('Promptitude is the first weapon, surprise three-quarters of a victory'), d'Estaing wasted a great deal of precious time.[1] It had taken him 33 days to reach Gibraltar from Toulon, and he was to take another 52 to reach America, for he insisted on putting his ships through exercises in mid-Atlantic. The sad truth was that, despite his exalted rank, d'Estaing's naval experience was very small. He had started life in the armies of the Maréchal de Saxe and was a soldier until 1759 when he was taken prisoner while serving with Lally before Madras. Released on parole, he spent the last year of the Seven Years War as a privateer, sacking British depots in the Persian Gulf and in Sumatra. At the peace he was allowed to transfer, aged 33, into the Grand Corps and within 14 months had been elevated to the rank of lieutenant-general and governor of the Leeward Islands.

D'Estaing boasted that like four of France's greatest sea officers, Duquesne, Duguay-Trouin, Jean Bart and Tourville, he had managed without the 'indispensable' training laboriously imparted to officers of the Grand Corps, but his fellow officers, seeing this most flagrant *intrus* elevated to the rank of vice-admiral (a rank equivalent to the English admiral), suspected that it was more for services rendered by his ancestor at Bouvines than for any distinction he had yet achieved in war. Disdainfully brave and cuttingly witty, d'Estaing had other crippling disabilities which the campaign was to reveal only too vividly. His mistakes over the next 18 months were to provide an object lesson in how not to conduct a powerful naval squadron, and his campaign was to be the epitome of the difficulties France found in providing at sea the same quality of leadership she had consistently found on land.

When the French sighted the Virginia Capes on 5 July the English had been able to prepare for him. Philadelphia and the Delaware estuary had been evacuated, Clinton was tucked into New York, and Howe's ships were safely locked behind the bar of Sandy Hook. The only chance the French had of their destruction was to navigate a shallow channel 23 feet deep. They needed 25 to get their biggest ships over, and despite the offer of an enormous fee from d'Estaing's own pocket the pilots refused to try. It is a rash commander who defies his pilots, and d'Estaing was not rash. Though Suffren in the *Fantasque*, seconded by d'Albert de Rions in the *Sagittaire*, was ready to try, on 22 July the French stood southward for Rhode Island. American visions of a second Saratoga as Clinton limped overland from Philadelphia had faded with the non-arrival of d'Estaing in May. A vision now of what was to happen at Yorktown, before the war had been brutalized by three more years of fighting, vanished with the French sails.

Washington's disappointment at Clinton's escape could, however, be reduced by the capture of Newport before the inevitable British reinforcements arrived. It was the seal to the huge inland bay to which Rhode Island acted as the stopper, and its capture would close its waters to English frigates and privateers. When General Pigot, commanding the British troops in Newport, saw d'Estaing's sails off Point Judith on 29 July, he assumed they could only be there because Howe had been defeated. But d'Estaing decided to wait for the Americans to arrive before attacking Newport and thus allowed Pigot time to sink blockships in the harbour and strengthen his defences to landward. The *Fantasque* and *Sagittaire* were sent in to destroy the six frigates in the bay, but their purpose was achieved for them by their captains who sank or burned them to avoid capture. Suffren sailed as near Newport as he could to identify the smoking hulks and to allow his crew to enjoy 'a spectacle which would have been more satisfying had we run any danger'.[2]

D'Estaing sailed through the middle passage, which Suffren had sounded for him three days earlier, on 8 August and began to land troops that afternoon. Towards evening the sea mist that had hung off the coast lifted enough to reveal the *Protecteur* and *Provence* running for the shore. Howe, reinforced by the first arrivals of Admiral Byron's squadron and by three ships from Halifax and Barbados, had come to Pigot's rescue. D'Estaing was taken by surprise but this time he was prompt. His men were immediately re-embarked and at 19.00 the squadron weighed and stood after the English with all sail set, even to studdingsails and royals. Howe gave way before him, hoping to lure the French far enough to sea to gain the weather-gauge. For 24 hours the two admirals danced an elaborate *pas de deux*, wooing the wind. But that element remained a capricious neutral and during the night of 11 August it rose to hurricane force so that over the next 36 hours all thought of combat was abandoned, and by 13 August the squadrons had lost contact with each other.[3]

When the French reassembled off Rhode Island, d'Estaing decided that he must now sail for New England. Byron's squadron had either arrived or was due at any minute, and his orders were not to risk his ships in uneven encounter. The American General Sullivan, seconded by Lafayette, wanted him to stay until Newport was captured, and when the French sailed on 22 August he published an Order of the Day which seemed to accuse them of desertion. D'Estaings were not bred to talk to rebels and the blunt American who defied the House of Hanover was not used to the honeyed refinements of a vice-admiral whose ancestor had helped to defeat King John of England at Bouvines in 1214. The alliance had got off to an inauspicious start.

The British had 'never longed to see the finest of women more
than . . . Admiral Byron' and by the time that wish was gratified
d'Estaing was securely anchored at Boston between Quincy Bay
and Nantucket, where Howe sighted him on 9 September.[4] No
one intruded except mischief. The French resented Sullivan's insulting Order, the Americans still felt abandoned on the point of
victory. Sailors came to blows in the trim New England streets;
supplies were mysteriously unavailable in the Arsenal. D'Estaing
offered to march overland to Rhode Island but refused to go to
sea now that Howe had been reinforced. Suffren chafed at the idle
days which reminded him of the time in 1759 when de la Clue
had been cooped up in Toulon for 18 months, for the English,
having recovered their freedom to move troops anywhere they
liked, 'leave us little hope of undertaking any major enterprise'.[5]
If he and d'Albert could take a couple of frigates and ravage the
Newfoundland fishing waters before the hurricane season, then
there might be something to show for the vast expense of this
expedition.

But until Washington soothed the comte's ruffled pinions,
d'Estaing was not going to move. For, unknown to both his allies
and his own commanders, d'Estaing's secret orders were to proceed
to the Caribbean as soon as he had lost numerical superiority off
the coast of America. When on 2 November a storm blew Byron off
the coast, he decided to sail. On 4 November he was at sea, heading
for Martinique, leaving Pigot invulnerable in Newport and Clinton
entrenched in New York. Despite a Congress resolution that the
Comte d'Estaing had behaved 'as a brave and wise officer . . . and
rendered every benefit to these States', they had gained very little
from his presence.[6] True he had kept his squadron intact, but
English losses from his presence were only five frigates and four
corvettes.

Washington knew very well that the French had not entered the
war out of sympathy with the American revolution. An absolute
monarchy would not ally itself with rebels unless there were real
gains to be had from so doing, and British sugar islands were
the pawns he must help the French to take as the price of that
alliance. But once the French entered the war, the English, too,
changed their plans. Secret Instructions of 3 May 1778 ordered
Howe to release ships for the reduction of St Lucia. Eleven days
after d'Estaing, Commodore Hotham, five ships of the line and

5000 troops sailed for Barbados. At one point the two squadrons sailed so close that three of Hotham's convoy were taken by French cruisers, but despite his 11 days' start, a journey shorter by 1000 miles and the absence of a convoy, d'Estaing reached Martinique only a day before Hotham sailed into Barbados on 10 December. Three days later the Barbados squadron under Rear-Admiral the Hon Samuel Barrington was anchored with Hotham's in the Grand Cul de Sac of St Lucia. By breakfast time the governor and his 80 regular troops had taken to the hills. The British were digging in round the Carénage harbour when at daybreak on 15 December d'Estaing's ships were seen making straight for the bay.

No one could fault his promptitude this time. As soon as an American privateer reported Barrington's presence in the Grand Cul de Sac, d'Estaing embarked the whole Martinique garrison and within 24 hours was off St Lucia. But the flag in the Carénage told him that once again he had arrived too late. During the night Barrington had anchored his ships in line across the bay, warped his transports within and waited for the attack. It came at 11.30 when d'Estaing sailed down upon him through driving rain; it was repeated at 16.00 hours. But the French came no nearer than three-quarters of a mile, turning along the English line and firing so high that several pieces of shot were recovered half a mile inland. Barrington was incredulous that the French with such superiority should still have treated his ships like Aunt Sallies, and Suffren seethed with muted rage on the deck of the *Fantasque*. There was no sandbar to protect the English this time, only their own staunchness and concentration, and these were just the qualities d'Estaing was unwilling to test by sailing down on them and risking the incapacitation of his leading ships.[7]

D'Estaing now transferred the action to the element he preferred and on 16 December put his men ashore. The attack on the British positions on 17 December was a ghastly failure. The ground was sodden, the powder wet, and every assault was beaten off with bloody loss. Suffren watched this folly with growing impatience until he could contain himself no longer. The squadron had been so denuded of men that it could barely fight Byron if he suddenly appeared. There was still a way to dispose of Barrington, 'by laying ourselves alongside his ships and anchoring at the top of their anchor buoys. If we delay they may escape, slip out under cover of darkness, leaving the troops to cover their retreat, and if we have weather again like the night before last they would fly away. As it is our ships being unmanned can neither sail nor fight. What happens if Admiral Byron comes? What will our ships do without crews or general? Their defeat will mean the loss of both the colony and the army. Let us destroy the squadron. The garrison would then have to surrender—que Biron vienne après,' he concluded in a phrase d'Estaing should have relished, 'il nous fera plaisir!'[8]

This was the language of Nelson but to sea sense of this kind d'Estaing was deaf. He hung off St Lucia until 22 December. On the 24th he formed two lines abreast and sailed down on the Grand Cul de Sac but tacked and returned to his anchorage. Two days later he repeated the manoeuvre, but it was without point. Then at 20.00 hours on 29 December, to Barrington's utter astonishment, the French returned to Martinique. An hour later the French governor came down from the mountains to surrender. Three years later Admiral Rodney was to sail from Gros Ilot Bay to victory at the Saints. 'If the Comte d'Estaing is ever given the baton of Marshal of France,' declared the wits of Fort Royal, 'it will be made of St Lucia wood.'[9]

The French returned to Martinique because Byron was in Barbados with 16 ships, but they did so with a bitter taste of defeat. The soldiers, stunned by the loss of so many of their comrades, murmured against the man who had led them to be butchered. D'Estaing would not challenge Byron without reinforcements, and the governor's sullen refusal to lend any more troops to be slaughtered for a dash on Guadeloupe rubbed the raw nerve of d'Estaing's proud and autocratic temper. For several days he sulked in his tent and resolved more firmly on inaction.

5. Grenada and Charleston, 1779

Now was the winter of Suffren's discontent. The campaign was in its eighth month and so far it had been a dismal catalogue of lost opportunities. The enterprise that had seemed so promising when it sailed from Toulon in April had dribbled away in miserable incompetence and wrangling. For this he had missed the promotion in Malta that he needed so badly, for, just before he had sailed, the new Grand Master, the Prince de Rohan, had offered him the next two-year command as captain-general if he could serve from January 1779. Suffren was sadly torn, but his desire for action prevailed. He asked Sartine to request the Grand Master to postpone the offer for two years or allow his younger brother, Paul-Julien, to serve in his place. De Rohan decided in the end to transfer Suffren to a richer commandery and to give the command to the protégé of the King of Spain.[1]

The Grand Master's decision reached Suffren in Martinique, and he replied with unconcealed bitterness. 'The wretched events that I have witnessed are enough to increase my regret at being so far from Your Highness. Could I only drive them from my mind ... They have shown how dangerous it is to put someone in command of a squadron who is not a sailor and is never likely to be one.'[2] To his widowed cousin in Provence, Mme de Seillans, he was more explicit. 'This campaign has been one long series of vicissitudes, good luck, bad luck and folly. I have served 35 years and seen a good deal but never so much of the last. You cannot imagine what idiotic manoeuvres have been connived at, what stupid, perfidious counsels have been given. I have earned few thanks for recently urging an attack by 12 of our large ships on seven of their small ones because they were defended by some guns on shore. I am utterly tired of it all and begin to regret not going to Malta instead.'[3]

There was a lot of activity over the next month but it was like the children's game of French and English, with ships slipping in and out of Fort Royal and Gros Ilot Bay, claiming to have chased the other home. Contempt for d'Estaing ran high among his enemies. ''Twould be a thousand pities if his Most Christian Majesty lose such a subject. I will not prostitute the word and call him officer,' wrote Governor Burtt of St Kitts to Samuel Barrington. 'I shall never expect to see the Art of War written by this Count.'[4] Suffren could have said the same. Meanwhile the French waited for their reinforcements when they would 'go and seek out the English, but if you ask me, it will be like the famous encounter between Harlequin and Scaramouche'.[5]

D'Estaing's twin object seemed to be to defend Martinique and to wear out the English on St Lucia. But, Suffren thought, 'the truth is that our General does not know what to do and has neither the will nor the ability to do it even if he did. We are at the same time starving our own colony and sooner or later hunger will drive us out.'[6] The English might have 25 ships across the water but he did not think they were well provided and he did not find Byron particularly frightening. D'Estaing, apparently, did.

On 5 June Byron had to leave St Lucia to escort a huge convoy clear of St Kitts and on 27 June, while Byron was working his way laboriously back against adverse currents, Toussaint la Motte Picquet sailed into Fort Royal with reinforcements. 'The convoy has arrived,' D'Estaing crowed. 'These words say all.'[7] Not quite. For his orders from France were to leave de Grasse in command and to return to France. But with the arrival of La Motte Picquet he now commanded 24 ships of the line, as many as Byron, if not more. He would go home by way of Barbados seizing what islands he could, hoping to challenge and destroy his rival. He would then go to Newfoundland and sack St John's before returning to France with at least one feather in his cap. After seizing the island of St Vincent, 30 miles south of St Lucia, he sailed from Martinique on 30 June, and the winds and currents that had been Byron's 'raw head and bloody bones'[8] carried him the 60 miles further to the south-west so that on 2 July he was off Grenada. Here was his chance to avenge the loss of St Lucia.

The governor of Grenada was an Irish peer, Lord George Macartney, who had been expecting his doom for several months. When he saw the Irish regiment of Dillon and the legionaries of Lauzun coming ashore at 04.00 hours on 4 July he knew he could make only a token defence. D'Estaing, wearing the cordon of St Esprit, marched sword in hand at the head of the assault, and at 16.00 Macartney surrendered at discretion. Grenada was French but all at once they were called upon to defend it.

Byron was off St Vincent when he heard of the attack on Grenada. The French were rudely awakened in the early hours of 6 July with the news that the English squadron was off the north point of the island. D'Estaing's ships were anchored in no sort of order in St George's Bay and over the next hour and a half they had to put their heads round and shake out their dew-sodden sails before Suffren, characteristically the first to be ready, led them out of the bay at dawn. The frigates meanwhile had discovered that Byron had only 21 line-of-battle ships to pit against d'Estaing's 24, and three of these were guarding a convoy of troops.

Byron for his part did not know that he was outnumbered—indeed he thought d'Estaing had only 16 ships of the line—and when he sighted the *Fantasque* at 05.00 he signalled a general chase. Barrington sailed down so impetuously that he had soon outstripped the rest of the squadron and Byron ordered him to sail instead for the French rear and sail up the French line, so that the rest of the squadron could follow and engage on the same tack. The three leading English ships took a fearful hammering from the French as they ran down the line, but worse was to hit three other vessels of the rear division commanded by Hyde Parker, which ran straight into the French van led by the *Fantasque* and were badly savaged by a concentration of fire from the whole line.

At 10.00 Byron had been fired on from the shore and thus knew that Grenada had fallen. He made signal for line of battle at two cables' distance but his squadron had difficulty in complying. Joshua Rowley, commanding the *Suffolk* in charge of the convoy, seeing how things were going, exercised the discretion allowed him by the *Fighting Instructions* and, followed by Captain Fanshawe in the *Monmouth*, sailed straight across towards the French van instead of following Barrington. The *Monmouth* outstripped the

Suffolk and was soon locked in deadly combat with the *Fantasque*. Between 11.00 and 13.00 the two ships disappeared into an acrid fog of gunsmoke. Suffren lost 22 dead and 45 wounded, among the dead a fellow Knight of Malta 'qui jouait si bien au pianoforte', he wrote in a rare note almost of self-pity. 'I was attacked in the position of honour not intended for me and for an hour and a half I bore the fire of two ships. Impartial testimony will say it was well done,' he told his far from impartial cousin in Provence. 'My enemies dare not say it was not.'⁹ But that night he led his officers in a toast to the captain of 'the little black ship', so called because the *Monmouth*'s gun-ports were painted black. He was to meet her again in battle six more times and to find her every time no less staunch.

Until this moment d'Estaing had remained on the defensive, but four English ships were too badly damaged to continue the battle while, apart from the *Fantasque*, none of the French ships had been much damaged. When at 13.00 the two lines parted, the French were immeasurably superior in numbers, power and mobility, and the almost incredulous vice-admiral had three courses of action from which to choose. He could encompass a general action between his 23 comparatively unmarked ships and the enemy's 18 still fit for battle. He could isolate and destroy Byron's convoy, which was virtually undefended. He could cut off, capture or destroy the four badly damaged and separated ships. He chose none. Suddenly alarmed by the distance between him and Grenada and by the disorder of his rear, he ordered his squadron to tack together and steer southwards for St George's Bay.

To Byron's astonishment they filed past two of the disabled ships, treating them only to a valedictory broadside, and in stately dignity and greatly improved formation (which showed the lessons learned in those *escadres d'évolution*) disappeared into their anchorage. Byron gathered up his wounded ships and returned to St Kitts. Had d'Estaing been less preoccupied with the safety of the newly captured Grenada and, perhaps, less respectful of the fighting qualities of his enemy, he might have beaten Byron decisively there and then, after which there could hardly have been a Battle of the Saints.¹⁰

D'Estaing claimed the victory, a *Te Deum* was intoned in Notre Dame in Paris and all France was overjoyed. But the British, though discomfited, had actually lost only one transport. Casualties on both sides had been roughly equal but the English had suffered more material damage. 'The General on land as well as on sea,' Suffren admitted grudgingly, 'has conducted himself with much valour. His victory cannot be disputed, but if he were as good a sailor as he is brave, he would never have allowed four dismasted ships to escape us.' Still, the English had taken a sad beating. 'Unless they receive very considerable reinforcements they will not show themselves again.'[11] To de Rohan in Valletta he wrote on 10 July: 'Grenada is the best of the British West Indies but it is very annoying that bad weather must now interrupt the course of our conquests.'[12]

The course of conquest was not quite over, for on 14 July Suffren and d'Albert mopped up the Union and Grenadine Islands. 'It is his one regret,' d'Estaing wrote to Sartine, 'that he has had only this opportunity to show with what promptitude and thoroughness he can carry out an operation of this sort.'[13] Five days later he joined the rest of the squadron off Guadeloupe and on 22 July they were off St Kitts in full view of Byron's ships anchored in a defensive line across Basseterre Roads. D'Estaing paraded once up and once down the length of the roadstead to see if the English were disposed to accept a challenge and, when he saw they were too damaged to do so, he sailed to Santo Domingo. From there he wrote a letter to the Comte de Vergennes, then in charge of foreign affairs at Versailles, a letter he might have done better to suppress. 'More noise than effect is too often the net result of a battle at sea. We were quicker in getting our boots on than the English after Grenada, but Admiral Byron had not finished his toilette. After having a good look at what we call at sea his wounds, which seemed to us pretty extensive, we did him the courtesy of waiting for him two whole days in his ante-chamber.'[14]

Two days did not, however, constitute a blockade, and his failure to stay until he had starved Byron into emerging could have been fatal had Byron been half a Rodney. As it was, the English admiral was a sick man. Worn out by constant fatigue and unremitting worry, he was prostrated by a putrid fever and on 23 July, the day after the French withdrew, he resigned his command to Hyde Parker. D'Estaing had won another victory of sorts.

From Santo Domingo d'Estaing should have gone home. But though his orders were now several weeks old, Sullivan's Order of the Day at Newport still rankled, and the disappointed anguish

of his fellow Auvergnat, the Marquis de Lafayette, at the abandon-
ment of the expedition against Rhode Island, nagged at his spirits.
He must strike one more blow for 'his very dear and great friends
and allies' to convince them of the value of French support. An
opportunity now offered.

Since his departure from the American coast the British had been
free to ship troops for the reduction of the southern states. Georgia
had been pacified and it was now the turn of South Carolina. In
July the state's American governor, Rutledge, begged d'Estaing to
mount combined operations against the British forward post at
Savannah. D'Estaing agreed and on 16 August he left Port au
Prince. He would stay off the Carolina coast just long enough for
the Americans to launch a swift attack, but he must be gone by
mid-September. His arrival on 31 August was a complete surprise.

With Benjamin Lincoln marching to meet him with 1000 men
from Charleston, d'Estaing prepared to put his troops ashore
and the position of the Hanoverian General Augustin Prevost in
Savannah became critical overnight. But on 2 September a storm
broke over the squadron and did such severe damage that it was
impossible for d'Estaing to consider a rapid departure. As Lincoln
took his time in coming, d'Estaing grew increasingly nervous. He
had left Santo Domingo with no information about the British
fleet and this was not the season to be hanging off an exposed
coast. Nevertheless the blow must be struck and on 7 September
he sealed the Savannah river. On 12 September his troops went
ashore but, without draught animals or wheeled carriages, it took
them four days to drag the artillery over the 13 miles to the city.
On 16 September he summoned Prevost to the arms of the King of
France (and, in omitting any mention of the United States, mortally
offended Lincoln). Prevost rejected the summons.

At that point Captain Hinrichs of the Jäger Corps was surprised
that d'Estaing 'who formerly, I believe, was a M la Resource', did
not storm 'this miserable sandpile' with bayonets, and was even
more surprised when the French proceeded to entertain the town
to a six-day cannonade before mounting an assault.[15] So was
Suffren, for everyone was worried about the lateness of the season.
He wanted to join in the attack when it came and have it over
with, but it was as well he was not allowed to, for the plans were
betrayed to Prevost. It was led by the vice-admiral with his usual
sang-froid and Saint Esprit, but his coolness turned to rage as he

fouled the stakes lining the Hanoverian trenches. He tore at them with his hands and teeth and was shot, first in the leg and then in the arm. When at last the attack faltered and broke, the French and Americans between them had lost 244 dead and 584 wounded in the bloodiest battle since Bunker Hill. It was not renewed. D'Estaing could delay his departure no longer and leaving not 'a single pistol as trophy to the English' he disembarked, leaving the loyalists to chant:

> To Charleston with fear the rebels repair,
> D'Estaing scampers back to his boats, sir,
> Each blaming the other, each cursing his brother,
> And—may they cut each other's throats, sir.[16]

A hurricane broke upon the squadron for the fourth time in 18 months on 23 October. Some of the ships limped back to Port au Prince, others to Fort Royal. D'Estaing on the *Languedoc*, both anchors cut and making six inches of water every hour, crawled in solitary agony across the Atlantic. If he had not captured a brig carrying British uniforms off the coast of France he and his crew would have landed at Brest on 7 December in rags.

Suffren was back in Toulon in the new year and there he paid off his crew. As he took leave of three officers who were later to sail to India with him, he could not congratulate them on a great campaign. True the *mocos* had shown themselves the equals of the Atlantic sailors. True, d'Estaing was brave if arrogant—so was he—and he understood why he withdrew from the irritable snubs of the Grand Corps into a disdainful hauteur. But while he could have a fellow feeling for the man who met hatred and contempt at every turn, he could not forgive the withdrawal from Sandy Hook, the desertion of Sullivan at Newport, the idling in Boston, the flimsy attack on Barrington in the Grand Cul de Sac, the unfinished battle off Grenada, the delay and dawdling outside Savannah. He could not know that d'Estaing's appearance at Savannah had so alarmed the English that they cancelled the reinforcements for Georgia and abandoned Newport so that d'Estaing 'had accomplished from 1000 miles away what he could not achieve by a close siege the year before'.[17] Above all he could not approve of secret orders which sent d'Estaing after irrelevant conquests in the Caribbean. All this was the negation of sea warfare. The long and dreary campaign, which had started with high hopes and ended now so emptily, was an object lesson in how not to do it.

The battle-hungry *capitaine de vaisseau* was no student of higher strategy. He could not see that the French priorities were to land their expeditionary force, distract the British fleet from the blockade of the American ports, and give the patriot armies more freedom of manoeuvre. To Suffren the freedom of the Americans was a lesser matter than a defeat at sea of the nation that had humiliated him at Lagos Bay and Finisterre. But he was uncomfortably right to realize that his fellow members of Le Grand Corps were mostly content to have fought off the British, for whom they felt an almost fearful respect, so that a battle that saved a convoy or survived an attack without sustaining serious loss was almost the equivalent of a victory. Indeed the French practice of taking the lee gauge, firing high and never allowing the enemy to get close enough to resort to rapid fire at point-blank range which was their speciality, while preserving their ships from injury, was fatal to decisive action.

Suffren was not to know that the British were feeling similarly disgruntled about their performance. In 1776 William Eden had written to Lord Sandwich: 'our Admirals prefer the destruction of defenceless towns to the defence of our most valuable provinces,' while Admiral Howe was criticized for exclusively attending the operations of the army.[18] And too many of the engagements with the French, owing to deficiencies in the British system of signals, had been merely inconclusive artillery duels. To Suffren, however, it was as if a century of disasters had taught the French nothing, for with splendid ships and exemplary seamen they could still not win battles at sea. If only he were in command . . .

6. Straining at the Leash, 1780–1

'The Commander de Suffren has given . . . outstanding proof of zeal and activity in every mission he has been given,' d'Estaing told the king, 'and of courage and ability in battle. He is one of His Majesty's finest officers and if he cannot be promoted at once, he deserves some mark of His Majesty's satisfaction.'[1] That was a pension of 1500 *livres*; as there were 39 captains senior to him in the list, His Majesty could do no more. Despite a growing perception in the Ministry of the Marine that only the promotion of younger officers with recent service before the mast was likely to pluck France from over 50 years of inertia, uncertainty and defeat, seniority was too strong a tradition to be outraged by the promotion of an officer only 51 years old.[2] D'Estaing's retort was 'as short as my request is great. M de Suffren unites in himself all military and nautical talents. He is an excellent and resourceful tactician, full of audacity and lust for action.'[3] To make him *chef d'escadre* now would be an incentive to able officers. France could do with some younger men in command. D'Estaing did not remind the king that he was the same age as the man he was generously supporting.

But it was still as captain that Suffren fitted out the *Zélé*, 74, in Toulon, preparing with d'Albert de Rions in the *Marseillais* to join the Spanish fleet at Cadiz. It took him from 7 March to 19 May to find sailors, for they melted away at the word of a long cruise. Pay was still outstanding from the long campaign of 1778–9 and men were readier to abscond without it than sign up again. His musters were completed by Corsicans and Maltese, good sailors in their own avocations of trade and piracy, but mercenaries. Suffren, to whom a ship was another sinew, preferred men of his flesh and bone. 'I am armed passably well for a fight, badly for navigation and very badly for a long campaign. I have so few really good sailors that if I lose any of those I have I shall be in real difficulties.'[4]

A long campaign seemed to be on the cards and that must mean he would again miss the chance to command the Maltese fleet. Would the minister compensate him by sending d'Albert and him down the African west coast on a freebooting expedition to recapture Gorée off the Senegalese coast? But de Rohan did what he was asked this time, and Paul-Julien was allowed to command in his brother's name. Thus the greatest sailor of eighteenth-century France was excused from commanding in person Europe's smallest navy.[5] Instead Suffren and d'Albert went to look for Commodore George Johnstone, who for some months now had been conducting a ruinous *guerre de course* from Lisbon on all allied shipping between Ferrol and Cadiz. But when they joined the Spanish command on 17 June, Johnstone had eluded them. An encounter was reserved in the book of fate for a later date.

For now, just as Suffren had feared, the Spanish Grande Almirante, Luís de Córdoba, had no plan. Gibraltar was the limit of his vision and for a month they did nothing. Then, when more ships arrived from America, the combined squadron went out to intercept the British West Indian convoys. On 9 August, 200 miles west of Cape St Vincent, they sighted a huge outward-bound convoy of 64 storeships, troopships and merchantmen, escorted by the *Ramillies*, 64, and two frigates. The *Zélé* started to chase at once; the English warships, being copper-bottomed, fled securely into the Atlantic, hoping vainly to distract their pursuers from the convoy. Of the 61 ships taken, the *Zélé* alone took 16 and it was the single most stupendous loss at sea the British could remember. When, 20 days later, the prizes, with 3000 men aboard and cargoes worth £1.5 million, sailed into Cadiz harbour, the event was acclaimed with more excitement than a victory and caused a serious depression on the London stock market.

Suffren, however, could not forget the ease, almost impertinence, of the escape of the *Ramillies*. Had the *Zélé* also been copper-bottomed, there might have been a chase with a different ending and, tantalized by the memory, Suffren urged Sartine on 9 August to copper the whole fleet without delay. Sheathing a ship's hull in copper preserved the bottom planking longer against the accretion of weed and barnacles and delayed the ravages of the teredo worm, which had sunk more vessels than storms at sea. A copper-bottomed ship sailed more easily in light airs and was more quickly careened. Lord Anson had first coppered the frigate *Alarm* in 1761, and over the next 20 years every ship in the British navy was sheathed.

The French copper-bottomed their first frigate in 1778, but by 1779 they had covered only three more; the cost of sheathing was high—anything up to 60,000 *livres* for a second-rater. Suffren urged a public loan to be repaid from the prizes copper-bottomed ships would take. The king could rework the copper foundries of Provence, buy copper abroad, re-open the Auvergnat mines, even send frigates to Dutch yards for sheathing. Any and every expedient must be tried, for unless French ships were copper-bottomed the British could always avoid action when outnumbered and never be outstripped when chased.

His passionate advocacy was one more voice in a cause half won, but the work was never fast enough for Suffren, so that across the sea miles between India and France came, two and a half years later, another desperate plea in his sprawling, illegible hand, for 'de bons vaisseaux et FREGATES CUIVREES'.[6]

Back in Cadiz, Suffren came once again under the command of the Comte d'Estaing. And when on 3 October the squadron returned from America with de Grasse and La Motte Picquet, all the naval expertise of France was gathered in one port with 28 French and 20 Spanish men-of-war. To that unplanned concentration of virtuosity and power there was to be no sequel. Suffren and d'Albert cruised from Cape Spartel to Trafalgar to see a convoy through the straits unmolested and on 7 November the French squadron sailed for Brest in battle order. They were in port before the end of the year. Suffren was now 52, he had participated in 23 cruises, commanded seven ships and fought in five battles. His rewards had been a pension from the king, captaincy-general (*in absentia*) of the Maltese galleys and a second enthusiastic report from d'Estaing. As the minister was unwilling to take any more action on the second than he had on the first, it was barely enough to keep him in good humour.

Then, in October 1780, there was a change of minister. Sartine in launching nine new ships of the line had overspent his budget by 20 million francs and the director-general of finances, Jacques Necker, demanded his resignation. The former police chief resigned to a merry jingle: 'J'ai balayé Paris avec un soin extrême, et voulant sur les mers balayer les Anglais, j'ai vendu si cher mes balais que l'on m'a balayé moi-même.' ('I swept Paris so carefully, but in sweeping the seas clear of English ships, I sold my brushes so dear, I have been swept away myself.') His successor was a former soldier, the Marquis de Castries, and almost the first paper he was to see crossing his desk was a memorial circulated by the Commander de Suffren to the Conseils de Marine at Brest, Toulon and Rochefort. Castries was impressed by what it contained.

None of his suggestions was revolutionary, just the fruits of practical observation. Every ship should be fitted with fire-pumps and a lightning conductor, a device of Benjamin Franklin's, tried and tested on American privateers. Like the English, each ship should have six (not three) launches to improve mobility in calm weather or in battle. (A fourth pinnace was agreed.) The Conseils did not agree that the second officer should command a gun-deck in battle rather than be by his captain's side. Suffren thought the danger of both captain and second officer being carried away together was too great, but the Conseils were right, for when Suffren tried it during his first battle under his own command the captain of one of his ships was killed just after giving an order which was never carried out because his second was on a gun deck and did not know what it was. Suffren wanted to experiment with a small mortar firing grape. Like many sea officers he had found the carcase shell more dangerous to the men who fired it than to the enemy (being a hollow iron shell filled with combustibles that ignited on firing), and a mortar on the poop-deck could do terrible execution in reply to the disciplined concentration of fire from British musketeers on board their men-of-war. Brest, however, favoured a swivel gun firing stone but Rochefort agreed that ships' launches could be armed with small-calibre guns to attack enemy launches towing prizes or casualties out of the line. Suffren meanwhile mounted two mortars on the Zélé.[7]

Water-softening chalk, leather-tanning acorns, how to deal with Barbary corsairs, copper-sheathing, and now this. 'But a fighting man should be distinguished by his deeds not by his writings.'[8] Castries, who had also heard of the commander's voracious appetite, asked him to dinner on 8 February 1781. They talked about his prospects. With 39 senior officers all expecting and no doubt receiving similar dinners and similar assurances, Suffren did not think much would come of his chat. India had been mentioned, but India was a long way away, and in the next 18 months he ought to be in Malta looking after his future there. He had missed too many opportunities in the island already to chase ever-vanishing trophies of war once more across the oceans of the world.

He returned to Brest in poor spirits, for two new *chefs d'escadre* had been appointed—'one a poor sort of fellow,' he told Mme de Seillans on 26 February, 'and the other has only held post command twice and then only to commit such acts of folly that he has had to be kicked upstairs . . . I would never ask for promotion at this price, but it is a strange irony that you can be promoted more easily if you are good for nothing.'⁹ How many times has that been said! All he wanted now was a good peace.

But peace was as elusive as ever; indeed, France had just acquired a new ally and a crisis. The British declaration of war on the United Provinces of the Netherlands had suddenly put the Cape at risk, hitherto a safe neutral staging port for Île de France (Mauritius) and India. Its loss would instantly sever France's lifeline to her outposts in the east. Castries had therefore a reason for mentioning India. French intelligence has reported as early as November 1780 that a British squadron was being fitted out for the Indies at Portsmouth. On 4 March 1781, Suffren was offered command of four ships and a force of troops to go first to strengthen the Dutch garrison at the Cape and then to join the squadron at Mauritius. As soon as he reached the Cape, he would enjoy the rank of *chef d'escadre*, thus leap-frogging most of those 39 captains above him in the lists. After 18 months he could return to pursue his interests in Malta. If he did not like the proposal, he could keep his present rank and sail with de Grasse for America.

'I am going to India,' he told his cousin on 18 March, 'in command of a division of five ships. M de Castries has given it to me with the best grace in the world.' There was only one small snag. By the same order the minister had also elevated Thomas d'Orves, commanding in Île de France, to the same rank. The Comte d'Orves was the senior officer, so Suffren would not be in command of the Indian Ocean squadron. But it was rumoured that d'Orves was a sick man. 'Between us we shall have 11 ships, and one small but happy chance could put me at the head of a fine squadron . . . I do not doubt that there will be a prize or two, so I could become rich.'[10]

The crew of the *Zélé* had already insisted on following him to his new ship before they knew where she was to sail, and on 2 February Ruyter-Werfusé went on board the 74-gun *Héros*, to the cheers of jubilant sailors, to take possession of her in the name of the Commander de Suffren. To her new crew, for the most part Provençals, their new destination might be America, India or the moon, but they would follow Suffren wherever he led them. On 18 March they knew it was to be India. There, so the story went, the whole continent was at war with the traditional enemy. Everyone would have a chance to shake the legendary pagoda tree and, like their commander, become rich.

PART II

Passage to India

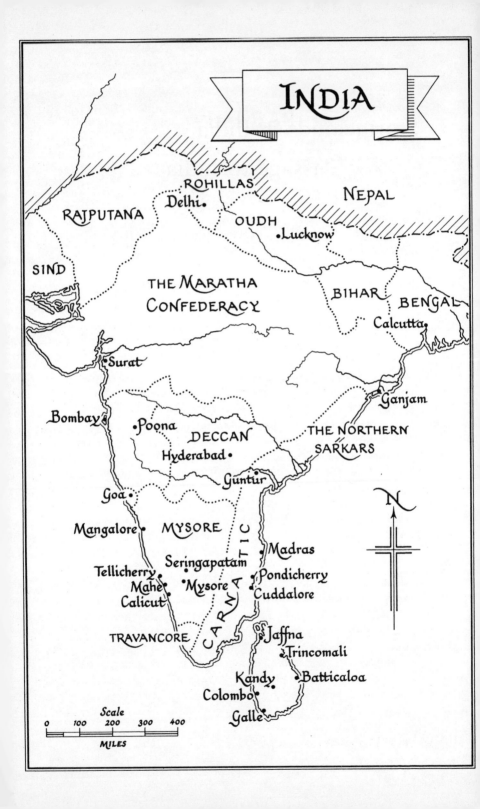

7. Stormclouds in India

Though the British had now maintained a presence in India for over a century, it was as a trading company, the basis of whose power was in the three presidencies of Fort William in Calcutta, Fort St George in Madras and Bombay. By treaties and conquest each presidency had built defences against the competing ambitions of Indian country powers who disputed control of parts of the sub-continent with one another under the shadowy suzerainty of the Grand Mughal in Delhi. John Company never felt entirely safe while the threat of French competition remained and this spectre returned at the outbreak of war in Europe in 1778. When, the following year, Company troops were smartly chastised at Wadgaon for interfering in the succession to the Peshwa of Poona, the mighty office of king-maker and uncrowned leader of the Maratha confederacy, that spectre took physical shape in the corridors of Versailles. There the ageing Marquis de Bussy could be heard talking of a triumphant return to the fields he had contested with Clive nearly 30 years earlier. In the event, the breeze with Poona blew itself out. Instead, the presidency of Fort St George blundered into war with the most dangerous potentate in India.

As soon as Warren Hastings learned of the declaration of war on France, he authorized Company troops to reduce the remaining French outposts in India. Chandernagore in Bengal fell without a shot; Pondicherry surrendered after a scrappy engagement at sea sent the French ships scuttling back to Île de France. Mahé on the west coast was occupied on 19 March 1779. But Mahé was not sovereign territory; it lay in the territory and under the protection of the ruler of Mysore, and he was deeply offended at this trespass. Haidar Ali had already in 1776 crossed swords with the presidency of Madras, and the select committee of Fort St George should have known that he was an opponent it was unwise to rouse.

Haidar Ali's career was a classic instance of the development of personal power. A Panjabi Muslim and son of a soldier of fortune, he had by methods very reminiscent of an Italian Renascence *condottiere* engrossed all the power of the Hindu Raj of Mysore into his alien hands. From a complaisant Grand Mughal in Delhi he wrung the title of nawab but, though he is known as the Nawab of Mysore, he was actually Nawab of Sera. By the skilful use of an army which had been tested against the European-led sepoys of Clive and Bussy and which was now armed with flintlocks and officered by deserters from Dupleix's sepoy regiments, and by a combination of calculated ferocity and cold intellectual treachery, he had built up the Raj of Mysore from a dependency of the Marathas to the foremost country power of South India. 'Revenge was profitable, gratitude expensive', and by assigning his objectives their true priority and by a policy of brilliant opportunism, Haidar Ali was now the most fearsome prince in India.[1]

His ambition was to create for himself and his descendants a kingdom covering the southern cone of the peninsula from the Arabian Sea to the Bay of Bengal. To the north he was confronted by the jealous hostility of the Maratha princes and the powerful Nizam of Hyderabad, both powers he was not yet strong enough to offend. But if he could engross the Raj of Tanjore, the rice granary of the south, and the Nawabi of the Carnatic which would give him title to royal estate, he would be the overlord of all south India and rival the medieval splendours of the kingdom of Vijayanagar. But the Raja of Tanjore was a client of the British and the Nawabi of the Carnatic in pawn to the money-lenders of Madras. As those money-lenders had at different times constituted the select committee of Fort St George, the presidency was so darkly and inextricably enmeshed in the monumental indebtedness of the nawab, Muhammed Ali Walajah, that it could not lightly contemplate a change of ruler. Haidar knew that the protestations of friendship from Madras meant nothing while Muhammed Ali was in hock to the English merchants there and that he would never be allowed to rule in Arcot unless he conquered it in war.

So when the Company soldiers insolently violated his territory to seize Mahé, this was what he determined to do.

Throughout the summer of 1780 he amassed an army in the intractable region of the Eastern Ghats, waiting for the auspicious moment to strike. It came on 23 July 1781. A few days before Suffren had sailed for Cadiz with d'Estaing, an army estimated at 86–100,000 men poured into the Carnatic. Its onrush was irresistible. Arcot, the scene of Clive's first great triumph, was soon invested and Mysorean cavalry sacked the temple city of Kanchipuram, only 46 miles from Madras. On 10 August Haidar's cavalry made a flying raid on the environs of the Mount itself. A month later, disaster struck. Colonel William Baillie, marching south to reinforce Fort St George, was trapped at Perambakan and overwhelmed. His defeat was greater than its scale suggested. The Company's allies, particularly the Nizam of Hyderabad, suddenly became deaf to appeals for help, while the French envoy to the court at Poona moved south to Hyderabad and began to advocate an alliance with the irresistible Nawab of Sera.

In Île de France the new governor, the Vicomte de Souillac, was hesitantly thinking about intervention. His squadron commander was Thomas d'Orves, just promoted to *chef d'escadre* along with Suffren, a year senior and so to be Suffren's chief. He, too, had fought as a *garde-marine* at Toulon with Suffren, and now commanded a pretty little squadron composed of his own 74-gun *Orient*, two 64s, *Sévère* and *Brillant*, the 50-gun *Flamand* and the 40-gun *Pourvoyeuse*. Unfortunately, the *Sévère* on her way to Île de France had passed off Madeira a squadron of six British ships bound for India, and the habitual fear of being caught outnumbered kept d'Orves willingly on the leash. Though in the course of 1780 he was reinforced by two more 64s, *Bizarre* and *Ajax*, bringing a detachment of the newly formed Régiment d'Austrasie under Maréchal des Camps Duchemin de Chenneville, to strengthen the defences of Port Louis, Souillac did not feel he could risk a challenge to the English. Now in Haidar's camp, the French agent to Poona, Piveron de Morlat, pestered him for action, proposing a treaty of alliance between France and Mysore, until the governor felt he could prevaricate no longer. He resolved on cautious action. D'Orves was to sail for the Bay of Bengal to reach the Coromandel coast when the north-east monsoon had blown itself out and the English squadron should still be wintering on the far side of India in Bombay—for there was no anchorage on the eastern coast except neutral Dutch Trincomali in which to shelter against the giant rollers and furious winds that struck the coast on or about 15 October and only blew themselves out by the end of January.

Once there, d'Orves was to establish contact with Haidar Ali. But at all costs he was to avoid an encounter with the English squadron, for if his ships were severely cut about there was nothing in Port Louis with which to repair them, and Souillac's first priority was to defend Île de France. Accordingly, d'Orves sailed on 14 October with several battalions of troops on board. But in the meantime the situation in India had changed dramatically. On 25 September the governor-general in council had decided that, in view of the distress of its sister presidency, Fort William in Bengal should send down by sea 15 *lakh*s of rupees and, more valuable than gold, its own commander-in-chief, the indomitable Irish general, Sir Eyre Coote.

Sir Eyre, like his compatriot, the Duke of Wellington, was one of those rare generals never to lose a battle. Negligent in dress, bizarre in manner, foul of tongue, a legend of greed, with his long nose and angular chin, close-cropped hair and stilt-like legs, he strode across the Indian scene like a warlock in uniform, distilling the elixir of victory from the ingredients of want, recrimination and despair. Often ill, always crankily sour, he possessed the meticulous genius of military organization and Napoleonic powers of endurance. Coote Bahadur was an old India hand. *Primus in India* with the 39th Regiment of Foot in 1735, he had served under Clive, defeated Lally at Wandewash, captured Bussy at Madras, reduced Pondicherry and become a colonel. On return to Britain he sat as MP for Poole from 1764 until 1770, when, still in pursuit of the fortune he feared would elude him, he returned to India. Warren Hastings, pandering to the general's obsessive fear of poverty, gave him a field command with allowances which added £18,000 to his annual salary of £1600, and sent him to Madras with the personal assurance that if he were in charge of the government of Fort St George he would give him unburdened liberty of action.

Liberty of action he took at once, unseating Governor Whitehill, suspected of having shares in a French privateer, and from his compliant successor he took full powers to subordinate all civil matters to his military needs. Fort St George was in no condition to stand a siege and the walls of Arcot had crumbled to surrender before the accuracy of French master-gunners. Haidar, he wrote to

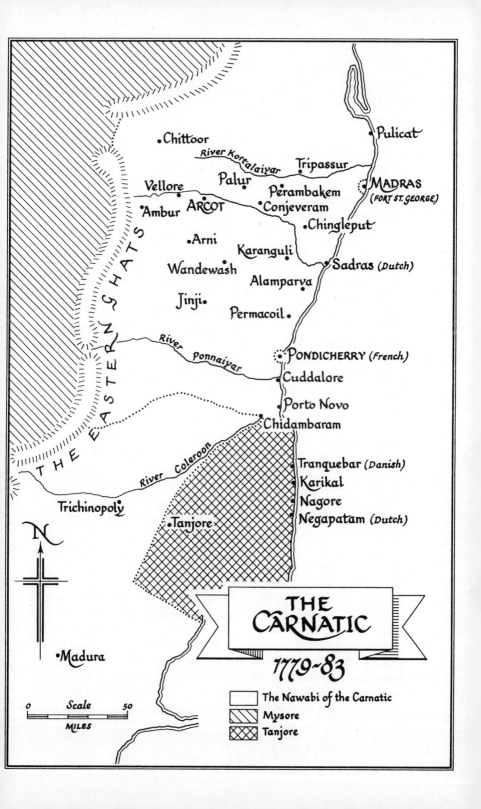

THE
CARNATIC
1779~83

The Nawabi of the Carnatic
Mysore
Tanjore

Hastings on 10 November 1779, 'has taken every measure which would occur to the most experienced general to distress us and render himself formidable ... His conduct in his civil capacity has been supported by a degree of political address unparalleled by any power that has yet appeared in Hindustan.'[2]

The fields round Madras had been turned into quagmires by incessant rain; tents, guns, rice and draught bullocks were nowhere to be had in the quantities he needed—for a bullock and its attendants consumed four-fifths of the load it carried, and to drive Haidar from the Carnatic he reckoned he needed 500 bullock-loads of rice a day for six weeks![3] He was never to have it. But he had one weapon that gave much comfort to the ladies of the presidency. 'His very name will strike those undisciplined hordes with terror!'[4] Armed largely with this, Coote marched out of Madras. Haidar was soon to recognize that the general had lost none of his old skill. On 24 January he relieved Wandewash. The nawab, however, merely gave way before him and, short as he was of food and transport, Coote could do little more than lurch after him. 'Our enemies have it in their power,' he wrote despondently to Hastings on 1 March 1781, 'to protract this war to a length of time we ought not to dare to look forward to, deficient as we must confess ourselves in those essential funds necessary to prosecute it.'[5]

On 27 January a more sinister shadow still fell across his spirits as d'Orves's squadron was sighted off the coast. Coote wasted no time. He marched at once for Pondicherry and destroyed all the *masula* boats or catamarans that could have brought troops ashore. But Haidar was in hot pursuit, so Coote marched south to draw him away from Madras. At Cuddalore he found only enough rice for three days when Haidar threw his army across his only escape route and six French ships of the line sailed out of the crystalline sky. He was cornered. A blockade of two, at most, three weeks would be enough to starve him into submission, but if Thomas d'Orves contrived to get some of his men ashore the end might be sooner.

But at this critical moment the French commodore lost his nerve. His supplies were running low and at any moment the Bombay squadron might appear off the coast. His orders were very strict and Haidar's invitation to him to stay off the coast could not be accommodated to them. To the nawab's cruel astonishment he declined. Haidar rejected the offer of French troops contemptuously for it was d'Orves's ships he wanted. 'As you have no authority to land troops we cannot accept them. We advise you to go back as quickly as possible to Île de France and return with 25 ships to capture all the English vessels at sea and with 6000 troops to fight on land.'[6] When the French sails disappeared over the horizon on 15 February, it was the third time that century that a French squadron had left the coast at a moment of crisis. In 1759 d'Aché had deserted Lally and the south was lost to Clive. Then only two years earlier, in 1780, Tronjoly had deserted Governor Bellecombe in Pondicherry. In both cases fear of an unequal encounter with the British squadron which might threaten their base at Île de France was a more important consideration, then as now, than the chance of an irresistible coup against the common enemy on land.

Coote had made a desperate attempt to break Haidar's ring of steel on 10 February. When d'Orves sailed he could write jubilantly to Warren Hastings: 'I need not take up your time with commenting on the conduct of the French admiral or describing the injuries we must have received if he had acted with common spirit. I may with safety advance that we are entirely indebted to his irresolute behaviour for the little security we now enjoy on this coast. He drew Hyder from Arcot with strong assurances of support and when he came near failed him in the performance.'[7] Souillac, forgetting that it was his order in the first place that had dictated the withdrawal, was bitterly reproachful. 'By the extraordinary obstinacy of M d'Orves ... we have lost the only chance we are ever likely to have of becoming masters of the Coromandel coast.'[8] The officers of the Austrasian regiment felt that he had dishonoured them. He had let the side down badly and ought to be replaced.[9]

Back in Île de France d'Orves learned instead from the corvette *Sylphide*, hot from Brest, that he had been promoted. The *Sylphide* also reported that he was to be reinforced by Suffren with five ships. Between them they would not have the 25 that Haidar had asked for, but with 11 they would be superior to the British squadron. But until Suffren arrived he was helpless. His cruise had exhausted all the supplies in Port Louis, his cordage was so frayed that his masts could scarcely bear sail and the first cases of black famine had been reported in the island of Bourbon. The *Sylphide* had also reported that an English squadron was bound for the Cape and India.

8. Porto Praya, 16 April 1781

The navy minister himself was in Brest when French intelligence reported that a tight little squadron of five ships of the line and four frigates commanded by Commodore George Johnstone and escorting 3000 troops was bound for the East Indies and for an almost certain assault on the Cape. Though it was said in London that his destination was Gibraltar and a *guerre de course* in Spanish waters, Castries was not going to take any risks. He added another 64, the *Artésien*, to Suffren's squadron and urged his instant departure. If Johnstone were sailing to join the British East Indies squadron it would then number ten ships. When Suffren reached Île de France, d'Orves would still, just, command a larger squadron than the English.

In fact Johnstone was never destined for the Indies. His first task was to capture the Cape, but then he was to detach only three of his ships for India and himself go to St Helena to escort the Atlantic trade. French intelligence had picked up deliberately false information intended to keep the Dutch East India squadron idle in Batavia waiting for an attack that never came. But it had the effect of galvanizing the French into action which was to upset the best-laid plans of the Lords of the Admiralty.[1]

Despite the shortage of copper sheathing, four of Suffren's ships were copper-bottomed: the *Héros*, 74 guns, pronounced unfit for war by her captain in 1780 on her first voyage, the *Sphinx*, 64, built in the 1750s, the *Artésien*, also 64, and the *Annibal*, 74, a splendid vessel which had carried La Motte Picquet to Grenada, sheathed only with difficulty as she nearly capsized in the process.

His fifth ship, the *Vengeur*, sister ship to the *Sphinx*, built during the Seven Years War for the Compagnie des Indes and pressed back into royal service, was not copper-bottomed. She had to be given a second hull of wood to slow down the inevitable corruption of her timbers on a long voyage and this took twice as long as expected because of the shortage of pitch and nails. The royal dockyards had never had to prepare so many flotillas for sea and their resources were strained at every point.[2]

Suffren's captains were a fellow Knight of Malta, the Chevalier de Cardaillac, a veteran with one arm like Nelson, commanding the *Artésien*. One of his cousins, *capitaine de vaisseau* Forbin, commanded the *Vengeur*. A former officer of the Compagnie des Indes, Trémigon, sailed the *Annibal*, and would have taken the squadron east had Suffren elected to sail west with de Grasse. The captain of the *Sphinx* was the only one of this band who was eventually to return to France in the same ship—a companion of the campaign to the Americas, du Chilleau, who had escorted Governor Macartney to France as a prisoner of war after the capture of Grenada. Of the rest, two were to die and one was to be cashiered.

Castries had obliged Suffren in everything but two things. He had declined to let d'Albert de Rions sail with his old friend, thus depriving him of a second in command he could trust, and as his 'eyes and ears' he allowed him only a 16-gun corvette, *Fortune*, which sailed more slowly than most of his men of war. The effects were not long in showing, but Suffren's expedition was a side-show for which the minister had already been generous enough. The great victories were expected across the Atlantic. By an extraordinary blunder the British Admiralty had directed a much larger force than de Grasse's to watch the Irish coast, so that de Grasse and Suffren could both lead their squadrons out of Brest undisturbed. In America the British had signally failed to cow the American armies in Virginia and it was to support them that de Grasse was bent. That move was to pay off, for as Cornwallis established his base in Virginia at Yorktown, he found himself unexpectedly invested by Washington and Lafayette on land and by de Grasse at sea. In October 1781, the British resistance crumbled; their temporary loss of sea control had sealed the fate of the British in what was to become the United States. Though Admiral Rodney was to recover that control and defeat

de Grasse at the Saints on 12 April 1782, a few hours by the sun
after Suffren had fought his second battle in the Bay of Bengal, the
main object of the war, the independence of the United States, had
been virtually achieved.

Furthermore all Suffren's ships were seriously overloaded, for
he was first to recapture and garrison the slaving station of Gorée,
off Senegal, then to leave troop reinforcements in both the Cape
and Île de France. His decks were thus crowded with 600 men
of the Régiment d'Austrasie, a company of the artillery from the
Régiment de Metz and 500 men of the Régiment de Pondichéry.
All were new recruits and for the whole winter they had kicked
their heels in port. Very few of them, moreover, had ever been
to sea and it was not long before they were incapacitated by
sea-sickness and scurvy.

On 15 March La Fine frigate left Brest with the latest orders for
Souillac and d'Orves. They were to take no independent action until
they learned that Suffren had arrived at and reinforced the Dutch
garrison at the Cape. Then on the 19th Dutch intelligence described
Commodore Johnstone's squadron with surprising accuracy. His
broad pennant flew from the Romney, 50, and with him sailed
the Hero, 74, under Captain Hawker, the Monmouth, 64, under
Captain Alms, the Jupiter, 50, under Captain Pasley and the Isis,
50, under Captain Sutton. There were also three frigates, Diana,
Active and Jason, two sloops, two cutters and seven transports
armed en flûte (that is, with guns on board but not mounted,
in order to make way for troops). The Dutch did not know
about the fire-ship and bomb-ketch, the 14 armed East Indiamen,
and 12 other victualling ships and transports. In fact Johnstone
commanded 47 sail and 446 guns, 124 of them on the armed
transports and 40 of them 18-pounder carronades, a new weapon
capable of doing great damage. It was a more formidable squadron
than the French suspected.

The unknown factor was George Johnstone himself. He liked
still to be known as Governor Johnstone from his brief tenure
of office at Pensacola in west Florida in 1763, and in truth he
was still more a politician than a sailor. His naval career had
been undistinguished. In 1748 he had steered a fire-ship away
from the squadron off Guadaloupe and his courage and skill on
that occasion were to save him nine years later when he was
court-martialled for insubordination and disobedience. Political

influence had made him governor of Pensacola. It also enabled him to sit in the House of Commons, where he styled himself the ministerialist expert on naval affairs and was quick to quarrel with anyone who contradicted him. In 1780 Suffren had sought him off the coasts of Portugal, where he led a *guerre de course* from a splendid town house on the Tagus in the intervals of wooing a noted Anglo-Portuguese beauty and enjoyed diplomatic status while he pursued and confused a secret peace approach to the court of Spain. His gubernatorial and diplomatic skills might be contemptible and he had never actually commanded a ship at sea before but if Johnstone were as aggressive at sea as on the floor of the House of Commons Suffren must look to his laurels.

Johnstone had hoped to lead a buccaneering expedition against Buenos Aires with two fellow Scots adventurers who had raised two regiments at their own expense to plunder the Spanish possessions in the South Atlantic, so that when his destination was changed to the Cape he was in a right ill-humour. He sailed from Spithead on 13 March, telling everyone that this latest change in his orders had cost him £100,000![3] On 16 March he was sighted off the Lizard. When on 22 March Suffren followed de Grasse's America-bound squadron out of Brest, Johnstone was almost at the Azores.

Suffren, now spared any diversion to retake Gorée, did what he could to reduce that five days' lead, but the faults of improvisation and haste began to take their toll. Two of his transports were lamed in a collision. Then the *Artésien*, provisioned for the short journey across the Atlantic, ran short of water and because progress was so slow there was not enough among the other ships to spare. The troops on board were decimated by sickness and it was clear that he must soon stop for water and repairs. The *Serapis* privateer was sent to the Cape to warn the Dutch that he would have to stop at the Cape Verde Islands. On 10 April he was 20 leagues from Hierro in the Canaries, still 1000 miles from his proposed port of call, and learned from two Portuguese fishermen that the British were still ahead.

That same day Johnstone reached the Cape Verde archipelago, entering Porto Praya on the largest island, São Tiago. This wind-swept island off the extreme western tip of Africa was neutral Portuguese territory, a poor haven of subsistence fishermen; not sure how much water might be available, he sent the *Monmouth* and *Isis* to the neighbouring island of Maio with two Indiamen and ten transports. Two of his ships had been detached for a cruise and would join him the next day and one of his frigates had departed for the West Indies. Before he really knew what was happening, the *Romney* had been hemmed into the bay by Indiamen, and even Johnstone began to think he had made a mistake. The *Serapis* had also called in at São Tiago and he now learned that Suffren was not far behind him, and also intended to call at Porto Praya for water. He summoned the ships from Maio, but when they came in on the 15th he allowed them to anchor where they liked.

Furthest into the bay were the victuallers and transports, with the *Romney* and the frigate *Jason* on the port side and the *Hero* behind the centre. The *Jupiter* and the frigate *Active* were to starboard, but the transports from Maio were outside them with the *Monmouth* on their port side. Three Indiamen lay beyond the *Monmouth* and somewhere, about a mile towards the easternmost point of the bay by which the French were bound to enter, was the *Isis* and beyond her still, near the Ponta Bicuda, the *Diana* frigate, the fire-ship and bomb-ketch. Anchored in this way they could neither protect themselves nor defend the convoy. Most surprisingly of all, he allowed 1500 men to go ashore with their officers to take 'the recreation of the shore'.[4]

Johnstone and his officers spent the early hours of Easter Monday, 16 April, dancing on the deck of one of the Indiamen and they were expecting another gala evening the following night. In the interim the commodore, thinking he ought to do something about the order of his ships, shortly after breakfast had himself lowered into a launch and at 09.30 was directing one of the storeships to move away from an East Indiamen to which it had drifted too close. At that moment the *Isis* signalled sails to the north-west and repeated the signal ten times.

From 9 to 16 April Suffren had made slower progress than ever. The *Sphinx* had to tow one of his damaged ships, while the lumbering of the other grew heavier every day. Off São Tiago the *Artésien*, being desperately short of water, asked to be allowed to reconnoitre Porto Praya. Suffren decided to sail straight in. He never expected to find Johnstone there for, if the English wanted an anchorage, they would surely choose St Helena. Anyhow, he had been towing a ship for four days so the English must be leagues ahead of him. So Cardaillac sailed blithely on, keeping close inshore, until he reached the Ponta Bicuda at 08.30 and

sighted the masts of the *Diana* and her companion ships. He
tacked at once and signalled four unidentified vessels ahead. A
few minutes later the look-out in the *Héros* saw them too, and
as Cardaillac edged out to sea he was able to see the English flag.
His second signal followed at 08.57, acknowledged by Suffren a
minute later. At 09.00 Suffren ordered the squadron to prepare
for battle.

Two minutes is barely time to consider the niceties of international
law but, like Boscawen at Lagos Bay, Suffren did not think reflection
necessary. He knew he had caught up with Johnstone's squadron
and there was no d'Estaing to hold him back as there had been
at the Grand Cul de Sac. And Johnstone had not, like Samuel
Barrington on that occasion, locked his ships into a dangerous line;
they were all over the place, given into his hand. At one stroke he
could destroy the squadron, save the Cape and preserve d'Orves's
superiority in India. His flag officer was so surprised that he hoisted
the wrong order of battle and had to change it at once. The *Héros*
took the lead and Cardaillac was ordered into third place. The
Sphinx, casting off her tow, and the *Vengeur*, both lying to the
rear, were ordered to make up the distance at all speed.

Johnstone knew that he was in mortal danger when the *Héros*
rounded the point at 09.30. The *Artésien* had not been seen and
surprise was complete. In the hazy heat of the tropical morning, all
his five men-of-war, his three frigates and endless transports and
Indiamen lay gently in the bay, sails furled and fishing lines out.
Suffren was intent on squeezing every advantage he could from the
shock and did not wait for the *Sphinx* and *Vengeur* to catch up. He
was determined to attack as soon as he could get into range and
hoped the ships following him would imitate their leader. It was
a rash hope, for this was the era of d'Estaing not of Nelson. The
gallant grey-head Trémigon, commanding the *Annibal* next astern,
could not believe that Suffren contemplated more than a foray.
This was a neutral port so he must be intending to spread fire
and confusion and then sail out again. To attack without forming
line, moreover, was contrary to the 1765 *Ordonnances*. So when
the *Annibal* rounded the point, her guns were still run back and
the sick, livestock and water-butts were still on deck.

Suffren ignored the cluster of minor ships round the *Diana*
and reserved his fire as the *Héros* sailed down the thick forest
edge of the convoy's masts for the heart of the mêlée. He saluted

The Battle of Porto Praya

16 April 1781

Shallow water 10 fathoms

Vengeur

Sphinx

Artésien

Annibal

Héros

Frigates

Vengeur

Nonmouth

Jason

Johnstone's Convoy

Romney

Isis

Héros

Sphinx

Annibal

Hero

Fortitude

Hinchinbrooke

Artésien

SANTA MARIA ISLAND

the *Isis* with a couple of shots from the larboard bow to call attention to his colours and sailed on the *Monmouth* in a hail of bullets from the troops still on the decks of the transports. He wanted to drop anchor alongside but his sails were still flying about in great confusion so that the spring on his cable did not hold when the ship was checked to bring up and, after colliding with a transport, he drove abreast of his flagship's namesake, the *Hero*. The *Annibal* followed only a few minutes behind, but in the terrible anger of the guns from the men of war and Indiamen alike she came on in a strange and ominous silence, for her men were still frantically clearing the gun-decks and running out the guns. The ancient veteran of the Indian seas on her quarter-deck, despite his disastrous miscalculation, remained imperturbable, and in the middle of the blazing inferno that surrounded the *Héros*, Trémigon executed a manoeuvre of such cool brilliance that even the sailors of the *Hero* and *Monmouth* had to cheer.

The *Héros* had drifted a little to leeward after her collision, and Trémigon steered the *Annibal* through the narrow gap that now appeared between her and the *Hero* and dropped anchor just ahead. Suffren paid out to prevent the two ships from fouling and now, bowsprit to poop, the *Héros* and *Annibal* shared the rage of the battle. But another 15 minutes were to pass before Trémigon could bring his batteries into action, and the silent ship was forced to endure the passionate violence of two armed merchantmen, two Company ships and the *Jupiter*, all on the starboard bow, and of the *Monmouth* astern. The *Isis* on the starboard quarter, the *Hero* to port and the *Fortitude* East Indiaman on the port quarter concentrated on the *Héros*, and men of the 42nd, 78th, 98th and 100th Regiments of Foot poured their shot on to the decks of both ships. Suffren calmly put on his brother's episcopal hat and ordered his gunners to redouble their fire. He had waited many years for this moment.

As soon as he had seen the *Isis*'s signal, Johnstone rowed back to his ship to give the alarm. But the masts of his transports formed such a thick palisade round the *Romney* that he could not see what was going on, so he set off again for the *Isis*. There he could see that the intruders were French and bent on mischief. As he returned to the *Romney*, he shouted up to the officers on the decks of the ships he passed to prepare for battle, but some of them had taken so little notice of his signals that they peered down at him and asked what he was shouting about. Fortunately for the British, Suffren had decided to take the point wide so that he could get a good view of the enemy, and that gave them time to see that his reception was hot. Johnstone, who was not afraid of a scrap, then shifted to the *Hero*, accompanied by General Medows who had pined to see a battle at sea since he had watched d'Estaing falter at the Grand Cul de Sac. Captain Hawker received them in the middle of the cannonade 'with as cheerful and affable civility as if we had come to dinner'.[5]

Suffren's other captains, Cardaillac in the *Artésien*, du Chilleau in the *Sphinx* and his cousin, Forbin, commanding the *Vengeur*, were taken as completely by surprise as Trémigon but lacked his experience and skill. Cardaillac did try to bring the *Artésien* up to take the *Hero* on both sides, but when a large ship loomed up on him from the artificial gloom he thought he was aboard the *Isis*. She was in fact the Indiaman *Fortitude*, fully as big as a man-of-war but lightly armed. Intending to board her by entangling her bowsprit in his fore-rigging and locking her in a fatal embrace, Cardaillac miscalculated the distance and succeeded only in bringing the *Fortitude*'s bowsprit into his backstays, so that both ships began to swing to leeward away from the *Hero*.

Afraid that his stays would snap, he ordered the bower anchor to be lowered so that he could tack and deal with her at his leisure but, before the order was carried out a stray ball struck him in the head, killing him outright. His second was where Suffren had said he wanted the second officer to be, commanding a gun-battery, and by the time he had reached the quarter-deck it was too late. The *Artésien*'s stays snapped and the *Fortitude* shook herself free. Without knowing what was happening and understanding that his dead captain had intended to board a ship, any ship, the poor lieutenant grappled with the *Hinchinbrooke* Indiaman in the mistaken impression that she was a frigate, and after a short tussle mastered her long enough to steal the British signals code. He ordered the *Artésien*'s cable to be cut, and the two ships in close embrace drifted out of the battle by 10.30.

Cardaillac had at least acted with the right intentions and his sudden death was one of those hazards that can always confound them. Forbin and du Chilleau missed their opportunities altogether. The *Sphinx* did have some excuse for being late into the fray as she had had to cast off her tow, but the *Vengeur* rounded the point only at 11.00, just as the *Héros* began her duel with the *Monmouth* and *Hero*. Forbin sailed straight for the little group round the *Diana* frigate and opened up on the fireship and bomb-ketch, both of only 8 guns. The 64-gun battleship then cannonaded the *Diana* but so briefly as to do her little damage. He then put his ship through her paces, so carefully described in the *Ordonnances*, bombarding the helpless transports as he passed and, to everyone's astonishment, completed a tour of the bay, floating before the wind and so out of the action, having contributed nothing beyond a series of lively but fruitless broadsides to the struggle of attrition raging between the *Héros* and *Annibal* and the *Jupiter, Monmouth* and *Hero* in the centre.

Forbin said afterwards that he had given the order to anchor as he passed astern of the *Héros*, but the noise had been so deafening that no one heard him. As he drifted on he came to the absurd conclusion that the water was too deep for his anchor cable, despite the visible evidence of stationary ships all round him, so he decided to luff and try again. This instruction, if it were ever given, was as inaudible as the first, and his ship just drifted on. Forbin may have been a blood relation of Suffren's but he had shown singular incapacity in fighting his ship and that to his cousin was unforgivable.

Du Chilleau was a gallant and enterprising officer but he, too, muffed his chances. The *Sphinx* was round the point at 11.15 but unaccountably did not anchor to leeward of the *Isis*, thus failing to relieve Suffren of her tiresome fire. Du Chilleau, too, was affected by a sudden mental delinquency about deep water and made no attempt to drop anchor anywhere, saying afterwards that he had failed to do so because of a sudden shift of wind. Instead, he ran among the merchant vessels, firing haphazardly at all and attempting to board one or two as he passed, raking the *Isis* once; then, firing rapidly at everyone he passed, he carried on round the bay until at noon he too was out of the battle.

From shortly after 11.00 hours until noon, the *Héros* and the *Annibal* bore the brunt of a combat now hopelessly uneven, and it was a savage experience for both captains and crew. At noon Suffren decided to end it. The sails and rigging of the *Héros* were torn, scorched or cut clean away, the masts so riddled with shot that they shook perilously and his halyards so cut about that he could not make a signal for the *Annibal*. His only course was to disengage and hope that Trémigon—whom he supposed to be still in command—would follow. As the great ship limped out of the action his men were able to repair enough rope to make a signal to the squadron to man their prizes and prepare to resume action, while Suffren was relieved to see his companion turn and follow. He had hoped to drive a large part of Johnstone's convoy before him but, as nearly all his stays and shrouds had been badly cut about and his masts were unsteady, he could only seek the safety of the open sea. The *Héros* had lost 32 dead and 55 wounded.

The agony of the *Annibal* had been fearful from the moment she slipped into place ahead of her leader. When at last she opened fire, she had many casualties to avenge. After half an hour Trémigon was mortally wounded. A cannon ball took off his leg and Morard de Galles was called up to take his place on the quarter-deck. The murderous cannonade continued while de Galles, himself wounded more than once by splinters, stood prominently on the deck, urging on the gunners and tempting death and destruction in the lurid midday darkness. At one time a raking volley carried off everyone on the deck except the young lieutenant and the ship's master. Another severed the halyards of his flag and carried it into the sea. The crew of the *Monmouth* thought he had struck and they cheered, but Morard, coolly calling for a napkin from the wardroom, climbed on to the poop-deck and nailed it to the mast. Then as he saw the *Héros* pull her head round, he cut his cable and, still firing both broadsides, began to follow her out of the inferno. His mizzenmast, however, was almost severed at the lower cap and, as he hoisted what shreds of sail he could, the strain was too great and it collapsed. Just as he was safely out of range, the mainmast toppled over with a resounding crash and had to be cut away into the sea. Shortly after, the foremast followed. By the time the *Sphinx* had slipped her a tow-rope, the *Annibal* had been reduced to a hulk, with 80 dead and 90 wounded aboard and her captain fighting for his life below.

As soon as the *Héros* disengaged, Johnstone slipped back to the *Romney* and called a council of war on the quarter-deck. 'Shall we,' he asked, 'cut and follow our blow by giving them battle again before they recover from their drubbing?' Captain Pasley of the *Jupiter* was all set to go but 'numerous difficulties were started against this gallant resolution'.[6] Johnstone declared that he then cut the council short 'and directed the men of war to cut and slip as fast as they could get to sea and follow up the victory'.[7] The words breathe a commendable sense of vigour and urgency, but in fact the battle had ended at noon and it was not before 14.40 that the commodore cut the *Romney*'s cable. At 15.00 Suffren thought the British were manoeuvring to form a line, but nowhere in his report to the Admiralty did Johnstone mention that two hours passed before he began to chase the French out of Porto Praya. Captain Pasley said that Captains Alms and Sutton, commanding the *Monmouth* and *Isis*, were against following the French and as they were both intrepid officers they would not lightly have advised against renewed action. The *Isis* had been savagely mauled, and perhaps Alms did not share Pasley's confidence in their commodore. Alms knew that they had to get first to the Cape and then he had to go on to India, and a scrappy action at sea could put both at risk. Johnstone put the best face on it. 'The action bordered upon a surprise and the service in which we were engaged rendered us liable to much confusion; yet upon the whole until the enemy were beat off I saw nothing on our part but steady, cool and determined valour. As soon as the *Jason* was out of the way the *Romney* was cast by a spring on her cable and went to sea under the acclamations of the whole fleet.'[8]

9. Race to the Cape

Despite all the huffing and puffing, Johnstone did not seriously intend to chase. He was clear of Porto Praya by 15.00 hours as Suffren was sailing slowly south-east at the speed of the *Sphinx* with the *Annibal* in tow. The commodore was to put the blame for his failure to force a renewal of the action on Captain Sutton, commanding the badly damaged *Isis* which was eventually dismasted by the manoeuvres she was forced to follow, and on the reluctant Captain Alms in the *Monmouth*. They both sailed so badly, he claimed, that he could not rely on them in any action, though his leading ships were ranging at two miles' distance from the French shortly after 17.40 (Suffren calculated that they never got within four miles and that even then their movements were very indecisive). When, six days later, having lost Suffren in the broad South Atlantic, he put Captain Sutton under arrest, it was on a charge of disobedience to his signals which had deprived him of an opportunity of improving the victory he had obtained.

The ensuing court-martial was to acquit the captain of the *Isis*. Johnstone should not even have waited for him to get into line.[1] He could see that the *Annibal* was helpless, the *Héros* seriously wounded and the crews of both exhausted. Against the *Vengeur*, *Artésien* and *Sphinx*, all of 64 guns, he could throw the *Hero*, 74, *Monmouth*, 64, *Romney* and *Jupiter*, 50 each, and three frigates. The *Romney* and *Jupiter* were both fresh and unmarked, while the *Hero* and *Monmouth* had sustained very little damage. Suffren had expected him to attack. Johnstone was stronger by one ship, he was in pursuit, his convoy was safe, his ships in tolerably neat line and ready for battle and, Suffren believed, he was an intrepid and resourceful commander.

Intrepid Johnstone may have been, resourceful he was not. Though at his hastily summoned council of war he learned that he had suffered comparatively mildly, he took so long to follow the French out of the bay that the *Sphinx* had already taken the *Annibal* in tow and the *Héros* had laid to and started repairing her damage. By the time he was out, the French had formed line of battle ahead. As the French men of war sailed south, their lights aglow in the tropical night to keep the English after them and not their convoy, the former governor of Pensacola realized that he had not made a rendezvous with his own transports. If he followed Suffren through the night, they could be in distress; if he returned to protect them, Suffren might get to the Cape first. 'I felt the cruel situation with an anguish which I never before experienced,' but he decided to return to Porto Praya.[2] The French, he was sure, must either send the *Héros* or the *Annibal*, or both, to the West Indies for repairs, or else make as a squadron for Brazil to water and repair, in either of which cases there was still a good chance of successfully completing the object of the expedition.

Such shallow reasoning did not do. His convoy was safe in Porto Praya and he had three frigates by which to communicate with it. He had lost only 36 dead and 130 wounded and most of these were on his transports. Considering how he had allowed himself to be taken so completely by surprise, he had been let off lightly. But unknown to Suffren, who expected him to be in pursuit, he was to take a fortnight to recover from the shock and left Porto Praya to see to the 'object of the expedition', so vital to the interests of his country, only on 1 May! When he called off the chase at 20.30 on 16 April the victory he had so readily claimed crumbled into dust. No amount of casuistry from Johnstone could disguise what was actually a defeat. The race and the Cape were lost. The audacity of the man whom the Indian sailors were to dub 'Admiral Satan' had won him his first battle.

Commodore Johnstone was not, however, without an understanding of publicity and, by turning back when he did, he ensured that his version of the 'victory' was the first to reach Europe. It caused consternation in Paris. Not only had Suffren violated neutral waters, but he had been badly beaten in the bargain. The only comfort the French could take from the reports was that nowhere had Johnstone mentioned either India or the Cape.

For his part, Suffren worried about his government's reaction to the violation of Portuguese neutrality. 'In all authors on international law, in Grotius, Pufendorff and Selden,' he wrote cautiously to Castries on 10 August, 'there is nothing to establish a consistent rule on how we should view territorial waters. Our *Ordonnances* are silent on this point.'[3] And well they might be. The British, on the other hand, had provided numerous precedents known to him personally. There was the occasion in 1758 when Captain Augustus Hervey had attacked and burned a French privateer within the territorial waters of Malta,[4] and then, of course, there was Boscawen's action at Lagos, as a result of which he had been taken prisoner of war. 'Add to all these reasons the great importance of what I attempted to do and sympathize with me for having failed to do great things with meagre means.'[5]

Eventually the truth trickled back. Castries was not worried about what Grotius, Pufendorff and Selden had not said. His Majesty had learned 'that you conducted yourself like a warrior and demonstrated your great abilities', and immediately confirmed his promotion to *chef d'escadre*.[6] This was 30 March 1782; by the time Suffren heard about it, 11 months later, his senior officer, Thomas d'Orves, had been dead for a year and he was preparing for his sixth battle. His Majesty would soon be considering his promotion to lieutenant-general. But to Mme de Seillans, Suffren was bitter. 'La Praya should have immortalized me. But I missed, or was made to miss, a unique opportunity. With my five ships I could have made the peace—and a glorious peace at that!'[7] A glorious peace was too much to have looked for from a chance encounter between two relief squadrons. At the best he could have deprived the East India squadron of the *Monmouth, Hero* and *Isis*, and so secured crushing naval superiority in the Bay of Bengal. That could have put the Honourable Company in real peril in India.

Like Johnstone, he could not help feeling that his captains had not given him the support he expected. In the early hours of 17 April, not knowing that the gallant veteran had died at 17.00 hours the previous afternoon, he wrote a note to the captain of the *Annibal* to rub a little salt into his terrible wounds. 'I must compliment you, my dear Trémigon, on the vigorous way you conducted yourself yesterday. This must be a ray of consolation to you in your present unhappy state. But nothing can console me for seeing so fine a ship, so well commanded, in no condition to serve.'[8]

Eighteen months later, Suffren was to regale his unwilling guest, William Hickey, with an account of Porto Praya. 'Had all my captains done their duty with the same ardour that the *Hannibal* and *Héros* did, it would have proved a woeful day for England. Three of the commanders for ever disgraced themselves, involving therein the noble families to which they were allied. These poltroons hung back and never brought their ships within gunshot of the enemy.'[9] And when he had got clear of the harbour and had set course for the Cape with the *Annibal* in tow, his commanders in a council of war on board the *Héros* pronounced 'my object impracticable and unjustifiably wild and chimerical. Two of the dastardly captains in particular said they could not proceed, not having water for more than 20 days besides which the state of the *Hannibal* made it impossible altogether.'[10] To this Suffren rejoined that he expected the *Annibal* to be new rigged at sea, while the water in the squadron would be shared among them all. 'If the entire quantity of the fleet would not afford a quart a day for each man then they must content themselves with a pint—nay, with half a pint, for to the Cape I would certainly go with the utmost despatch.'[11]

Either William Hickey's or Suffren's memory was at fault, for there was no council of war, but the rest is more or less accurate. Suffren took the unprecedented decision to tow the *Annibal* all the way to the Cape without advice. As for the 'dastardly poltroons', his cousin Forbin and the hapless du Chilleau, he asked the minister to recall them in disgrace. On 24 November 1781, the minister anticipated this request in a letter that Suffren did not receive for a year. He was to send back to France any captain against whom he had complaint, for 'there can be no respect or consideration for those who dispense themselves from obedience'.[12] By the time this permission was in Suffren's hands, Forbin was on his way home and du Chilleau had fought himself back into favour.

Yet neither Forbin nor du Chilleau was wholly to blame. Inept they certainly were on this occasion, but Suffren had expected too much of them. To abandon their cherished traditions and follow him into the heart of a mêlée, to leap from tactical orthodoxy into daring opportunism with no more than a signal, was a test

most sea captains of the day would have failed. Suffren should
have foreseen that he might find Johnstone at Porto Praya and
kept stricter battle order in waters through which his opponent
had already passed. He should never have allowed Trémigon to
clutter his decks with water barrels. In short he should not have
assumed that the two veterans in the *Annibal* and *Artésien* would
understand his intentions by instinct. Had either of them been his
colleague from 1779, d'Albert de Rions, when between them they
had mopped up the Union and Grenadine Islands, the result might
have been different.

For if Suffren had learnt to be a great fighter, he had not
learnt how to get the best out of his fellow captains. He may
have learnt—from his apprenticeship of defeats, dismays, lost
leadership and abandoned opportunities—the virtue of instant
offensive action, but to expect his colleagues, ordinary sea captains
of the formal school, to undergo an instant conversion to its merits
during their encounter with Commodore Johnstone was an error of
the first order. Sadly he never learned how to make them wiser. He
had more than his share of pride of caste and his irascible temper
could demand only that those who failed him were broken, not
instructed and reformed. As they grumbled and intrigued against
his restless bad temper, they became his enemies.

Suffren may have believed, like Nelson after him, that the
principal object of naval activity was the destruction of the enemy's
ships, but when Nelson saw Brueys in Aboukir Bay he 'would
sooner have thought of flying than attacking the French in their
position',[13] had he not been confident that his captains would
know exactly what to do. Porto Praya was too novel an experience
for French captains. Novel, too, was Suffren's iron determination
to continue his journey, even though it meant towing the *Annibal*
all the way. Few other commanders would have cared to do it,
knowing the need for urgency and feeling uneasily the hot breath
of pursuit in the mild Atlantic winds that blew them south.

At dawn on 17 April there was, comfortingly, no sign of
Johnstone but Suffren learned that Trémigon and Cardaillac were
dead, along with 80 in the *Annibal*, many more than the casualty list
of the *Héros*. Between them they had 145 wounded. The *Vengeur*,
on the other hand, had lost only two dead. The prizes had also
escaped. There was nothing to show for the battle but the *Annibal*
at the end of a tow-rope. 'If I had only had a couple of frigates,'

he told the minister reproachfully, 'they could have manned seven or eight of the ships which sailed out of the bay and must have surrendered.'[14] But he had only the *Fortune*, and next to useless she had been, even though commanded by a member of the family that had once ruled Cyprus.

But there was no time for recrimination. The *Annibal* must be new-rigged at sea and to everyone's astonishment the job was completed in eight days, with a spare topmast in place of the mainmast and a topgallant yard borrowed from the *Héros* to carry a sail. Almost as remarkable was the surgery performed on the *Héros*, for between the 17th and 21st the carpenters sent up her main topmast, fixed a splint to the mainmast and main yard and rigged a jury mast for the mizzen yard until, on the 24th, she was able to take her turn in towing the *Annibal*. But by 15 June the tow-rope had broken so many times that Suffren ordered her to finish the journey under her own sail. At last, after an agonizing crawl through equatorial calms, they sighted the thin plume of cloud that marked the great ridge of Table Mountain. It was 20 June, and to cries of 'Vive le Roi!' Suffren could fly his *chef d'escadre*'s broad pennant from the masthead of the *Héros*.

The Dutch flag was still flying from Lion's Head, but there was a mysterious silence on shore. And there was no sign of recognition from Simonstown on the morrow. It was only at 16.00 that Suffren saw the prearranged signal that told him the Cape was still in Dutch hands. Two hours later the commandant of Simonstown came on board to explain that they had all been so convinced that the French were British that they had hurriedly packed up their houses and either fled into the countryside or hidden behind closed shutters. The race was won, but there was no time to celebrate. The British might still appear at any moment and Suffren had a garrison to put ashore and sick and wounded to recover. The *Annibal* came limping in on 22 June when Suffren marched overland to Cape Town with the detachments from the Regiments of Austrasie and of Pondicherry and the 100 gunners from Metz. They were sadly needed. The garrison of 400 men had fled into the citadel as soon as his ships were sighted. Few of them had ever fired a shot in anger and, had they wanted, they could not have done so since the 12 pieces of ordnance in the fort were unserviceable. Governor van Plattemberg was a distant, reserved man, thought to be pro-British, but if he was he showed a pathetic anxiety to be saved from them and seemed genuinely pleased to see his allies.

There was little beyond the fears of the governor to keep Suffren in the Cape. The arsenal could provide only nine spars for his ships and none big enough for the *Annibal*, and he had to have trees felled specially. He would leave as soon as he was watered, but that was not likely to be for some time as the fountain at Simonstown could fill only 80 barrels a day. While waiting, he replaced his two dead captains. Morard de Galles was given the *Annibal* as he had deserved, for 'there had been no example in the three wars of our century of a vessel, in the state in which the *Annibal* then was, being saved'. To the *Artésien* he promoted the second officer of the *Sphinx*, Pas de Beaulieu. As his own flag-captain he appointed Ruyter-Werfusé, who had sailed with him in the *Zélé* and *Fantasque*, for as *chef d'escadre* Suffren no longer commanded only the *Héros*.[15]

Then at 17.00 hours on 22 July an agitated message came from van Plattemberg. The English had appeared off Saldanha Bay, about 50 miles north of the Cape, whither the governor, as soon as he had received news of Johnstone's expedition, had sent five Indiamen to hide. Four more were anchored, out of sight he hoped, in Hout Bay, and in this way he had planned to deprive Johnstone when he sailed into Table Bay of nine certain prizes, rich with cargoes from Batavia, Negapatam and Trincomali. By a stroke of fate that seemed almost to unnerve the wretched governor of the Cape, the former governor of Pensacola had made his first landfall at the very place where a prize fortune lay unprotected. Suffren refused to be drawn. He would not sail until repairs to the *Annibal* were completed. If Johnstone were to seek him in False Bay, he would find him as ready to do business as before. But the Indiamen were lost.

Commodore Johnstone had not lighted on Saldanha Bay by accident. As he idled south from Porto Praya there was a hot debate on what he should do next. The soldiers, reckoning that the Cape must now be re-garrisoned, demanded to be taken to Ceylon. The sea captains wanted to go to the River Plate and see what they could find there. Then, on 9 July, the frigates *Active* and *Jason* reported that Suffren was at the Cape but that there was unprotected shipping in Saldanha Bay. Johnstone, still nagged by his lost dream of £100,000 prize-money from filibustering in the

Plate, decided to go for it, and the soldiers reluctantly agreed to join the 'sheep-stealing and marooning party'.[16] The Dutch tried to fire their ships, but too late; as it happened, only four were richly laden and two foundered on their way back to England, so that, when the prize-money of the other two was adjudged to the crown, the commodore got very little from the expedition after all.

Meanwhile, on 23 July, Johnstone's convoy had appeared off Table Bay, throwing the town into panic and dismay. 'The drum beat the men to arms, the troops assembled, but everyone just weeps and wails.'[17] Suffren, learning that they were transports not warships, refused to budge, hoping that Johnstone would still try the odds of battle in Table Bay; but if the commodore had a penchant for quarrelsome fighting, he was not going to risk his prizes in a second affray with Suffren. He would as well think of attacking Paris! Instead, on 27 July, General Medows accompanied his men on to the *Monmouth* and three other Company ships and set off for India. Johnstone then cruised for a while in case Suffren's convoy was still at sea until, on 6 August, he sailed for St Helena. From there he went to Lisbon and married his dashing beauty, Charlotte Dee, 'a fine woman,' thought William Hickey, 'but rather masculine both in person and in mind'. He thus 'condemned himself to misery for the rest of his life, his Portuguese bride proving as arrant a termagant and tyrant as any unhappy husband was tied to!'[18]

None of this was known to Suffren, but when Johnstone left suddenly he suspected that he might have detached some of his ships for India. If that was so, Suffren must waste no more time. On 2 August Morard de Galles in the *Annibal* was ordered to take the convoy to Île de France. The *Fortune* was to precede them to the island and commandeer a mast for the still-stricken battleship. The rest of the squadron, watched discreetly by the *Active* frigate, escorted the four Indiamen from Hout Bay to Table Bay where, on 14 August, the Feast of St Louis, Suffren gave a dinner for the governor and a supper, ball and fireworks for the garrison. It was to be his last social occasion for two and half years.

After a week of fitful calms and wild winds, Suffren sailed on 27 August, leaving Table Bay and the Cape to the protection of the Irish Captain Conway and the Regiment of Austrasie. On 4 September he caught up with the *Annibal* and his convoy. At Porto Praya the first of a lifetime of old scores had been paid off and the

humiliation of Lagos Bay avenged. In the east there was an empire
to be recovered, but at Port Louis he would revert to being second
in command. Castries had tied a leash to his collar which he must
surely tighten at the news of Porto Praya. Suffren could be forgiven
a frisson of disappointment.

10. Onward to India

In Île de France, Souillac and d'Orves waited impatiently for news. The island was reputed to be a tropical Cythera—the legendary abode of mainly non-wedded love—and had already been dubbed by Bernardin de Saint-Pierre *la nouvelle colonie de Vénus*. He also called it a haven for bankrupts, ruined libertines, swindlers and other scoundrels, 'who, chased out of Europe for their crimes and out of the East by our misfortunes, tried to rebuild their fortunes on public ruin'.[1] Disturbed as a rule only by hurricanes, the life of perpetual holiday was now menaced by uncertainty, for the colony depended on trade and slaves; the trade had been interrupted by fear of the British squadron and the slaves were hungry. Black famine had been reported in the neighbouring island of Bourbon and the garrison was on the alert for a slave rebellion. All this because the lifeline to the Cape was threatened.

If the Cape *had* fallen to the enemy, and if the British squadron on the India station *had* been reinforced, then Souillac knew that it was only a matter of time before they took Île de France. With that dismal prospect the garrison and squadron waited in listless torpor. On 10 July *La Fine* frigate arrived from France with new orders for d'Orves. As soon as he had learnt that the Cape was safe he was to sail to meet Suffren and to prevent reinforcements reaching the British squadron. But if he heard nothing about the Cape, he was to stay where he was and sail again for India only when Suffren arrived. Parting with every piece of serviceable cordage he could lay hands on, d'Orves despatched the *Consolante* to Africa with a message for his colleague. If Suffren could not come at once he should send back in the frigate every item of ship's stores she could carry. Without them, d'Orves was paralysed.

The *Consolante* and the *Fortune* passed each other on the high seas but, before de Lusignan reached Port Louis on 6 September, the colony's spirits had plummeted even further. Two of Suffren's convoy had sailed in with news of Porto Praya, closely followed by a Danish merchantman who could not believe that with his damaged ships Suffren could possibly have beaten Johnstone to the Cape. The cloud that hung perpetually over the mountains above Port Louis began to creep into the town.

The arrival of the *Fortune*, however, threw the island into a fever of excitement. Souillac, who as a lieutenant 22 years earlier had worked the top-deck guns with Suffren in la Clue's ill-fated *Océan* at Lagos Bay, began to hope that within a month of Suffren's arrival the squadron might be at sea and d'Orves could redeem his promise of help to Haidar Ali. But if the prospect fired the governor and the ailing admiral, it was not pleasant news to the officers and men who had now been in the island for six months and felt no compelling desire to exchange the earthly paradise for the rigours of the Coromandel coast. The iron hand of famine on the point of removal, their first interest was to revive the trade from which they expected to make their fortunes.

Île de France was so far from France that the expense of maintaining a proper base had been too great for the Ministry of the Marine to meet. Port Louis was a fine sheltered bay and a safe anchorage from the Indian Ocean's many storms, but the island's economy was required to be self-sustaining, and it was not. Its inhabitants could not live off sugar and they were dependent on mainland Africa for meat and vegetables. The local *armateurs*, who fitted out ships for trading in the dangerous waters of South Asia and Africa, were required to equip their merchant vessels for war but tried to balance the needs of privateering with the lure of profits from trade; monoculture had led to the destruction of trees tall enough to supply masts and a squadron of warships only competed for scarce local resources against the vital carrying trade. The alliance with the United Provinces meant that the Cape and Ceylon were safe so that the island did not feel threatened by the English from India. It was a safe haven for occasional forays into the Bay of Bengal, but it was neither equipped nor physically capable of providing for the needs of an exhausted and battle-damaged squadron.[2]

Moreover the sea captains idling in Île de France had on the whole done pretty much as they liked under Tronjoly, and his successor, Thomas d'Orves, was a sick man, dragged down by the climate and approaching death. Two were veteran officers of the Compagnie des Indes but the rest were true members of the Grand Corps, conservative in their ideas and very conscious of their rank. They did not like what they heard of Suffren and when at last, on 25 October 1781, the *Héros* anchored alongside d'Orves's *Orient*, they had decided that the new *chef d'escadre* should be put firmly in his place before he started to throw his weight about.

Almost as soon as the newly arrived officers had come ashore, a delegation, led by Bernard Marie Boudin de Tromelin, captain of the *Brillant*, and consisting of two other fellow members of the Corps, Maurville de Langle, captain of the *Flamand*, and Saint-Félix, commanding *La Fine* frigate, came to ask why so fine a ship as the *Annibal* had been given to a lieutenant. Tromelin had served for several years in the east under Tronjoly and had actually been promoted captain in 1777 before Suffren himself. He was a distinguished mariner, whose name is still carried by a small island he had rediscovered off the coast of Madagascar in 1776, and he had been responsible for the dredging of Port Louis so that it could now harbour, even if it could not provision, the largest French squadron to have been seen in these waters. He had now been 16 years in the island, giving good service to his monarch, and by sheer seniority he considered that the ship should be his. Indeed d'Orves had promised it to him. Moreover, Morard de Galles, undoubtedly a gallant and enterprising officer, was ranked twelfth in seniority in the joint squadron and had already served under Tromelin in the *Normande*. It was insupportable that an officer so junior should command a 74 and that Tromelin, third in seniority, had to be content with a 64.

Maurville de Langle, whose *Flamand* mounted only 50 guns, demanded one of the 64s and Saint-Félix asked for something more than a frigate. When d'Orves asked Suffren for his views, the new Admiral was short. 'The command of the *Annibal* became vacant by death and I have filled it. It is no longer free.'[3] But d'Orves was not the man to stand up to unpleasantness; in the interests, he thought, of harmony, he weakly revoked the promotion of

Morard de Galles which he had already confirmed. Suffren was
disgusted. Tromelin may have served 35 years in the same Corps,
but to Suffren he was contemptible. When the two met at dinner
that night Suffren refused to recognize the officer who came up to
make his excuses for the part he had played that morning. 'I do
not know you.'[4]

It was a snub the affronted captain was never to forget. Suffren
was to put it down to the lilies and languors of Venus's new
colony. 'Despite the great operations that await us in India, only
apathetic languor and indifference reigns here, wholly revolting
to a man who professes any patriotism. The military spirit has
been forgotten—but what can you expect from the indulgence of
commanders and the independence and insubordination of their
subalterns, who look on this place as their patrimony and do what
they like by making their senior officers afraid of them? Nearly
everyone has a wife or a regular mistress. The ladies are charming,
life is comfortable. There are all the delights of Calypso's island
without the presence of Mentor. Many have made their fortunes
and become proud and factious.'[5]

The most particularly proud and factious were soon to find that
they had misjudged their man. He was very soon to doubt their
fitness to command. Had they not crossed him from the beginning,
he might not also have believed them capable of treason. D'Orves
was still fit enough to know that they had all got off to an
inauspicious start and eagerly fell in with Suffren's plans for an
early departure for India. Suffren was not too impressed by this
sign of energy. He could not always be at his side, especially at
sea. 'The gentlemen of India want only cadets to serve with them.
This place is another Capua. No one leaves it of his own free will,
for everyone wants to be either Governor or General!'[6] But leave it
they must, for the former *procureur-général* of Pondicherry, Piveron
de Morlat, now the French agent at the court of Haidar Ali, had
a draft treaty ready, under the terms of which the nawab would
undertake to meet all the expenses of a French expeditionary force,
lending it moreover 12,000 foot and 4000 mounted troops. The
ultimate prize would be a *jagir*, or territorial grant, worth 20
million rupees a year, and all the present possessions of the British
on the coast, including Madras. If the lamentable impression of
d'Orves's untimely withdrawal from the coast in February was to
be removed, the French must arrive at once.

Indeed, d'Orves wrote to Castries, 'I shall be extremely put out if the first news I send you is not of the combat I shall seek with such vigour that I have no doubt it will end in our favour . . . It will be essential to capture Madras and, once the British squadron has been defeated, I shall be able to proceed to its conquest. Several reasons induce me to want to keep my station off India for a long time . . . Only indispensable necessity will force me to return to Île de France.'[7]

That sounded remarkably like the voice of the sick admiral's new alter ego, who made sure he was never far from his side. Souillac, too, seemed fired by new energy. Duchemin must command an expeditionary force larger than the 1000 men he had promised Haidar, something more like 5000—a motley selection from the various forces in the islands, topped up by 500 black slaves offered the equal prospects of freedom or death. They might not be hand-picked veterans from the finest regiments of France but the Europeans among them almost matched in numbers those thought to be in the Madras army. If the Dutch in Ceylon played their part, the expedition might arrive in India with sufficient supplies for six months and if it left in November it could be on the Coromandel coast before the British squadron returned from Bombay.

November was to prove too soon. The damage of Porto Praya had to be repaired, the *Annibal*'s new mast to be fitted and enough cordage found to rig the squadron. Six months' supplies, too, proved to be a mirage. They had not come with Suffren and they were not to be found in the islands. The Dutch in Ceylon could not be relied on so Haidar Ali must assume responsibility for them. In the meantime Suffren set himself to find what there was in Île de France itself.

Tillette de Mautort, a young lieutenant in the Austrasian grenadiers, followed the admiral's activities with approval. He too wanted to be off to India to improve his fortunes. 'There was very soon an unaccustomed bustle in the workshops and yards. M de Suffren was everywhere. The inhabitants, in admiration of his active spirit, supported him with all their power. One sent lengths of timber to the yard, another with those of his slaves who had any skills. The *colons* of Bourbon sent rice, maize and corn. But, believe it or not, all the obstacles he met came from those captains who were here before he arrived . . . They were astonished at the way M de Suffren ordered them about so imperiously and held them responsible for the delays they saw fit to make in carrying out his instructions. They intrigued sullenly against him and tried, with little success, to subvert the junior officers and leading seamen. All they gained from this was general contempt and obloquy for wanting to upset the operations of a man for whom everyone was filled with admiration.'[8] Yet, despite his unceasing activity, the squadron was ready to sail only on 6 December. That it was ready at all was almost wholly due to Suffren's energy and to the sense of confidence his presence had inspired.

Haidar was still in the Carnatic, impatiently waiting for the promised expeditionary force. That much was known on 29 November when the sloop *Diligente* returned from India. With that news, d'Orves made the last effective decision of his life: the squadron would sail for Ceylon by a new route, pioneered only a few years before by the Comte de Grenier in *La Belle Poule*; it was not the shortest route but it was swifter. The ships would let the winds take them across the Indian Ocean as far as the Indonesian archipelago where, at about longitude 90° and latitude 6° north, they would bear west and approach Ceylon from the south. In this way they would spend less time in equatorial calms. Duchemin could be put ashore at a prearranged place with Haidar Ali before the English knew they had arrived.[9]

The squadron that put to sea at 07.45 hours on 7 December was the largest the French had ever assembled in the east. D'Orves's broad pennant flew still from the *Orient*, not the equal of the two other 74s, *Héros* and *Annibal*, but a powerful ship for all that. Tromelin commanded the *Annibal*, Maurville the *Artésien*, Saint-Félix the *Brillant*. Du Chilleau and Forbin kept their 64s, the *Sphinx* and *Vengeur*; the two Compagnie veterans, Bouvet and la Pallière, the *Ajax* and *Sévère*. La Landelle commanded the third 64, *Bizarre*. A newly promoted lieutenant, Cuverville, had replaced Maurville in the 50-gun *Flamand*. There were three frigates. The best of them, *La Bellone*, arrived from France on 21 November, commanded by Villeneuve de Cillart. But Cillart had set off with two ships in convoy and lost them off Africa to the frigates *Active* and *Jason*, so that he arrived under a cloud which thickened as the campaign progressed. *La Pourvoyeuse*, 40, now commanded by Morard de Galles, was large enough to be used as a transport and as tough and resilient as any ship afloat, but she was not a fast sailer. *La Fine*, Suffren's torch-bearer from Brest,

with 36 guns, was commanded by Perrier de Salvert, a young
lieutenant in the Suffren mould: brave, dashing and single-minded
in action. He had also married well, no less than the daughter of
France's most distinguished tactical theorist and the founder of the
Académie de la Marine at Brest, Bigot de Morogues. In addition
there were three corvettes: *La Sylphide*, 16, *La Subtile*, 24, and
La Diligente, 10. *La Fortune* stayed at Île de France to carry
despatches. Besides the seven transports and the *Toscane* hospital
ship there was the fire-ship, *Pulvériseur*, commanded by a young
man who, as Admiral Villaret-Joyeuse, was to show something of
the Suffren touch 12 years later at the Glorious 1st of June.

The intendant of Île de France was glad to see the proud and
factious sailors go. 'De tous ces bougres-là, je puis vous assurer
qu'il n'en reviendra pas la moitié' ('I can assure you that only
half of that lot will ever come back.')[10] He was to be unpleasantly
surprised. If Perrier de Salvert and 1000 men did not make the
return journey, nine captains did before the year was out, three
under arrest, all in disgrace. Save for the Compagnie officers and
those who had been baptized in the fire of Porto Praya, the captains
were largely untried men, and in the next 18 months they were
to be tested to the limit. Few were to emerge with credit. Of
those who did, one was the factious Saint-Félix who, despite
his caballing and a piqued withdrawal to Île de France after
the fourth battle, returned before the end of the campaign and
in 1793 was promoted vice-admiral of the Revolutionary Levant
fleet. Two others, Cuverville and a lieutenant in the *Flamand*,
Trublet de Villejégu, became *contres-admiraux* (rear-admirals) at
the Restoration but, with Villaret-Joyeuse, they were the only ones
to survive the storm with honour. The ordeal by fire and water was
to be too strong for the rest.

It was a slow crawl under threatening stormclouds, sighing for
air, but, once over the line, the squadron picked up wind and
was off Sumatra by mid-January. By a stroke of luck they fell
in with an unidentified vessel and, using the codes taken from
the East Indiaman *Hinchinbrooke* at Porto Praya, Suffren tried
to lure her closer. But he could not read her reply to his signals,
and when the French did not respond she sheered off, only to
be sighted again and chased. After a resistance long enough to
satisfy honour, she surrendered on 22 January and proved to be
the 50-gun *Hannibal*, on her way to Madras, copper-bottomed

and in good trim. Less good was the news that she sailed only
two weeks ahead of the *Sultan*, 74, and *Magnanime*, 64, escorting
a convoy of men and munitions for Fort St George. Suffren had
met the *Sultan* at Grenada. When these two ships, along with the
Hero, Monmouth and *Isis*, joined the British squadron, the French
would no longer have the advantage of numbers.

Speed was now of the essence. The French must put Duchemin
and his motley expedition ashore—probably no more than 3000
men in all, more than Haidar was expecting, if less than Souillac
had wanted to send—before they fell in with the British squadron.
Then they must seek it out to destroy it before the reinforcements
arrived. The *Hannibal* became the *Petit Annibal* (but we shall
continue to call her by her English name) and was pressed into
line. Suffren wanted her to go to his own second officer, Ruyter-
Werfusé, but seniority intervened and Ruyter had to be content
with the *Bellone* frigate while Cillart got the prize. He consoled
himself by thanking the English for the gift of two Hannibals.[11]
And by the news that Thomas d'Orves was really too ill to remain
in command. The *maladie compliquée* from which he had suffered
so long had now so sapped his vitality that on 3 February he joined
the sick in the *Toscane*.

When Suffren read the admiral's letter of resignation to the
captains assembled on the *Héros*, they heard it with mixed feelings.
D'Orves had been a complaisant commander, only too willing to
be advised and easily convinced of the need for caution. Suffren, on
the other hand, had little regard for their opinions and no interest
in their advice. He expected instant obedience to his orders, in
the framing of which they were not expected to share. Three of
them were already in his black books following Porto Praya and
another three, including Tromelin, who now became his second in
command, had offended him deeply at Île de France.

To show how little he proposed to use the council of war as
a forum of equals, he informed them bluntly that he no longer
proposed to sail to Ceylon, on which they had all decided in
Souillac's presence in Port Louis, but to make straight for Madras
before the British should have a chance to retire under the guns
of Fort St George. This was not the time, he informed them
coolly, to prescribe any order of battle. He expected 'that the
valour and ability of each officer would permit him to adopt any
action suggested to him by the state and position of the enemy's

squadron'.[12] He did not rule out an attack on the British ships, even should they be safely within range of the shore batteries. It was now only a matter of hours before they sighted the Coromandel coast and every ship must be ready for action. The days of Tronjoly and d'Orves were over.

Two days later Tromelin was handed the instructions he was to follow in the event of action. They were unequivocal, in the form of an order, and the proud and resentful captain's temper was further soured. Like Admiral Mathews at Toulon, the first sea battle that Suffren had witnessed, he was to seek out the enemy with a spoiled and angry colleague in sullen command of the rear division.

PART III

The Duel of Giants

11. Admiral Hughes

What no one in the French expedition knew was that the British squadron had not actually wintered at Bombay and that the power of the Dutch as collaborators in both India and Ceylon had been gravely damaged. The desperate situation in which d'Orves had left the British in February 1781 had significantly eased in his absence. Haidar had ravaged the Carnatic and his huge army still swarmed like angry locusts up and down the province, but none of the garrison towns, except Arcot, had fallen and, though Coote had been immobilized for long stretches by shortages of rice and cattle, the nawab had been unable to claim a victory of any substance. When the British squadron returned at last in June 1781, the English in Fort St George felt that with their backs to so stolid a wooden wall, their prospects of survival were pretty bright.

Its commander, Vice-Admiral Sir Edward Hughes, KB, was certainly stolid, in almost every way unlike his nervous, splenetic and demanding comrade in arms, Sir Eyre Coote. A sea officer with an impeccable sense of public duty, cool in his bearing, generous in his sentiments, impartial in his behaviour, his phlegmatic calm and serene confidence inspired a genial trust in everyone who met him. He was no stranger, either, to the citizens of the presidency, for between 1773 and 1778 his commodore's broad pennant had flown from the *Salisbury* as commander-in-chief of the East Indies squadron. Under instructions then to co-operate with the Honourable Company in any action upon which the supreme council in Fort William agreed (as long as it did not infringe the articles of peace referring to the French settlements in

India signed at the Treaty of Paris) he kept his station off Bombay during the first brush with the Marathas. When Haidar Ali went to war, a certain nephew to Captain Suckling, then a lieutenant on board the frigate *Seahorse*, experienced his baptism of fire against the warships of the nawab at Mangalore.

In May 1778 Hughes was relieved by Commodore Vernon and returned to England and promotion. But in July of the following year he was reappointed to his old station and knighted. With the navy heavily committed to North American and European waters, the Admiralty wanted a man in India who would not badger it for ships and men it had not got. Lord Sandwich, leafing through earlier reports, found one by Sir Hugh Palliser in 1773. Edward Hughes, he read, 'will not wander out of the path that may be prescribed for him to follow any schemes or whims of his own, nor never will study to find fault with his orders, but always how best he may execute them in His Majesty's service'.[1]

Everyone knew that he was not a man to get easily excited. His so far rather undistinguished career had emphasized the qualities of attention to detail, tenacity and courage. He was a stickler for the right forms and would not allow himself to be betrayed into making a mistake through haste. He was, moreover, a man in whom the milk of human kindness was not easily curdled—though it was certainly to be soured in the months ahead—and the care he took of his men, while it did credit to his heart, also incurred him the reputation of mollycoddling. The French sailors, hectored and bullied by the intemperate furies of Admiral Suffren, mocked him with the soubriquet of 'Mother', or 'Mère Hews'. His own seamen, so the French learned from prisoners, called him goodwife 'either because he was advanced in age or because he talked too much'.[2]

He was in fact 62, immensely fat and intemperate in his appetite for both food and tobacco. 'A short, thick-set man,' according to another William Hicky, this one the editor of the *Bengal Gazette*, 'his skin fits remarkably tight about him; he has very rosy gills and drivels a little at the mouth from the constant use of quids.'[3] Sir Joshua Reynolds did not flatter him when he painted his portrait at the end of the war. There he stands, four-square upon the strand of the Coromandel coast in full uniform, his paunch forcing the brocaded waistcoat to bulge like a hopsack, his snubbed button nose set in fleshy cheeks, well-fed, sleek and complacent.

William Hickey, genial lawyer and memorialist, dined on board the *Superb* in 1783 when the tables on shore were reduced to a little mutton and claret only. 'Our gallant admiral,' he was told, 'took great care to provide himself with a professed cook, and usually employed both a French and an English one.' His chief performer on that occasion was the Frenchman, for the English cook had been killed in action, but despite the nationality he was to see 'one of John Bull's favourite dishes in all its glory'.[4] Even Dolly's could not have surpassed the flavour of the beefsteaks he was served. No wonder the admiral's nickname was 'Hot and Hot' since he was so 'remarkably fond of and always doing complete justice to this truly English dish'.[5]

'Hot and Hot' with his beefsteaks and quids and 'Admiral Satan' with his bouillabaisses and cheroots, both men with their paunches, dewlaps and tobacco-stained teeth, and their five fearful and inconclusive battles to come, might almost have been the prototypes for Tweedledum and Tweedledee, but unlike those timid and querulous twins both men were inexhaustible in energy and indomitable in courage.

Sir Edward, moreover, was a 'safe' admiral, unlikely to do anything tactically eccentric or rash, and his seamanship was faultless. His ships, by and large, were well-drilled, his signals always clear and consistent. Yet there has never been a HMS *Hughes*, unless one counts the 36-gun Company ship transferred to the Royal Navy during the Napoleonic wars to cruise with Admiral Sir Edward Pellew in the East Indies. It was unfortunate for his immortal reputation that he was shortly to be confronted by a genius of uncontrollable energy and bold tactical originality.

If Hughes never shirked action and never wavered before the ferocity and unexpectedness of an attack, he was never able to gain an advantage which subsequent hesitation did not lose. Unlike his approaching rival, he was not prepared to stake all on an intuition or hazard all on a bold stroke. Time and time again Hughes was to miss his chances from a fractional caution and, in the improbable war upon which he was soon to find himself engaged, he was always slower, by a critically small but vital margin, than his rival. Nevertheless, in the ordeal to which Suffren was about to subject them, the sailors of His Majesty's squadron were fortunate to be commanded by a sailor of the calibre of Sir Edward Hughes.

He arrived for his second tour of duty off Madras in January 1780, to command five line-of-battle ships. His flag flew from the *Superb*, 74, built at Deptford in 1760. Commodore Sir Richard King flew his broad pennant from the 64-gun *Exeter*. Two other 64s were the *Eagle* and *Worcester*, Captains Ambrose Reddall and Sir Charles Wood, and Peter Rainier commanded the 70-gun *Burford*. His frigates were the *Seahorse* (Nelson no longer aboard) and *Coventry* which posted between Bombay and Madras. The little squadron was in its turn to be a nursery of future admirals for, besides Commodore King and Captain Rainier, the commander of the *Seahorse* was Lieutenant Thomas Troubridge, 15 years later to form one of Nelson's 'band of brothers'.

Hughes and Coote had their brushes—who would not at some stage clash with Sir Eyre?—but on the whole the two knights understood each other. The prickly general had to accept that the squadron was there not at his convenience but to destroy any French squadron that might appear in Indian waters. He might be short of bullocks but Hughes could not be expected to clutter up his gun-decks ferrying cattle up and down the coast. Coote's men were kept alive by the rice which the squadron's presence permitted Bengal to send down in convoy, but the safety of the rice convoys could not be put above that of His Majesty's ships. Coote, too, could not expect Hughes to keep constant vigil off the coast, for no squadron chose to weather the north-east monsoon and Hughes expected to be back in Bombay before it broke. He had accordingly passed the winter of 1780–81 in the western presidency and, because the hulls of so many of his ships were much destroyed by worm, he had given them a thorough refit. He was, therefore, not to be back off the Coromandel coast until June. On 11 June, between Porto Novo and Madras, he met the sloop *Nymph* with two important items of cargo from Britain: packets announcing the declaration of war on Holland and the new governor of Madras.

Lord George Macartney had not spent long as a prisoner of the French after the surrender of Grenada to d'Estaing, being exchanged under cartel. The Company directors in London were at that moment looking for a new governor of Fort St George who would make a change from the carpetbaggers who had for so long disgraced the Mount and presided over what was little short of 'a set of licensed plunderers, who, scarce equal to the honest arts of commerce, grasped in idea imaginary sceptres and disposed of kingdoms not their own'.[6]

Macartney certainly came from a different world from that of the Rumbolds and Whitehills. Scion of an Irish barony, educated at Trinity College, Dublin, member of parliament in, successively, London and Dublin, ambassador extraordinary to St Petersburg, chief secretary of Ireland and latterly captain general of the Caribbees in Grenada, he was handsome, gracious, witty, gifted with a sardonic intelligence and master of the turned phrase which had beguiled the ear of Catherine the Great. He was also a consummate politician. Though the son-in-law of Lord Bute, he had the entrée to Holland House; as chief secretary of Ireland he had won the friendship of the Irish 'patriots' Henry Flood and Charles Lucas. He was extravagantly well-qualified to transform the presidency of Fort St George from the worst to the best governed in India.

But what he found when Sir Edward delivered him to his beleaguered presidency was a half-starved fortress surrounded by a waste of charred hovels and untilled plots. If he was to hold this against the French, his first objective must be a feat of diplomatic finesse to end the debilitating and unnecessary war with Haidar into which, he moralized sternly, the greed and ineptitude of his predecessor had blundered. But it needed more than finesse to divert the angry nawab from his designs on the Carnatic. 'The Governors and Sirdars who enter into treaties,' Haidar replied to his first overture, 'return to Europe after two years and their acts and deeds become of no effect.'[7] There was nothing to be expected from that quarter but continued war.

Coote, meanwhile, plodded doggedly after the elusive victory which might give his ragged nerves and exhausted soldiers a respite. Food was always short, bullocks non-existent, but on 1 July 1781, among the shifting sand-dunes of Porto Novo, he at last pinned the nawab down to a pitched battle and won. The victory raised morale but little more, for Haidar re-formed his scattered troops and Coote had no resources with which to follow up. 'We are more like beaten than victorious troops,' he wrote morosely to Macartney.[8] But his sting was powerful and Haidar bore off. He allowed Bengal reinforcements to join the wily general and was defeated again, at the very place where his men had cut up Colonel Baillie's force at the beginning of the war. Slowly the tide turned. Haidar was worsted a third time and Coote's laurels lay thick about his brow. But he would have exchanged them for dry weather and rest. He had to be lifted bodily from his horse after days in the saddle and carried prostrate from fever and exhaustion in a litter while rain turned roads to quagmires and streams to raging torrents. Horses, camels, bullocks and elephants died by the roadside and his soldiers, thin as drumsticks. were carried off so fast that what he commanded from behind the curtains of his palanquin was 'more like a field of battle than a line of march'.[9]

Lord Macartney now felt it was time for him to enter the war. His orders were to reduce all Dutch settlements in India and Ceylon, but Coote resolutely refused to add to his enemies. But even he could not deny that the sturdy fortress of Negapatam, garrisoned by Dutch and Malay troops, unmarked by war, and reinforced by Mysoreans, would be a direct threat to Madras. It would give Haidar his outlet to the Bay of Bengal and, with its secure anchorage and abundant fresh water, be the obvious destination of a French expedition. Edward Hughes, too, wanted to see it in British hands before he left the coast on 16 October. When, on 3 October, another future admiral, Captain Gell, sailed into the Madras roads in the 68-gun Spanish prize, now HMS *Monarca*, with the news of Porto Praya, Governor Macartney, reiterating that 'the overthrow of Indian princes is among us a slighter justification . . . than advantage over European enemies', and the admiral between them overbore the reluctant commander-in-chief.[10] On 22 October Hughes landed 827 sailors north of the port. The Mysoreans took to their heels at the first onslaught of the blue-jackets who stormed their redoubts, cutlasses in hand, and on 12 November, after an honourable interval, the Dutch capitulated.

Macartney now turned his ambitions to the even more important harbour of Trincomali. In British hands this Ceylonese harbour, capacious and sheltered from the monsoon, would render unnecessary the long winter haul round to Bombay which kept the squadron off the coast for six months. In French hands it would enable the enemy squadron to winter only a day or two's sail from Madras and to strike a mortal blow against the presidency before the British could get back from the west coast.

In spite of this overwhelming logic, Coote continued as antipathetic to adventure across the water as he was to any outside the Carnatic, and while the three men haggled over priorities the monsoon broke upon the squadron as it rode off Negapatam, tearing the sails to ribbons and snapping its anchor cables. Throughout December Hughes had to wrestle with the deadly surf and with winds of over 100 knots, but towards the end of the year they abated and on 2 January 1782 the squadron sailed with 200 coolies who had never handled a weapon and another 100 warriors 'composed of all the outcasts of all the corps at Negapatam'.[11] But they were enough. The Dutch governor at Trincomali had no stomach for a fight, and one assault by Hughes's blue-jackets was enough. On 11 January he, too, surrendered with the honours of war.

Eight days later Mr Proctor, Company agent at Palamkottai, reported the latest news from Haidar's darbar. A French fleet was expected daily at Point Galle on the south-west coast of Ceylon, of between 10 and 11 ships of the line and escorting 3000 French troops. A French agent had already arrived at Colombo and taken possession of a first draft of rupees on the Dutch regency. But then the information went astray. The object of this expedition was not Pondicherry but Bombay! And there was one other, purely temporary, inaccuracy; the squadron was led by a certain Knight of Malta, the Commander de Suffren, the same gentleman who had performed at Porto Praya and the Cape. Admiral Hughes had done well to keep the coast!

12. The Battle of Sadras, 17 February 1782 (1)

The strong currents and southerly winds brought Suffren on to the Coromandel coast further north of Madras than he had intended and when, on 6 February, he sighted the eyelash fronds of palmyra palm lining the lagoon near Pulicat he knew that his arrival would not be a secret for long. Every country ship he met, most of them laden with rice, had been carefully taken for the last two days and the cargoes and crews transferred to his transports, but soon he had no room for any more rice and was forced to sink ships as he met them. But not every ship he sighted was either taken or sunk, and the news that he had appeared off Pulicat was, as he feared, soon in Madras. On 7 February he learned that Hughes was on his way back from taking Trincomali.

Sir Edward had received no news of Suffren since the Cape and shrewdly feared that he was nearer the Bay of Bengal than he knew. He wasted no time at Trincomali and hurried back. Alone of his reinforcements, the *Monarca* had joined him, but he had no idea where the *Monmouth, Isis* and *Hero* had got to. Trincomali, moreover, had nothing more than shelter to offer his storm-racked ships, so that he would be altogether better off under the guns of Fort St George, especially since he feared that the French were in better shape and superior numbers. The same winds that bore Suffren north took him home, and he was safely in Madras roads on the 8th. The next day, to his inexpressible relief, the three ships for which he had been waiting joined him.

Hughes was seldom the favourite of that capricious neutral, time, but on this occasion, more by chance than good management, it was on his side. For the *Monmouth, Isis* and *Hero*, which had parted from Johnstone on 27 July, had taken a month to reach Madagascar and then, against seasoned advice to take the route across the Arabian Sea to Anjengo on the south-west coast of India in Travancore—which was what Hughes expected them to do—they had crawled up the East African coast instead. By the time they were off Arabia there were so many men down with scurvy that James Alms in the *Monmouth* called a halt for another month to put them ashore. Expecting to find Hughes at Bombay, he sailed straight down the west coast of India, put in at the presidency, watered and then, with scurvy once more rife, set off for Madras. Had Hughes lingered at Trincomali, the trio, weakened by sickness and the long voyage, might have sailed straight into the jaws of the French squadron. Their escape was providential for, if Proctor's intelligence was true, Hughes would have had only six ships to do business with 11. Had Alms fallen in with the French, that number might have been 14.

Suffren knew from the country boats he had taken that Hughes had six ships, not five and that he was expecting three more from Johnstone's squadron. According to Captain Christie of the *Hannibal*, he was also to be joined by two more ships from England. So it was imperative to sweep down the coast to catch him on his way back from Ceylon before these reinforcements joined him. But sweep down the coast he could not. From the moment he sighted land the wind dropped and he was helpless in the grip of a dead calm. When Thomas d'Orves died at last on 9 February he was consigned to the sharks with all the dignities of his rank, including the three cannon salutes which Suffren wished he could have spared so as not to advertise his presence.

For eight exasperating days the admiral was forced to whistle for his wind and as he did so the chances of a quick and cataclysmic engagement with the enemy evaporated. Suffren therefore decided that he should use the time to make contact with Haidar Ali. Within six hours of d'Orves's death, the Mysorean emissaries who had come to Île de France went ashore with Duchemin's aide-de-camp and messages for Piveron de Morlat. The French agent should tell the Nawab that the army would go ashore at Porto Novo—now that Negapatam had gone, the only point on the coast he still controlled.

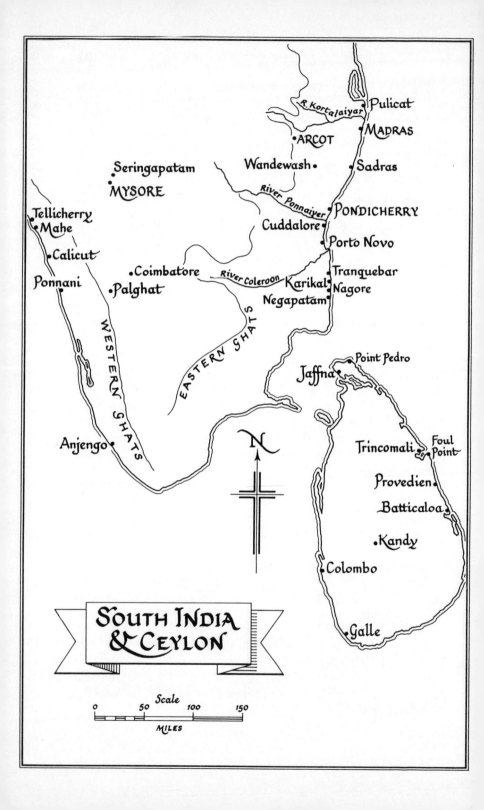

R. Kortalaiyar
Pulicat
•ARCOT
MADRAS
Wandewash•
Sadras
Seringapatam
MYSORE
River Ponnaiyer
PONDICHERRY
Tellicherry
Mahe
Cuddalore
Porto Novo
•Calicut
•Coimbatore
River Coleroon
Tranquebar
Ponnani
Palghat
Karikal
Nagore
Negapatam•

WESTERN GHATS

EASTERN GHATS

Point Pedro
Jaffna•

Anjengo

N

Trincomali
Foul
Point
Provedien
Batticaloa
•Kandy
•Colombo

Galle

SOUTH INDIA
& CEYLON

0   50   Scale   100   150

MILES

D'Orves's death allowed Suffren to remedy one of the injustices of Île de France. Morard de Galles was given his command at last, transferring from the *Pourvoyeuse* to the *Hannibal*. This time Suffren followed the order of seniority so that la Pallière took the *Orient* and Cillart the *Sévère*. Ruyter-Werfusé moved from the *Bellone* to the *Pourvoyeuse* and Pas de Beaulieu took over the *Bellone*. But he refused Tromelin's request to be allowed to exchange the *Annibal* for the better armed and provisioned *Orient*. The veteran felt the snub keenly, though Suffren had been entirely good-tempered and polite in his refusal, since seniority (and he was indisputably the most senior officer under Suffren) had governed the other changes.

No sooner had these changes been made than on 14 February the wind suddenly freshened and the squadron and convoy started to move south. The distance between Pulicat and Madras was quickly devoured and at 13.00 hours they were in full view of the watchers on the walls of Fort St George. Then, as suddenly as it had risen, the wind dropped, and for the whole afternoon the two squadrons faced each other across three or four leagues of open sea. *La Fine* counted nine battleships and two frigates, and when Suffren ordered his ships to anchor at sunset he knew he must do his business with Sir Edward Hughes before the two other reinforcements arrived.

Sir Edward, for his part, viewed the prospect of an engagement with little enthusiasm. All his ships had been at sea a long time. Five of them had endured the monsoon and were growing foul below the waterline. His reinforcements were almost unmanned by scurvy. He was in no state to challenge 11 ships, all of which he had every reason to believe were in spanking trim. But if Suffren's convoy carried an expeditionary force, then it was his clear duty to engage and prevent it from being put ashore. Sir Eyre Coote was sufficiently alarmed at the prospect to agree to the loan of 300 men of the 98th Regiment of Foot. Otherwise his imperturbable sang-froid must take the place of another battleship.

He had no intention, however, of fighting on a lee shore. When on 15 February he saw the French set their course upon him in line of battle, with the wind fresh but not strong from the north-east, and the *Héros* in the lead, he moved his ships under the guns of the fort, each with a spring on her cable so that they might bring their broadsides to bear more effectively on the French if they attacked.

When Suffren saw the tightly locked line, he knew that with the wind so feeble no attack was possible. At 11.00 he anchored four miles out to sea and summoned his captains on board the *Héros*. For three hours the squadrons lay almost parallel in uneasy confrontation while the 300 men Coote had promised paraded on the waterfront and the walls of Fort St George were thick with spectators, passing the hours before dinner in their sprigged muslins and frock-coats, waiting for something more stimulating than coffee.

'It is not without distress, gentlemen, that I see myself forced to propose for today that battle should be postponed.'[1] The man who had criticized d'Estaing for not attacking Barrington in the Grand Cul de Sac wavered sadly before the inevitable, but d'Estaing then had 12 ships to Barrington's seven and the expeditionary force he carried had only the limited objective of recapturing St Lucia. Upon Duchemin's successful arrival depended the goodwill and continued support of Haidar Ali and, with that, the ruin of Britain in India. However much he kicked against those considerations of higher strategy which had so often paralysed the power of French ships, Suffren had to accept the remorseless logic of the situation. So did all his officers, with the exception of the spirited Perrier de Salvert, who thought Haidar Ali would be more impressed by a battle.

Suffren's council of war ended soon after 14.00, and at 14.30 the French ships weighed anchor and sailed south-east in two columns under an easy sail. Hughes prepared to follow them at once. By his reckoning, they could have only two objects: either to attack Trincomali, which was in no state to defend itself, or to put troops ashore. He must obstruct both. The select committee in continuous session in Fort St George decided to go to bed, having informed Warren Hastings in Calcutta that there must certainly be an engagement on the morrow. They had the firmest hope that, despite their inferiority in numbers, the issue would be favourable to British arms.

In that firm hope they slept while the two squadrons sailed through the night, Hughes hauling his wind to the north-east breeze to try to gain the weather-gauge. Suffren, seeing Hughes follow him, feared for his convoy which had not yet put its cargo of troops and munitions ashore. To ensure its safety, he ordered Ruyter-Werfusé in the *Pourvoyeuse* to shepherd the transports so that they sailed between the land and the squadron, which would mark its position by flares.

'Par une bêtise incroyable', Ruyter bungled it. In the course of the night, miscalculating the speed with which the wind was carrying the convoy forward, he allowed it to sail too far ahead of him as he hung back to keep in signal distance of the *Héros*. When he tried to catch it up, he found himself alone in the inky blackness without a light or a sail to guide him. At dawn the sea was ominously empty. Uncertain what to do for the best, Ruyter decided to make for the rendezvous at Pondicherry. He had in fact sailed through and out of the gap that he had allowed to yawn between the squadron and the convoy, and he was not there to see Admiral Hughes sail, quite unknowingly, straight into it.[2]

All Suffren could see at dawn was *La Fine* grappling with a prize, but at 06.00 the frigate made a signal of ten warships to the west-south-west. He could not, at first, believe it, but the painful truth was only too soon obvious. Somehow during the night Hughes had overhauled him and must even now be flying down upon his convoy. He could no longer bring about the combat to suit his own convenience. He must rescue the expeditionary force.

The general principle at sea, where the elements are always unreliable, that action is preferable to inaction, had justified Sir Edward's decision to sail after the French. Now only three leagues from the enemy's convoy, with his copper-bottomed ships bearing down fast on the troop transports, he could do them irremediable damage before Suffren caught up with him, and might even frustrate any landing. The speed and certainty of his action was in the tradition that Suffren admired, though he was to smart from it. In the mêlée the British took six prizes, one of which had 300 men of the Légion de Lauzun aboard and most of the expedition's ordnance. Suffren could tell in the soft powdery light that his convoy was in trouble, but it was not until 17.00 that he came close enough for Hughes to call off the chase and form line of battle again. In the few minutes of daylight left, the two rivals sailed south-east, four and half miles apart under easy sail, flexing their muscles for their first encounter.

Throughout the night of 16/17 February, *La Fine* kept a close watch on Hughes and when morning dawned cloudy, with a slight wind from the north-east and the promise of sudden squalls, Suffren still had the wind of Sir Edward. But this advantage was not to

The Battle of Sadras

17 FEBRUARY 1782

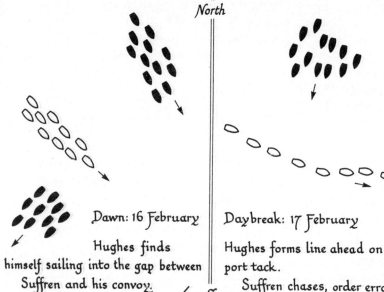

North

Dawn: 16 February

Hughes finds himself sailing into the gap between Suffren and his convoy.

Daybreak: 17 February

Hughes forms line ahead on port tack.

Suffren chases, order erratic.

West

S

East

WIND

Artésien
Ajax
Bizarre
Sévère
Hannibal
Annibal
Vengeur
Sphinx
Exeter
Orient
Héros
Isis
Hero
Worcester
Flamand
Monarca
Superb
Eagle
Burford
Brillant
Monmouth

4.00–7.00 pm: 17 February
The Battle of Sadras.

prove as valuable as it should, for in order to maintain his line through the hours of darkness he had ordered each of his ships to light her three stern lights. The vessels in the rear had taken this for a signal to turn into the wind altogether, so that at dawn the French line straggled out of alignment to the east, with the rear division many degrees north-east of the leading ships and the *Artésien* in particular very far behind.

Throughout the morning all his efforts to tighten up his line were thwarted because the rear ships sailed so badly and because the gusts of wind from the north-north-east kept blowing them out of line. But if these squalls bamboozled the French, they also prevented Hughes from gaining the weather-gauge and they drove Suffren down upon him faster than he had expected. Soon after noon he could defer preparing for action no longer. Accordingly he bore up in line abreast and stood to leeward, ordering his rear ships to close on the centre, keeping only two cables' distance between them to prevent any attempt to break his line. In this position he was able to hold his opponents off for another four hours while Suffren's impatience grew to fever pitch.

'My uncoppered ships sailed so heavily and several others so badly, that I should not have been able to attack at all had I not taken the lead.'[3] Seeing Hughes flying before him, two ships lighter than he, he recalled the tactic of an earlier Sir Edward when, off Cape Finisterre, Hawke had sandwiched the French line between his fastest ships and one by one reduced them to surrender. Collecting his coppered ships into the van behind the *Héros*, he determined to repeat the tactic, ordering them to engage only at pistol-shot range. At 15.00 he signalled the *Annibal*, *Ajax* and *Flamand* to double on the enemy's rear to leeward.

Hughes was now in a very uncomfortable position, retreating before the wind with his rear ship, the *Exeter*, straggling far behind and, as far as he could see, the French bearing down on him in irregular double line abreast. At 15.40 he knew that he could evade action no longer and signalled his squadron to form line of battle ahead at two cables. The irregular double line abreast was in fact only a badly ordered line in which Suffren was massing his copper-bottomed ships in the van. Sir Edward expected to find himself engaged, ship for ship, the length of his line, and for this he was prepared. The signal from the masthead of the *Héros* was for close engagement. And if Hughes deduced this, so too did most of

Suffren's captains, including the commander of his rear division, Tromelin.

Suffren, for his part, expected Tromelin to act on the instructions he had been given 11 days earlier, carefully outlined in a friendly and uncharacteristically diplomatic letter. 'The British capture of Trincomali and Negapatam, and perhaps of all Ceylon, requires us to work for a general action. If we are fortunate to find ourselves to windward of the English—who will only have eight or nine ships at the most—my design is to double on their rear division. If your division is in the rear, you will observe from your position how many ships will overlap and order them to double. If on the other hand we find ourselves to leeward, yet our ships by crowding all sail are still able to double on the enemy, then provided they are not attacked, or if attacked then only feebly or at a distance, you will order them to tack and double to windward. Whatever the circumstances, I ask you to order your division to take what action you shall believe to be the best to achieve the success of the engagement.'[4]

The French had the wind. Their 11 ships were opposed by nine and a general action was about to begin. The odds were in their favour and Suffren hoped at a blow to drive Hughes off the coast. He was never so dependent as now on the intelligence and enthusiasm of his captains, who must deduce their actions from his own. As they were all traditional line sailors of the conservative school, this was an assumption as bold as the tactic he was about to adopt.

13. The Battle of Sadras (2)

Shortly after 16.45, closely followed by the *Orient*—indeed so closely that at one stage her gunners were firing into the flagship—and by the *Sphinx*, *Vengeur* and *Hannibal*, the *Héros* moved up the English line, past the *Exeter*, *Monarca*, *Isis* and *Hero* until she came alongside Hughes's own flagship, *Superb*. There she stopped and, despite the signal flying from her masthead to approach within pistol-shot range, held off a little to prevent the four leading British ships from tacking and doubling on her from the other side. While the wind blew from the north-east, these ships were obliged to be impotent spectators while Tromelin and his rear division took a course to the leeward and subjected the five ships of the English rear to a combat from both sides. Before the *Worcester*, *Eagle*, *Burford* and *Monmouth* could pull their heads round and join in, the *Exeter*, *Monarca*, *Isis* and *Hero* would be battered into submission. It was a bold plan and Hughes could do nothing but bear up staunchly to receive the attack.

But it was to be Porto Praya again. Tromelin, like Trémigon, was a very ordinary captain. Unlike Trémigon, he did not make up for his lack of imagination by ready courage and the superb handling of his ship. For Tromelin, like Richard Lestock at Toulon in February 1744, Suffren's baptism of fire, was consumed by a bitter dislike of his commanding officer. He chose to understand his orders of 6 February to mean that he was to order his two unengaged ships to double on the English rear only when all nine ships of the English line had been engaged. Now, unexpectedly, he found himself at the head of six ships, one of which, the *Artésien*, was too far away to be effective. The signal for close engagement could not mean what it said, for Suffren in the *Héros* had not engaged closely. Waiting for the *Héros* to continue up the line, he merely repeated Suffren's signals.

Whether through turpitude or incapacity, Tromelin now threw away the victory which it lay in his power to win, and by preserving the line he had been taught to revere he held five ships back from taking any effective part in the battle. Only Saint-Félix and Cuverville realized what should be done. First the *Brillant* then the *Flamand* turned to leeward of the *Exeter*. When Bouvet also tried to move the *Ajax* out of the rear division, he was promptly ordered back into line by Tromelin, whom he meekly obeyed. The *Brillant*, moreover, ran into a volley from the *Artésien*, firing fiercely and erratically from a long way off. The shot cut her top-braces and, momentarily helpless, she swung round to present her stern to the broadsides of the *Exeter*, which raked her savagely for several minutes.

The heroes of the action were, undoubtedly, Commodore King and his crew. Though the attack on the *Exeter* was more wild than erratic it was fierce enough to reduce her through two hours of battle to little more than a hulk. But throughout the ordeal her fire was constant. Sir Richard needed all his British phlegm to bring him through, for just as the *Flamand* bore down on him in support of the *Brillant*, a ball struck his flag-captain Reynolds as he stood beside the commodore on the quarter-deck and splattered his face with brains and blood. Still reeling from the shock, King stumbled into the ship's master coming to report another French ship bearing down upon them.

'What is to be done?' cried the master in his agitation.

'Done?' echoed King wiping his face with a handkerchief. 'Why, there is nothing to be done but fight her till she sinks.'[1]

Towards 18.00 hours a squall from the south-east paid round the heads of the English van and Suffren was himself in danger of being caught between two fires. The contest between the *Superb* and *Héros* had been waged without quarter but also without result, and the broadsides exchanged between the *Orient* and the *Hero*, the *Sphinx* and the *Isis* and the *Vengeur* and the *Monarca* had put neither side into any real difficulties. Suffren knew that the battle could not now be won. Hauling his wind, he stood to the north-east, leaving Hughes to continue on his original course. The

Flamand continued to batter the *Exeter* in the failing light until the *Monarca*, her next ahead, and the *Worcester* and *Eagle* in the van pulled round to her assistance, when Cuverville broke off to join the rest of the squadron. At 19.00 Suffren rallied his ships and stood before the wind on a starboard tack while Hughes escaped into the night.

Suffren was beside himself with baffled fury, 'uttering violent imprecations against those who had so essentially failed in their duty'.[2] Almost certain victory had degenerated into a bloody fracas. The *Exeter* was, it is true, reduced to a hulk and bore out of the battle ten of the 32 English dead and 45 of their 95 wounded; the *Superb* had five feet of water in her hold and was severely wounded in masts and rigging, but how much more terribly would the English have suffered had all his ships done their duty! Only Saint-Félix and Cuverville had behaved properly, the first all the more so as he had doubled on the *Exeter* without being ordered to do so. At least he knew how to fight—which was more than the other intriguers from Île de France had shown themselves ready to do. It could hardly be coincidence that of the other captains who had done their duty, la Pallière, du Chilleau, Forbin and Morard de Galles 'who commanded the little *Hannibal* as he did the big *Annibal*, and as he will do always—very well,' only Pallière had served under d'Orves. Tromelin, Landelle, Maurville, Bouvet and Cillart had distinguished themselves by their failure to fight.[3]

To the minister he was cautious. 'I have complained of no one for it would be dangerous to upset these gentlemen, who have been spoiled by the extreme indulgence of M d'Orves and are not at all used to being commanded. I shall have to keep them, for among the junior officers there is no one to replace them.'[4] (He was far more restrained than Admiral Rodney who, watching a similar manoeuvre fail for the same reasons at the Battle of Martinique on 17 April 1784, called it 'the dastardly behaviour of a fleet which called itself British'.)[5] But if Saint-Félix and Cuverville could be rewarded by a pension or higher pay, it might encourage their fellow captains to imitate them.

His casualties, moreover, were nearly the same as the British—30 dead and 100 wounded. The enemy, forced to fire into the wind, had fired high and cut his five ships about aloft and wounded topmasts. As for the rest, when Landelle reported neither damage nor casualties, but a hole in the rudder of the *Bizarre*, it was immediately ascribed to a cannon-ball. An indiscreet carpenter, however, declared that it was merely the work of old age, whereat the mockery of the squadron was complete. For several days those serving on board were asked if they needed caulkers to stop their shot-holes, surgeons for their wounded, liniments, dressings. Landelle scarcely dared appear on deck and skulked in his cabin.[6]

Hughes expected the French, with their decided advantage of wind and numbers, to resume the battle on the 18th, but Suffren never contemplated doing so. The events of the 17th had demonstrated with dispiriting clarity the calibre of the men he commanded. Tromelin he knew to be very cold, very correct, very imperious, 'a man who has always been an enemy born to whomever is in command and who would be in despair if things went well. He is skilful in ruses to mask his misdoings. It is both dangerous and disagreeable to have such a man in his place.'[7]

Bouvet he felt he had to dress down severely. The zeal and ability of the old Compagnie veteran had been particularly recommended to him, 'but yesterday's example of subordination [to Tromelin's order to rejoin the line] showed you in your real colours. You little know what it has cost us, retiring when you should have engaged.' Then taking pity on the grizzled head hung in shame, 'I shall take care to see that you are not exposed to such a disagreeable situation again.'[8] Had Castries allowed d'Albert de Rions to sail with him to India, the *Monmouth*, *Isis* and *Hero* would never have escaped the inferno of Porto Praya and Admiral Hughes might even now be his guest in the *Héros*. The minister must send him a competent officer to fill that role. Until he did Suffren must be all things to himself.

Hughes was, in fact, nowhere to be seen at dawn on 18 February, as he had withdrawn to Trincomali to repair the underwater shot-holes that menaced three of his ships, as well the damage to the *Superb* and *Exeter*. So Suffren determined to look for his convoy. Some of it he found at Porto Novo on the 23rd and four others had taken shelter with the Danes at Tranquebar. The *Toscane* hospital ship had run foolishly into Negapatam and been captured, a sad loss for with her went his surgeons and all their medical supplies which could not, like guns, powder and shot, be easily replaced in India. Of the six ships that Hughes had taken, all but one had escaped. When the *Bellone* did not find the rest of the convoy at Pondicherry, Suffren had to assume that she had gone to Ceylon, and though it hurt him to do so he relieved Ruyter-Werfusé of his new command for failing to keep her under closer watch.

On 24 February, Duchemin and Suffren went ashore at Porto Novo, where Piveron and Haidar's *vakils*, or agents, were waiting for them. The fanfaronade of broadsides which had announced the arrival of the French was described to their waiting allies as a victory, but Sadras was, and everyone knew it, only a drawn battle. There was some justice in the decision by the supreme council at Fort William to celebrate the capture of one French transport and the silencing of French guns after two and half hours by a squadron inferior in numbers. Warren Hastings wrote comfortingly to Hughes that the combat 'must excite in the minds of all the powers in India a confirmed opinion of the unrivalled military character of the English nation'. Considering the hopes pinned on the French fleet by Haidar Ali, then a drawn battle was as good as a victory. 'We regard your action with the French fleet as the crisis of our fate in the Carnatic, and in the result of it we see the province relieved and preserved and the permanency of British power in India firmly established.'[9]

Even as he wrote a French army was marching on Cuddalore.

14. Haggling with Haidar Ali

Warren Hastings had always taken the French threat more seriously than his fellow presidents, while Macartney from the moment of his arrival in Madras had refused to treat it with the seriousness it deserved. If d'Estaing had been France's most senior and valued admiral, what had the former governor-general of the Caribbees to fear from this Admiral de Suffren? Anyhow, if there were French troops on their way to India, they must surely land on the western coast as 'they would be starved on this!'[1] If only the 'uncontrollable and impractical' Coote could be persuaded to relax his despotic and querulous preoccupation with the Carnatic and take guidance from Macartney, he might score a few real successes against Haidar. Look at what a bit of imagination had done at Negapatam and Trincomali! So off went Hugh Boyd, his personal secretary and a fellow Trinitarian from Dublin, to the King of Kandy on a secret embassy to contrive the victory that Coote seemed unable to win.

The proposal Boyd carried was for a joint offensive against the Dutch, who had driven the king from the coast and now confined him closely to the highlands. Once the Dutch had been expelled from Ceylon, the British and their Sinhalese allies would then mount a second front on the Malabar coast and take Haidar from the rear. This brilliant coup would at once secure Trincomali, stop Hughes nagging for reinforcements, bring a large and rich island under the protection of the Honourable Company and give Coote a reprieve from the endless campaigning in the Carnatic which was steadily killing him. 'We only want a little plan,' Macartney wrote to his fellow Celt, the unamiable Sir John Macpherson and the

governor-general's most active critic on the supreme council in
Fort William, 'but it is . . . impossible either to concert or pursue
while the present general remains with us . . . The notion of the
king's commander has operated so strongly on his pericranium
that I can't help thinking it was a powerful ingredient in his late
apoplexies.'[2]

The news of Sadras fired the governor's natural optimism. True
he was having difficulty with General Medows, who had refused
to take any command in India and sailed instead with James
Alms in the *Monmouth* to watch the battle at sea he had still
not witnessed. It seemed also to be true that the French had
established contact with Haidar who had turned south, clearly
to meet an expeditionary force at Pondicherry. If Macartney could
get Medows and Coote to work together, then, even if it landed, it
should cause them little anxiety. But four days later the situation
took a dramatic turn for the worse. While Hughes and Suffren
had been locked in battle off Sadras, Colonel Braithwaite and
the Tanjore army were cornered on the Coleroon. For 25 hours
his 2250 men had sustained an enveloping attack until, at noon
on the 18th, his square cut open by French mercenaries led by
the Savoyard Henri de Lallé and by the horse of Haidar's son,
Tipu, he surrendered. Tanjore and its rice fields were cut off and
when by ensuing posts the governor heard that the French were
going ashore at Porto Novo, even his ebullient spirits began to
droop.

Fortunately for the governor's drooping spirits the general
commanding the French force was a man of stubborn and
unimaginative caution. Castries had never intended Duchemin de
Chenneville to do more than defend Île de France. The business
of India was to be entrusted to the arch-wizard of the Deccan,
the Marquis de Bussy, and to a European army. The decision to
send Duchemin to India had been Souillac's, taken on his own
authority. His arrival served the important purpose of steeling
Haidar's resolve to continue the war, but it also meant that the
first regular French troops to land in India were commanded by
an officer who bordered on the incompetent.

He showed his quality from the start by refusing Suffren's advice
to seize Negapatam while Hughes was still licking his wounds
after Sadras. His first priority was to ensure the nawab's formal
adherence to the terms of the treaty which Souillac had drafted

on 11 November. Duchemin cannot be wholly blamed for wanting to ensure that his army was supplied with the 5000 head of beef and the 3000 sheep a month on which his European troops were to march and the six *lakh*s of rupees quarterly which would pay among other things for their women and their drink, but he was to show an obstinate failure to understand the reluctance of an Asian prince to commit himself too firmly before he had tested the quality of the men for which he was being asked to pay so handsomely.[3]

Haidar received the French emissaries on 3 March and sent them back with the promise of a *lakh* of rupees to be going on with. 'If the general trusts in me, he will not be disappointed.'[4] The French mercenaries in his service, however, warned them that the nawab might be rich but the war had cost him dearly already and the Carnatic was a waste. As a result Duchemin wanted neither to trust in the nawab nor to land a single man; but Suffren could not hang off shore indefinitely in an exposed anchorage without knowing where his convoy had got to. He insisted that the hesitant general believe what he was told and land his troops. With considerable reluctance Duchemin ordered his expedition ashore on 10 March and, hoping that a more senior officer might succeed where the first emissaries had failed, he sent his greedy brother with his aide-de-camp back to Haidar's camp. They saw the nawab on the 23rd: the haggling was prolonged and stubborn, but Haidar would not agree to any advance on one *lakh* of rupees. If he was to give more, the French must account for it and must engage not to withdraw from the alliance should France and England make peace. And Duchemin must guarantee that the French would always be superior to the British on land and sea.

The French commander agreed to these monstrous terms, having neither the competence to do so nor the intention to comply with them; all he wanted was the money. But he was soon to learn how unwise it was to rely on the generosity of an Indian prince. His repeated requests for cash before he did anything antagonized the nawab, who had still not forgotten the French defection the year before. A quick attack on Negapatam would have been more likely to unlock the store than continued inactivity. Yet the wretched French general was in an unenviable position. One *lakh* of rupees, even had he received it, would not have gone very far. Coote needed seven *lakh*s a month for his own army of 2000 Europeans and 5000 sepoys and it was costing the French interest at 36 per cent to raise a loan from the money-lenders of Tranquebar.

All this reminded Suffren dangerously of what had happened with d'Estaing at Savannah. While he waited off Porto Novo for Duchemin to complete his tortuous and impolitic negotiations, Hughes was refitting at Trincomali. Though the other half of his convoy was reported safe and sound at Galle, he needed its supplies. But it was now Duchemin's turn to call the odds. The negotiations with Haidar were being conducted on behalf of both the squadron and the expeditionary force, and the departure of the fleet before the treaty was signed would make Haidar less willing than ever to pay up.

Suffren could see the power of this argument but when he learned on 12 March that Hughes was back off Madras he knew he could not stay where he was. It took another five days to convince the nervous general that he must go, and by that time a whole month had passed since Sadras. His only gain in that month was the *Chaser* sloop, taken by the *Bellone* on 1 March. With 12 *lakh*s of rupees from Bengal she was a serious loss to Hughes, but with money in hand Duchemin was persuaded to let the admiral go in search of his convoy on 24 March and scored his first—and, as it happened, only—success of the war.

Cuddalore was a tiny British outpost, ill-defended by crumbling walls and a garrison of 400 sepoys and five European gunners under Captain James Hughes. Offered the honours of war if he capitulated, and sack by the Mysoreans if he did not, he accepted the pleasanter alternative on 8 April. Cuddalore was a poor place but it commanded a series of small creeks sufficient for landing supplies. They were also sluggish and malarial and their waters brackish, so the French soon began to drop with dysentery. Duchemin moved up to Manjukuppam, a few miles inland on higher ground, where he bivouacked among the ruins of the Company's neo-Palladian villas and orange groves, still blackened from their devastation by Haidar's men the year before. The march from Porto Novo in the humid heat of an Indian summer had been an atrocious experience for the soldiers from Europe who had never undergone anything like it, and most of the spirit for a great and noble adventure was sweated out of them before the month was over.

Cuddalore was a trifling capture compared to that of Negapatam but it was a beach-head of sorts. Haidar, however, was not impressed. His officers had been disconcerted by Duchemin's close and persistent enquiries about his honorarium, while junior French officers had assiduously put it about that 'in France they were very *grands seigneurs*, relations or favourites of the king, and that everything really depended on them and not on Duchemin, who was a mere soldier of fortune of the lowest caste in Europe'.[5]

Their intention was patently obvious both to the disgusted Mysoreans and to the embarrassed French mercenaries in their service. The rage to make a fortune had showed itself before they left Île de France and they had only embarked to intercept some of that legendary *bakshish* that had made the fortunes of men like Bussy in happier times. The nawab could see no reason to be more generous. So far the expedition had cost him one *lakh* for the army, 30,000 rupees in presents for Duchemin, 10,000 for his brother and 2000 for his ADC—all for Cuddalore. Had he known the French wanted it, he could have taken it for them on his way down to meet them at Porto Novo.[6]

One of the constant features of the naval conflict that had now begun in the Bay of Bengal was that both sides were desperately short of frigates. They were the eyes and ears of the fleet, the outriders, news-bearers, heralds and messengers. Frigates could take messages during a battle from the commanding officer to a captain out of sight of signals, or report progress at different points of the line. (Indeed after the Battle of the Saints, the French ordered their admirals to repair to a frigate in order to conduct a battle, as it were, from a safe observation post.) They could keep a watch on the movements of the enemy squadron, and undertake a quick filibuster into enemy waters. They could chase off the enemy's frigates, hunt privateers or behave like them, take messages between the fleet and the army, carry despatches, be sent off to fetch spares. A squadron like Suffren's operating so far from base needed plenty of frigates for all these purposes. He was to cry in vain in this campaign for more frigates, especially copper-bottomed ones.

Sir Edward Hughes, too, never had enough at his command, only the *Coventry*, which had to keep her station off the Malabar coast, and the 16-gun *Seahorse*, if we do not count the *Nymph* sloop, to match against the *Bellone*, *La Fine* and *Pourvoyeuse*.

As a result, the two squadrons sailed largely in ignorance of each other's movements. When Suffren left Porto Novo on 24 March, he knew that the coast was clear only because of overland reports of Hughes's arrival at Madras. The whole squadron had to go in search of his convoy because he had no frigates to send. He had somehow to raise money and, though he had already raised 15,000 pagodas, or 120,000 *livres*, from the sale of 14 ships at Tranquebar, the Dutch had given him no credit. So he had to take prizes and, as Castries had given him no frigates, he had to hunt in pack. And that was how he missed 11 important prizes.

From the moment he had taken Trincomali, Hughes had been worried about its meagre defences. By starving it of reinforcements Coote and Macartney between them seemed resolved to hand it over to the French. In exasperation he delivered his ultimatum on 13 March. He would sail in ten days' time and he must be given troops for the protection of the port. The reluctant commander-in-chief agreed and on 23 March the admiral sailed with troops and stores for Trincomali. He had been a week at sea, working down inshore against light winds and northerly currents, when he met his reinforcements: the *Sultan* and *Magnanime*, their convoy of seven ships carrying 1800 men of the 78th Regiment of Foot, the East Indiaman, *Hinchinbrooke*, so briefly the *Artésien*'s prize after Porto Praya, and a small French prize, the *Necker*. They had been ordered to India as soon it was known that Suffren had left the Cape and, like the *Monmouth, Hero* and *Isis* before them, they had dawdled on the way, largely because they had towed the *Necker* all the way from St Helena. When he learned this, Hughes was furious. 'Had these ships been conducted with common prudence and the least attention to the orders they were under our superiority would have been decisive [at Sadras].'[7]

Now that they had eluded Suffren at least, he determined to land the sick and scorbutic at Trincomali rather than Madras, 'without seeking or shunning the enemy',[8] for he shrewdly guessed that Suffren would not delay in making an attempt on the port. Indeed the normally timid governor of Colombo had written to the French as early as February proposing a joint attack. The fact that the letter took from February to June to reach Suffren did not mean that Hughes had sailed too soon. For he had guessed rightly, and Suffren, freed from Duchemin's obsessive greed, had recovered his sanguine spirits.

'I am in a superb position,' he wrote on 1 April to his landlocked cousin in Provence. 'I command 12 ships of the line, but—there are plenty of buts. I am afraid M de Castries will grant my request to be recalled after 18 months, for nowhere else could I be employed so brilliantly.'[9] It was in this ebullient mood that at noon on 8 April, off Point Calymère in Ceylon, he read the signal of the *Brisson* transport reporting 14 sail to the north-north-west. He followed them through the night. The next day he was in no doubt that they were Hughes's squadron.

At once, taking the lead in the *Héros*, he set off in pursuit. Hughes, knowing on the 8th that he had been sighted, hoped to reach Trincomali first. Short of 600 men despite the 300 Coote had lent him, and with the *Sultan* and *Magnanime* loaded with sick, he thought better of not shunning battle. But the wind was fitful and some of his ships sailed so poorly that, as the two squadrons flew south in Indian file through the 9th, 10th and 11th, Suffren was gaining on him all the time. On 10 April Salvert in *La Fine* captured a brig carrying Macartney's secretary with the tale of his sorry mission to Kandy. He had waited long in the courts of the king, but His Majesty had shown no desire to exchange the Dutch for the English as overlords. Suffren knew now that the Dutch no longer feared an uprising in the island so that, with a garrison of only 60 European and 400 native troops, Trincomali still hung at the end of a rope. He had only to drive Hughes off the coast to pluck the prize.

15. The Battle of Provedien, 12 April 1782

Suffren might have forced action on 10 April had all his ships been copper-bottomed, but his rear division was lagging behind. When the two squadrons reached the latitude of Trincomali the following morning, Hughes made a valiant effort to dash for home, setting studdingsails and beating to quarters, but the wind failed him. Realizing that he could not make it, he turned south at sunset and tried to work his way to windward of the French. But during the night he misjudged his course and at dawn on 12 April he was uncomfortably close to shore, while Suffren's coppered ships were eating up the seven or eight miles between them. At 09.00 Hughes bowed to the inevitable and ordered his ships into line of battle ahead on the starboard tack at two cables' distance from each other. The French were bearing north by east, about six miles behind with the wind north by east. The chase continued until 12.15 when they bore away to engage.

Suffren had difficulty in locking his ships into line so that he could benefit from having 12 to Hughes's 11. The *Héros* moved from the lead to the centre, as he had decided on a tactic that his captains must understand, a parallel action, ship against ship, the rearmost only to double. The air was close, the sky threatening and there were squalls of rain from the north-east, and behind the leaden clouds a storm was lurking. The two squadrons were now six or seven miles from a small coral island known by its Dutch name of Provedien, and 30 miles south of Trincomali. Both commanders knew that the fate of the port hung in the balance.

The Battle of Provedien

· 12 April 1782

North

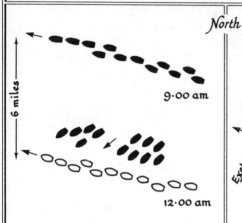

9.00 am

12.00 am

Forenoon of 12 April

Suffren closes on Hughes, having the weather gauge and with the English dangerously close to shore.

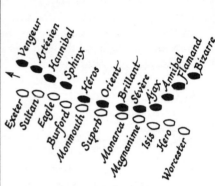

1·00 – 1·45 pm

First stage of the battle. French have formed crescent.

West ═══════════ WIND ═══════════ East

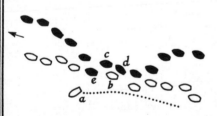

3·45 pm

The *Monmouth (a)* is beaten out of line and the *Superb (b)* is covered by the *Orient (c)* and *Brillant (d)*. The *Héros (e)* has drifted into the English line. At this moment wind from the north enables Hughes to disengage.

Ships' Captains at the Battles of Sadras and Provedien

ENGLISH ◯	FRENCH ⬤
Exeter ~ King	Vengeur ~ Forbin
Sultan* ~ Watt	Artésien ~ Maurville
Eagle ~ Reddal	Hannibal ~ Galles
Burford ~ Reynier	Sphinx ~ du Chilleau
Monmouth ~ Alms	Héros ~ Suffren
Superb ~ Hughes	Orient ~ Pallière
Monarca ~ Gell	Brillant ~ Saint-Félix
Magnanime* ~	Sévère ~ Cillart
Wolseley	Ajax ~ Bouvert
Isis ~ Lumley	Annibal ~ Tromelin
Hero ~ Hawker	Flamand ~ Cuverville
Worcester ~ Wood	Bizarre ~ Landelle
	(* Did not fight at Sadras)

South

Suffren's foremost ships were in range shortly after 13.00 hours, sweeping down in an arc, the *Vengeur* and *Artésien* in the lead, followed at a distance by the *Hannibal* and *Sphinx*, then the *Héros* and *Orient* in the centre and the rest of the uncoppered ships, the *Brillant*, *Sévère*, *Ajax*, *Flamand* and *Bizarre*, tailing away at ever increasing distances. Despite all his efforts to keep his line close, the two leading ships had stretched too far ahead and when they exchanged their first shots with the *Exeter* and *Sultan*, Forbin in the *Vengeur*, suddenly disconcerted by the distance between him and the rest of the squadron, luffed in order to expose the *Exeter* to his broadside instead of bearing down upon her. The *Artésien* followed suit, with the result that both ships held off at a distance. Suffren, determined this time on decisive action, ordered them at once to resume their original tack and made straight for the British centre himself, ignoring their first shots of greeting until, at pistol-shot range about 13.45, he made signal to open fire.

Despite all his signals, his slowest ships were well to the rear of where they should have been and, following the letter if not the spirit of Suffren's orders, the captains all luffed at the same instant as those ahead of them. Thus the French line formed a curve; at one extremity were the *Artésien* and *Vengeur*, at the other the *Bizarre*, *Ajax* and *Sévère*, and as a result they were too far from their opposites in the British line. The *Héros* and her next astern, the *Orient*, alone were in pistol-shot range. In the next 15 minutes first the *Hannibal* then the *Sphinx* closed in, Morard de Galles bringing his 50-gun ship down upon the 64-gun *Eagle*, being wounded in the arm at once. Du Chilleau's *Sphinx* engaged the 70-gun *Burford*.

Gun for gun, the British had the greater weight in the van—64 versus 64, 74 versus 64, 64 versus 50 and 70 versus 64—but Suffren had concentrated his greatest weight in the centre for conflict with the *Monmouth*, 64, *Superb*, 74, and *Monarca*, 68. For his own attentions he had singled out the flagship of his rival once again; their first shots were exchanged at 13.40 and in those first few minutes shot from the *Superb* severed one of the braces of the *Héros* and, unable as a result to back her topsails in time, she carried on to fetch up alongside the *Monmouth*. Once again Suffren found himself ranged against the 'black ship of Grenada' and so close did he come, making the signal again for all ships to engage at pistol-shot, that James Alms thought he was about to be boarded.

Alms luffed up to rake his attacker, backed his topsails and engaged the *Héros, Sphinx* and *Hannibal.* For nearly an hour and a quarter he held them off. Twice the *Monmouth*'s colours were shot away and had to be nailed to the stump of the mizzenmast. Seven guns were dismounted, Alms was struck in the face by splinters, two musket-balls went through his hat, his hair was set on fire, his coat torn between his shoulders and one of its skirts shot away.[1] The wheel was twice cleared and only two people were left on the quarter-deck. Hughes in the meantime found himself locked with the *Orient,* and Gell in the *Monarca* with Saint-Félix in the *Brillant.* All was hell and confusion in the centre when, just before 15.00, the *Monmouth*'s mizzenmast toppled overboard, to be followed shortly after by her mainmast which crashed over the larboard quarter and caused her to drift slowly out of position.

Though the *Superb* was now ablaze, Hughes determined to do what he could to help her and, by hauling close to the wind, edged to the windward of the *Héros* which was too cut about to prevent him. But a violent explosion in the *Superb* pulled her up short and the *Orient* and *Brillant* moved up in support to put themselves between the two flagships. The shock of their guns forced Sir Edward to give way and rejoin his line, passing to leeward of the *Monmouth,* now drifting down the French line, the helpless victim of a broadside from each of the seven ships she passed.

At 15.40 Hughes found himself driving dangerously close to the shore, and when the wind continued far northerly without any sea breeze he had to take immediate action to avoid running on the reef. He signalled his ships to wear and haul their wind in line of battle ahead on the larboard tack, still engaging the enemy. The movement was made in perfect order, but when Suffren followed suit the difference between the sailors in the two squadrons was demonstrated with disconcerting eloquence. His order was executed without the same admirable despatch—by the *Vengeur* and *Artésien* too slowly, by the *Ajax* the wrong way round, so that she was blown temporarily out of the action. At the same moment the mainsail of the *Orient* caught fire and her crew was fully absorbed in extinguishing it.

RIGHT. Le Chevalier de Suffren, by the Swedish portraitist in Paris, Alexandre Roslin. The portrait shows Suffren before he grew very corpulent and was probably done while in his 40s and enjoying his first commandery. Roslin often painted from other people's sketches and this shows a more romantic-looking Suffren than the more realistic portraits of 10 to 15 years later.

RIGHT. Vice-Admiral Sir Edward Hughes by Sir Joshua Reynolds. (National Maritime Museum, Greenwich.)

ABOVE. Suffren being received at the camp of Haidar Ali Khan. Already – it is July 1782 – Suffren in uniform looks, to use his own words, like 'a hog in armour'.

LEFT. Lieutenant-General Sir Eyre Coote, commander-in-chief in India, a brilliant sepoy general who, like his countryman, the Duke of Wellington, never lost a battle. (Attributed to H Morland. National Portrait Gallery, London.)

ABOVE. The Battle of Cuddalore, 17 June 1983, the last of the five ferocious battles between Admirals Suffren and Hughes, actually fought after peace had been signed in Europe. (Musée de la Marine, Paris.)

BELOW. 'Indians from the Coast of Malabar by a Mediterranean shore', by Henry Tresham RA. The inscription identifies the shore as Malta and the subjects 'as being brought over by Admiral Suffrein'. (Original in India Office Library, London.)

LEFT. Pierre-André de Suffren, a bust commissioned by the Estates General in the Hague from France's leading sculptor at the time, Jean-Antoine Houdon, and now in the Mauritshuis. The immense dewlaps do not diminish the air of vigorous authority depicted by the artist.

BELOW. A sample of Suffren's handwriting. A signed letter to Grand Master de Rohan from Martinique, 3 January 1777, in which he complains about the West Indian campaign. The Archives the Knights Hospitaller in Malta, MS 1242.

During the interval before the resumption of battle, the *Hero* cast a rope to the *Monmouth* and towed her out of danger without hindrance from Maurville de Langle in the *Artésien*, to whom Suffren was shouting through his speaking trumpet orders to intercept and reduce the hapless vessel. At 17.30 the foretopgallant yard of the *Héros* fell and, his ship temporarily unmanoeuvrable, Suffren moved to the *Ajax*. From Bouvet's quarter-deck he could now see how close to shore both squadrons were.

Hughes sounded 15 fathoms at 17.40 and ordered his ships to prepare to anchor and, though Suffren's rear (now his van) was safely out of range, his centre ships were still perilously close to the enemy. The firing continued until after dusk when, according to Sir Edward, 'the enemy's squadron drew off in great disorder to the eastward and the engagement ceased'.[2] Matters were not quite as simple as that. In the fading daylight, murky with driving rain from the north-east, the *Orient* and *Héros*, the latter almost helpless from the state of her standing rigging, had been forced to drop anchor in seven fathoms, so close to the English ships that they could hear the English sailors shouting across to one another. They were also too close for safety to the razor-sharp reefs of coral on to which they had all but driven and which now threatened both squadrons impartially. Nearby the *Monmouth* tossed dangerously in less than four fathoms, grinding her timbers against the coral at every swell of the sea, and most of Hughes's ships were too preoccupied with their own safety to take much notice of the French in their midst.

From the deck of the *Ajax* Suffren ordered *La Fine* to tow the *Héros* out of the mêlée before total darkness fell. Salvert was able to pass a rope to the stricken ship, but before he could pull her clear the lowering storm clouds had so reduced visibility that his frigate brushed against the *Isis* and caught her bowsprit in her shrouds. For several minutes no one on deck knew what had happened, only the men aloft realizing that they had run into an Englishman and hacking away at the ropes, while in the confusion a number of British prisoners on *La Fine* cut for freedom. Running to the quarter-deck, Captain Lumley bellowed through his speaking trumpet that if the French gunners fired a shot he would blast *La Fine* out of the water with his lower batteries. When he received no answer but a stunned silence, he thought Salvert had surrendered and prepared to send men aboard. At that moment the *Orient*, blundering out of her own unpleasant position in casualties' corner, sliced through the tow-rope and in doing so plucked the frigate free from her dangerous entanglement.

Moissac, left in sole command of the *Héros*, now despaired of rescue and, putting a spring on his cable, he whistled for the wind that might, if it changed direction, swing him clear or turn him head on to the enemy if at daybreak they bore down to take him. But at 21.30 a breeze blew from the south-west and, cutting his cable, he sailed clear of the enemy to anchor alongside the *Ajax*. Through the rest of the night the two squadrons lay at anchor, not sure what was to happen next. 'Six hours of bad weather,' Hughes wrote in his diary, 'might lose us the squadron, but my sole consolation was that the enemy would suffer the same fate.'[3]

At dawn on 13 April the two rivals viewed the disorder of their opponents, separated by about two miles. Hughes's glass showed him the French 'in much disorder and apparent distress, but they had lost no lower masts'.[4] Both squadrons were frantically employed in repairing their damage, each uncertain of the intentions of the other. Would Suffren renew the attack? Would Hughes try to rescue the *Monmouth*? The safety of that vessel was now Hughes's chief concern, for Captain Alms was in no state to defend himself. The British casualties had been 137 killed and 430 wounded and the *Monmouth* alone accounted for 45 of the dead and 102 of the wounded. Though these were not as high as Sir Edward's on the *Superb*—he had lost 59 dead and 96 wounded—the *Monmouth* was more extensively damaged.

No French ship had been as badly savaged. Most of them, however, had been badly cut about aloft and their casualties, more evenly distributed among the squadron, had been, with 139 dead and 351 wounded, little smaller than those of the British. Only the *Vengeur*, to which Suffren now shifted his flag, had escaped comparatively unhurt, with only two wounded men on board. The ferocity of this battle may be gauged by a comparison with the British losses at Trafalgar, when the casualties in the two 100-gun battleships, the *Victory* and *The Royal Sovereign*, were, respectively, 59 and 47 killed and 102 and 94 wounded.

It took Suffren until 16 April to complete his repairs, and only then could he contemplate a renewal of the conflict. But he was not sure he enjoyed a commanding position. 'We are still in presence,' he reported to the minister, 'and are going to have a third affair.

Afterwards I do not know what I shall do for we shall probably have no more spars, cordage, powder or shot. We are anchored in very bad water two thirds of a league from the shore and only half a cannon shot from the English ... There are few examples of a conflict like the one we have just had and the squadron has lost about 500 men, half of whom are dead and dying.'[5]

Though the *Monmouth* was disabled, the *Superb* crippled and it was open to him to attack Hughes where he lay, he decided against renewing the battle. The English were anchored alongside a reef and an attack on a squadron in such a position called for greater seamanship in his captains than he could command. Until he was reunited with his convoy he was, moreover, short of ammunition. His casualties were high and he needed to rest his exhausted crews, while short as he was of 12 topmasts and with nowhere nearer than Île de France to refit he could not risk incurring more damage to his ships. He had now fought two battles within six weeks and he had no Trincomali to which he could go to repair the damage and rest his men. If he were forced to leave the coast after a third battle, the nearest place to go to would be Malacca; and if he had to do that, the English would lose no time in reducing the rest of Ceylon. Hughes, moreover, was better manned than he.

But this reasoning was all specious. Had he made for Trincomali, Hughes must have followed him and a third battle would have ensued. He could not know that, by the time Sir Edward returned to Madras, scurvy had reduced his musters to half-strength. The real reason for his decision not to do so was the one he put last. 'To try such a thing with any hope of success there must be both capacity and will, and assuredly I have tried these enough not to want to hazard them on one throw.'[6] His cousin Forbin in the *Vengeur* and Maurville in the *Artésien*, commanding his two fastest ships, had failed him badly. Tromelin had once again shown either malice or incapacity by not seeing that the rear engaged closely, though, when he eventually came into action in the latter part of the battle, his ship had fought well. Landelle in the *Bizarre* had not doubled on the English rear as ordered. Had they all fought like Pallière and Saint-Félix in the centre, Hughes might have lost the *Monmouth* and been forced off the coast, leaving Trincomali for the taking. 'If in this squadron we do not change five or six, that is half, of the captains we shall never achieve anything and perhaps miss every opportunity that offers.'[7]

He abandoned his station off Provedien with great reluctance. The sloop *Diligente* was sent down the coast to summon the convoy waiting at Galle to meet him at Batticaloa, where he hoped the Dutch could take his sick and wounded ashore. But in case Hughes gave him a chance to attack, he waited off the island for two more days. Sir Edward was not to be tempted. On 19 April Suffren threw down the gauntlet unmistakably and sailed down on the enemy in line but, seeing the English unmoved, and unwilling to sail too close to the reefs, he tacked at 15.00 hours, nagged by a new thought.

Hughes's unwillingness to accept battle from the start and his refusal to pick up the challenge now were suspicious. He was no less strong than Suffren; could he be expecting reinforcements, before the arrival of which he would take no risks? More masts, cordage, powder and shot were important, but more important was the need for a base nearer than Île de France. And he was not now master of Trincomali because half his captains had fought only half a battle. The victory that still eluded him, moreover, would have had an importance far beyond the tactical advantages of France in India for, unknown to Suffren, 12 April 1782 was a fateful day for France's navy. On the other side of the world, his friend and former fellow Knight of Malta, Admiral de Grasse, had surrendered his sword to Admiral Rodney after the Battle of the Saints. The sword of Sir Edward Hughes, but for the incompetence of Tromelin, Maurville and Forbin, might have been a partial consolation for this terrible defeat. It was not in Suffren's nature to forget or to forgive.

16. The Marquis de Bussy

Suffren took 11 days to get to Batticaloa, but there he met his convoy at last and on 1 May he watered and started to put his sick ashore. Hughes, he learned, had returned to Madras on 22 April. At Batticaloa Suffren also found the *Pulvériseur* with despatches from Souillac. He read them with astonishment. The governor of Île de France required him to return there instantly to await the arrival of the Marquis de Bussy and his expeditionary force. If he could have contemplated leaving India before Provedien, now it was unthinkable. No matter what great designs were afoot in France, his place was in the Bay of Bengal if there was ever to be an ally for the great Bussy to meet or a landing place at which to go ashore.

The French government had resolved finally to send an army to India in the summer of 1781, but the orders were sealed only when it was known that the Cape was safe and Île de France had been garrisoned. At long last the lucubrations of successive governors of Pondicherry and the proposals of numerous military adventurers in the service of the Indian princes had crystallized into a set of royal instructions. After 22 years of luxurious retirement, Charles Joseph Patissier, Marquis de Bussy, was to return to India. The former uncrowned ruler of the Deccan was 63 and a martyr to gout, but his 'knowledge of Asiatic politics and his success during the last war in India' persuaded the king to appoint him commander-in-chief of all forces by land and sea in India.[1]

No one contemplating his extraordinary career dared dispute that Bussy alone was the man who could complete the destruction of the

English upon which Haidar Ali was already engaged unassisted. Certainly his 20 years in India read like an oriental romance: the tale of an impoverished heir to a marquisate who sailed east to seek his fortune and who rose to be the effective ruler of the great central plateau of India that formed the Nizamate of Hyderabad and is roughly marked today by the state of Andhra Pradesh. He showed unusual qualities for the role of *éminence grise* to an Indian prince—a flair for languages, military acumen, great personal courage, decision in the face of panic, an acute penetration of the Indian mind and, above all, a pliant and subtle duplicity which proved too much for the enemies who wished to poison his monarch's mind against him and indispensable to the prince who protected him.

After eight years in Hyderabad, where Salajat Jang was totally dependent upon both his counsel and the army which he had drilled into a formidable fighting force indisputably loyal to himself, colossally rich, apparently unmovable, Bussy and his splendid empire were destroyed by the jealousy of France's commander-in-chief in India, Lally de Tollendal. Lally despised him for a fortune-hunter and ordered him to abandon his careful neutrality in the Deccan and to march to his assistance in the Carnatic. At Wandewash in January 1760 he was captured by Sir Eyre Coote during the engagement that broke the French challenge in India. Salajat Jang was instantly deposed by his brother, Ali Khan, who exchanged gifts with the British and occupied the dazzling edifice that Bussy had left. With France's hold on the Deccan gone for ever, Bussy retired to England and captivity. He was released on parole and bought an estate in France, where he lived in seclusion, fighting off recurrent attacks of malaria and gout. From time to time he went to Paris to advise on Indian affairs, and in the autumn of 1777 he was formally invited to submit a plan for a renewed invasion of India.

From his experience of the various alliances available, Bussy would have preferred the Marathas and an attack on Bombay. At no time did he show any enthusiasm for Haidar Ali, partly because he distrusted and disliked the man, partly because he thought that with Haidar as an ally French chances of an alliance also with Poona and Hyderabad were prejudiced. But if France were to win allies at all, she must ask for no territorial reward in India (he was later to be horrified to hear of the terms Duchemin had been instructed to demand) and her expeditionary force must be so strong in men and money that it could be independent of local support. In his view that meant a force of 9000 European soldiers and a budget of ten million *livres*. The British, he estimated, had 9000 European troops in India and their 70,000 sepoys would be offset by the armies of France's Indian allies. The Marathas only took, never gave, money and it would be fatal to have to depend on the generosity of so shiftless an ally as Haidar Ali. Demonstrably strong and transparently disinterested, only then could the Marquis de Bussy hazard a return to the scene of his early triumphs.

His minimum conditions could not be met. Castries promised him 6–7,000 men, naval superiority—which meant substantial reinforcements for Suffren—and five million *livres* in cash. For the other five million he must look to the Dutch. Bussy accepted these terms wryly. At this price and strength, he warned the minister, he could promise neither an attack on any major British establishment nor an Indian ally. But in order to make the most of what he found, he demanded and was given absolute command as lieutenant-general of all forces in the east by land and sea. The naval squadron must be required to subordinate its operations entirely to those on land and be always ready to lend him men. Once again the pernicious doctrine that ships were inferior to soldiers was written into orders and the brilliant opportunism of a Suffren subjected to the megalomania of a Bussy. But the new lieutenant-general was to find that his troops did not come up to the number that Castries had promised. He was ordered to sail with 4000 of the 7000 he had expected. The rest, it was piously believed, were waiting idle in Port Louis.

For the royal instructions were sealed on 11 November 1781, in blissful confidence that the men and ships at Île de France were still there. Parallel despatches to d'Orves, Souillac and Duchemin ordered no expedition to leave the island until the great man himself arrived so that the terror of his name could make a suitable impact on the enemy, to be followed at once by the decisive blow against Bombay or, if Haidar were still at war—'hardly to be hoped for'—against Madras.[2] Everything was to be done to make it possible for Bussy to select a landing on the west coast, the king even writing into his instructions every objection to a campaign in the Carnatic: the indifference and unreliability of the Dutch, the caprice of the monsoon, and the duplicity of Hyderabad. Only if Haidar were actually investing Madras and if Negapatam were still in Dutch hands was a landfall on the Coromandel coast to be chosen. Otherwise the object was Bombay, to be attacked if possible before Sir Edward Hughes was back from his station off Madras and, if Montigny in Poona had been able with the promise of Bussy's return to tempt the Marathas into an alliance, by an irresistible coalition on land.

These were the astonishing arguments that Suffren read off Batticaloa. Except for the news that Bussy was coming with men and, more important, ships, they seemed quite irrelevant to the situation of May 1782. Instead of a broadcast declaration that France had no territorial ambitions in India, Duchemin had asked for and obtained the slippery promise of lands worth 20 million rupees a year and, far from operating independently of Indian money, the French expeditionary force was humiliatingly tied to the purse-strings of the Nawab of Sera. If he was astonished, his former comrade at arms, Souillac, had been deeply embarrassed. The despatches effectively countermanded the orders he had given Duchemin on 15 November, only four days after the king had sealed his instructions for Bussy in Paris. But as Haidar was not actually investing Madras, and as he was not Bussy's preferred ally, then perhaps it would not matter so much if Suffren returned to Île de France. By the time Suffren had returned, the first of Bussy's ships would have arrived and he could be back off the coast, refitted and reinforced, in April.

This was plain nonsense, and the recall was unworthy of a captain of His Most Christian Majesty's navy. Suffren, moreover, had a very good precedent for refusing the order to return, outrageous as much to his tactical as to his diplomatic sense. D'Estaing, instead of leaving Martinique for France as instructed in 1779, had sailed westwards to Savannah and, in Suffren's not wholly impartial view, more was now at stake in India than d'Estaing had ever hoped to achieve in America. To abandon Duchemin, perilously weakened by sickness and inertia at Cuddalore, would be to expose Haidar to the whispers of a negotiated peace and Ceylon to capture by Sir Eyre Coote. To imitate Tronjoly and d'Orves and to abandon the coast now would surrender whatever advantage he had gained from his two battles and leave the Bay of Bengal uncontested to his rival.

The fact, too, that most of his captains could not wait to return to the fleshpots of *la nouvelle colonie de Vénus* merely added spice to the irritation of his resolve. A long letter from Saint-Félix received after Provedien was followed by a visit from the captain of the *Brillant* as soon as he had anchored at Batticaloa. Saint-Félix was convinced, and so were his fellow captains, that a return to Île de France was now the only right thing to do and the admiral should call a council of war. Suffren, disgusted to find so brave an officer the spokesman in an unworthy cause, was short. 'One calls a Council to find out what people think. As you have told me what they think, I see no need to call one.'[3] But he thought better of it. Knowing that they must sooner or later learn of the contents of Souillac's despatch, he summoned them all on board the *Héros*. There he left them in no doubt about their future. Since they had dared to cabal behind his back, they had forfeited any right to an opinion. He was giving them their orders.

The proceedings were short and sharp. 'I have, gentlemen, only a few words to say to you. I have decided to remain in India and you know why as well as I. What, perhaps, you do not know is the tenor of His Majesty's general instructions which dictate what we should do. I know them by heart and they run like this: "The wisdom of His Majesty does not attempt to determine any particular operation. He knows that, 4000 leagues away, it would be unwise to do so, and he limits himself as a result to informing M le Comte d'Orves that the inactivity of the squadron is what he principally forbids." '[4] Then, tiring of this elaborate persiflage, he flung out a challenge. 'It would be better to sink the squadron under the walls of Madras than to retire from before Sir Edward Hughes. If any one of your men believes I am capable of such an act of cowardice, let him come and tell me and I shall tell him what I have decided. You may inform your officers and men that these are my orders.'[5]

As he understood the tactical needs of the war so well it is sad that he could not share his understanding with his captains. But the opposition of Thomas d'Orves's former comrades had now become a personal matter. The Tromelins and Saint-Félixes, like the la Clues and Tronjolys before them, were too set in their ways to learn that war at sea was a serious and often decisive factor in the births and deaths of empires. If France ever hoped to wrest the control of India from the British, she would first have to destroy the squadron of Sir Edward Hughes. He sensed, too, that in the easy camaraderie of the mess-cabin the senior had infected the junior officer, and his combustible temper crackled at the hint of intrigue. He dismissed the captains from his state cabin as unworthy of hearing the arguments he now patiently rehearsed for Souillac in Port Louis.

He would need 45 days to go to Haidar and explain his departure and another 40 days to sail to Île de France. Then he would need more time to careen and another 30 days to return to India. Total: 160 days. Six months lost and God alone knew what the enemy might do in the meantime. Hughes, whom he had already beaten twice, would neglect no opportunity to say that he had been beaten himself. True, several ships were sadly in need of repairs and many of his men were wounded and sick, but two crossings of over 1200 leagues was not what they wanted. What they wanted was a base in India, and Suffren was determined to get one. Souillac should instead send everything Suffren needed to Galle, including any copper-bottomed vessels no matter how small. The squadron would not leave the coast.[6]

Souillac wasted no time being affronted. If Suffren left the coast, he explained to the minister, then Haidar Ali would make his peace with the British and Duchemin's troops would count themselves very lucky if they managed to escape to Ceylon. 'The brave decision by M de Suffren may save India and prepare for the success of M le Marquis de Bussy.'[7] That gentleman would need all the luck he could get. For if he expected whole-hearted co-operation from the Dutch, he was going to be disappointed. Dutch policy was to do as little as being at war permitted to annoy the British, and by inaction to preserve Ceylon from a British-fomented insurrection in Kandy. Their failure to hold on to Trincomali and Negapatam and their obstinate insistence on being paid for everything they supplied from Batticaloa and Galle only strengthened Suffren's resolve to keep the coast. It was as important to put some spine into Falck at Colombo as to bolster the belligerence of Haidar Ali. In the event, however, nothing was to justify his decision to stay where he was more than the news that any hope Souillac might have had of seeing Bussy at Île de France in April was the product of unthinking optimism.

On 4 January 1782 the 60-gun *Saint-Michel*, Captain d'Aymar, left Cadiz with Bussy on board, bound for the Canaries. With him sailed the 74-gun *Illustre*, the *Consolante* frigate, the *Lézard* cutter and three transports. There they were to join a joint squadron from Brest, one bound for the West Indies, the other for the East Indies. Bussy and his little flotilla arrived at the rendezvous, and so did two ships from Brest carrying his heavy artillery, but the rest were driven back to Brest by Admiral Kempenfelt. As the marquis was impatient to get on, he did not wait for the rest of his expected convoy and left the Canaries on 16 January. He was to gain little from his impatience. The *Illustre* was such a bad sailer and the weather so unhelpful that, by the time he should have been at Île de France, he had only reached Table Bay. There he decided to wait for the ships that had not joined him at the Canaries while the Dutch governor, obsessed by fear of a British attack, begged him to leave at least half his force behind to defend the Cape.

Disillusionment was not long in following. After several days of great talk, the *Marquis de Castries* arrived with Bussy's artillery but also with the depressing news that his escort had been driven back to Brest. A packet from Île de France also informed him that d'Orves was dead and that the expedition he was supposed to lead triumphantly to India had already sailed. Then, to cap everything, Bussy himself fell ill and could not move for nearly two months.[8] At last, agreeing reluctantly to leave nearly 1700 men at the Cape on the understanding that they should be sent on as soon as reinforcements arrived, he sailed for Île de France on 28 April. His last action at Cape Town was to ask the Dutch governors in the East Indies to have his five million *livres* waiting for him, and he reached Port Louis on 31 May. The bills went ahead to be presented on a bankrupt community.

A second attempt to support Bussy was made on 11 February, when de Guichen led out a second convoy including four ships of the line for India: two 74s, the *Fendant* and *Argonaute*, and two 64s, the *Hardi* and *Alexandre*, together with the *Cléopâtre* frigate and *Chasseur* corvette. On board 35 transports were 2500 men and massive supplies of the materials of war. This time they were luckier. All but one small transport, picked up by the *Sceptre* on her way to join Hughes, reached the Cape on 19 May. But if they had escaped the British, they had not escaped the scurvy. It was to be a long time before Peynier, leading the convoy in the *Fendant*, was able to join Bussy in Île de France.

A third and last attempt was made to complete the expedition on 19 April, but on the 23rd Admiral Barrington was in full chase

and ten of the transports and two of the escort were taken. The
rest returned disconsolately to Brest. These then were the proud
reinforcements for which Souillac had thought fit to recall the
squadron from India. A limp and tardy lot, and Suffren was to
fight another battle before he had sight of any of them and two
more before Bussy himself arrived. Meanwhile Lord Sandwich
had not been idle. As soon as he picked up word of Bussy's
projected departure, he resolved to reinforce Sir Edward Hughes.
On 22 January Commodore Sir Richard Bickerton hoisted his
broad pennant in the 80-gun *Gibraltar*. She was a splendid Spanish
prize, taken only in 1780, and with her were to sail seven other
line-of-battle ships, two frigates and nearly 4000 troops 'with all
despatch to Fort St George'.[9]

17. Keeping the Coast

Bickerton's relief squadron sailed on 5 February 1782. Apart from the *Gibraltar* there were two 74s, the *Cumberland*, seven years old and with Ushant, St Vincent (1780) and the relief of Gibraltar on her battle honours, and *Defence*, built in 1763, the *Cumberland*'s companion at St Vincent; three 64s, the *Africa* and *Sceptre*, both brand-new, and *Inflexible*, one year old. There was one 50-gun ship, the *Bristol*, built in 1775, with the scars of Charleston on her timbers. The two frigates, the *Medea*, 28, and *Juno*, 32, were new, and, most important of all, every ship in the squadron was copper-bottomed.

It was a deadly and superior force, to which Peynier's little relief squadron, one of which had to be condemned on arrival at Port Louis, could not compare. Commodore Bickerton himself had assisted at the 'Lagos affair' in the fire-ship *Aetna*, at Ushant in the *Terrible*, and at the second relief of Gibraltar in the *Fortitude*. If this experienced sailor, with ships either well-weathered or repaired, were to reach the Bay of Bengal before either d'Aymar or Peynier, he could swing the balance decisively against Suffren and his battle-weary squadron, while the *Gibraltar* with her massive tonnage, her crew of 700 and the carronades on her quarter-deck, was a mighty engine of destruction which no ship at Suffren's disposal could equal. And there was no Kempenfelt or Barrington lurking off Plymouth to pounce upon him.

Suffren's luck, however, was in, for Bickerton's passage was bedevilled by misadventure. On the night of 11 February he was unaccountably separated from both the *Sceptre* and *Medea* and, after crawling through light equatorial winds, reached Rio de Janeiro only on 29 April to find that these two ships 'to my utter astonishment and concern' had left for Madras on the 21st. Scurvy, moreover, had begun its deadly work among the troops on the transports and an alarming number of those who were allowed on shore fell victim almost at once to the special maladies of the Rio stews, so that he was forced to linger there until the end of May.[1]

It was September before he reached Bombay and much had happened while he was on the high seas. For the lordly dispositions of the Courts of St James's and Versailles were largely irrelevant to the daily uncertainties of the sub-continent. Both Suffren and Hughes expected to be reinforced but they knew neither the day nor the hour nor the form it would take. Lord Shelburne wrote to warn Sir Eyre Coote on 6 July 1782 that Bussy was on his way, when Bussy was already in Île de France, and Coote received the news only on 27 January 1783, when Bussy was on his way to Ceylon. Bussy himself learned that his convoy had been dispersed only when he was at the Cape and had already decided to leave for Île de France. Hughes did not know that Bickerton was on his way until the *Sceptre* reached Madras on 13 July, and when he left the coast in October he actually passed him off Ceylon without knowing it.

War may be an option of difficulties, but it was clear to both admirals that they must stay off the Coromandel coast for as long as possible and lose no chance to beat the other off it. Both buoyed themselves up with the hope that one would destroy the other before his relief arrived. Suffren, after the bitter disappointment of Provedien, was pitting all on a third and conclusive encounter. At Batticaloa, waiting for his convoy to join him from Galle, he set himself to bringing this about.

The *Bellone* brought the transports in at last on 16 May, 15 days after Suffren had anchored there, and with them a Dutch storeship loaded with munitions and a prize which sold for half a million welcome *livres*. His position was still critical. Greater men than Tronjoly and d'Orves would have had every excuse to return to Île de France, and to his captains the resolve to stay and try the odds with Sir Edward Hughes for a third time seemed foolhardy to the point of self-destruction. He had admitted almost as much when he had sent his list of requisitions to Souillac: at least, and at once,

1200 men, 12 topmasts, anchors, cables, cordage of every kind, medicaments, surgeons, jury masts, oars and, above all, powder and shot. 'For we have no more than a third of our ammunition left for a single battle.' He impressed lascars and bought 'kafirs' but they were poor substitutes for Europeans. 'Send me everything you have.'[2] Last but not least he asked for ships. Any fast sailer, copper-bottomed, would do very well, even the English prize he had sent back carrying his despatches. He bullied the Dutch into giving him what he knew they had in the way of artillery and he commandeered the ammunition on board two transports bound for Batavia. His only comfort was the news that Hughes was in a worse plight than he.

Sir Edward had anchored in Back Bay on 22 April, his crews reduced to half-strength by sickness and a death-roll from battle and disease of 380. The health of the 1462 sick and wounded, moreover, was not improved by a serious scarcity of fresh meat and vegetables, and forage parties had to wander far from the security of Trincomali into hostile country. By 1 May, 110 more of his sick had died. Nevertheless he hoped to have rested and recovered enough of the 800 survivors to man his ships by the end of the month. 'Until this is effected,' he told Macartney, 'the squadron is in no condition to proceed on any service.'[3] The *Sultan, Magnanime* and *Monmouth* had, each of them, scarcely 30 fit men aboard, and every artificer in the squadron was employed in rigging up a new mainmast for the last and in repairing the masts of the others. If the convoy expected from Malabar attempted to sail round to the eastern coast he could not protect it. 'Be the event what it will,' he concluded flatly, 'I am conscious of my having done everything in my power for the public service.'[4]

Suffren could, it was true, rely on the listless support of the Dutch but, even so, his energy in preparing his own scarred and weary squadron for sea was more marked than his rival's. Hughes allowed his captains, whom he trusted, to work at their own speed and he gave them a liberal timetable. Suffren had to rely on his own vitality to overcome the obtuse inertia of his own officers and his greater enemy—time. For the third battle must be fought before Hughes was reinforced.

On 1 June Hughes gave an indirect hint that he would be at Trincomali for some time to come. Three ships from Batavia, loaded with ships' stores and 400,000 *livres* in cash, put their noses into the mouth of Trincomali harbour. Discovering their mistake just in time, they turned and fled. They were not pursued. Such a wink was as good as a nod to the impatient Suffren, and he decided to risk the passage past Trincomali to Cuddalore, land the artillery he had borrowed and in return borrow some soldiers from Duchemin to man his ships. He would then return to Ceylon. Everything hinged on Hughes. If he could then be lured away and beaten, Trincomali might soon be French. If Hughes was determined to stay put until reinforced then, without d'Aymar and Peynier, Suffren must acknowledge that he could not keep the coast. But Sir Edward had shown that he was not the sort of commander who wished to avoid battle, and if Suffren trailed his coat sufficiently the gallant admiral must surely emerge from his lair.

Suffren sailed on 23 July and was off Trincomali the next day. When *La Fine* reported that the English were under sail but at anchor below the fort guns, Suffren sailed on north. On 5 August he was at Tranquebar, where he met the two Batavians which had nearly sailed into Hughes's clutches, and for the next 15 days he kept Danish waters, transferring stores from the Dutchmen and buying biscuit. While he was there, unknown to Macartney, the governor of Fort St George decided to send a small reinforcement down the coast for the army in Tanjore and for the garrison at Trincomali. It comprised six Company ships, and Macartney failed to order them to keep well out to sea, in case the French were off the coast, and failed to warn Hughes that they were coming. On 1 June the little flotilla was inadvertently split and on the 7th the *Artésien* and *Sphinx*, cruising with the *Bellone* and *La Fine*, fell upon three of them. One, with a cargo of muskets and field ordnance, was an easy capture. Another, carrying 44 guns, should have been another but Maurville, commanding the *Artésien*, called off the chase just as he was within reach of his prey.

When Suffren heard what had happened, he flew into a stupendous rage. For a second time Maurville had failed in his clear duty. 'Kindly explain to me why you allowed yourself to abandon chase without the consent of your chief.' Did he say he had seen no signal to chase from the *Sphinx*? Since when did a captain need a signal not to abandon an enemy on the point of capture? If he thought he needed one, which he did not, why did he not ask for one? The disgruntled officer replied *en propos indécents,*

en reproches audacieux and sealed his fate. Suffren decided that at
the first opportunity he would be sent back to France in disgrace,
for it was now dismally clear that only by the most drastic action
could he recall some of his captains to their senses.[5]

It was a saddening and embittering experience, but there was
comfort on the 10th when the *Resolution*, a coppered vessel of 16
guns in which Captain Cook had made his second and his third,
fatal, expeditions to the South Seas, was taken by the *Hannibal*.
More followed on the 20th when *La Fine* brought in a 16-gun
Indiaman loaded with artillery and powder for Colonel Nixon in
Tanjore. The two Company prizes were armed as privateers and
the *Resolution* was sent to Porto Novo with letters for Haidar.
That same day Suffren anchored off Cuddalore.

What he found there was dispiriting: Souillac had sold his
miserable expeditionary force for a preposterous sum, and so
far it had achieved nothing beyond the capture of this wretched
watering-hole. Coote had been prevented from marching south to
mop it up only by a diversionary move on the part of the Mysorean
army against Madras, but now he had decided that, provided he did
nothing to bring the two allies together, they would surely fall apart.
But while Coote waited for the inevitable result of this ill-made
match, Macartney found him more cranky and sluggish than ever,
'no longer what he was, soured by disappointments, grown old,
impaired in his health, jealous and fractious'.[6] It was very difficult
to stay on good terms with him, and everything added fuel to
their differences: the 'supreme powers' Coote claimed, above all,
bullocks, Company troops, money, even Muhammed Ali, Nawab
of the Carnatic, who persisted in addressing Sir Eyre and not Lord
Macartney as his saviour.

All this time General Medows refused to take any command
in India and the only person to whom he could turn was 'old'
James Stuart, a one-legged Company colonel without a king's
commission who was almost as cranky as the commander-in-chief.
Still, Haidar Ali and the French had not joined by 12 May. 'They
treat one another as sharpers and seem afraid to co-operate,' he
told Macpherson in Calcutta, 'but it will probably soon come to
a Union'.[7]

Any hopes that Haidar might be persuaded to come to terms
had now receded with the promise of Bussy and his thousands.
Macartney believed that he had come very close to it. 'The defeat

of many Baillies and Braithwaites,' he was reported to have said in darbar, 'will not destroy [the English]. I can ruin their resources by land but I cannot dry up the sea!'[8] But that hint of remorse was all the comfort he received. Peace with the Marathas had at last—17 May—been secured at Salbai but had yet to be ratified by Calcutta and Poona. By the treaty the Maratha Peshwa was to encourage Haidar to relinquish his conquests and make peace with the English and his sworn enemy, the Nawab of Arcot. All he was to be promised in return was that they would leave him in peace. Haidar was correctly informed of the contents of the agreement by his spies, and was not impressed. He had had such a guarantee before and it had proved worthless. Now at last the elusive victory for which he had played such high stakes was at hand. He had assembled the largest army ever seen in the south and at Vilnoor he had been joined by Duchemin and his French regulars.

The French were awed by their encounter with the moving and articulate mass that had been the scourge of the Carnatic, and impressed 'by the beauty of the troops composed of so many different nations, the order which reigned in the nawab's camp and, above all, by his intelligence and mighty resources. He alone gave all the necessary orders to his ministers for the direction of this great machine and for the provisioning of a camp of 100,000 combatants, of whom about 60,000 were cavalry. His army, including camp-followers, numbered 300,000 but he made no special distribution of supplies. He saw to it that the bazaars were daily supplied with the necessities of life, with clothing and with entertainment. Even curios, which no one would have expected to find in the middle of an army, could be bought there. What a head! What a genius!'[9]

The author of this panegyric, Lieutenant Mautort of the Régiment d'Austrasie, accompanied Duchemin to the nawab's darbar on 22 May. Marching under an escort of dragoons with silver-tipped lances, through great pavilions the size of houses and covering in all an area of a quarter of a league in circumference, they entered Haidar's tent past six pieces of cannon ready primed, the gunners standing constantly by them with fuses lit to blast intruders to eternity. They found the nawab enthroned above his ministers ranged on cushions at his side, and from the light of the torches, the diamonds and rubies in his turban, the gold thread in his silken cloak, he glittered like a statued saint before whom the

French general and his officers bowed thrice. Censed with perfume and aspersed with rose-water, they sat on rich cushions exchanging courtesies and sampling fruit, *pan* and sweetmeats at his feet for over an hour.

Mautort was left in no doubt as to the nawab's authority. 'Such a great silence reigned in the assembly that only those persons who were being questioned could be heard to speak.' The ceremonial concluded with gifts. Duchemin received a diamond ring worth 50 louis, his junior officers rather less valuable trinkets, and as soon as the distribution was over the nawab left abruptly.

All these courtesies could not hide his disappointment with his allies. Though their arrival had temporarily interrupted his constant and devious pourparlers with the Madras agents, the unsigned treaty and unpaid cash still poisoned relations between them. And nothing had been said at this darbar about money. It was to take another five days' haggling with his *vakils* for the French to persuade Haidar to part with the *lakh* of rupees he had originally promised and a *lakh* did almost nothing to relieve the parlous conditions of the French troops. When Haidar marched off to Killenur on 29 May to meet Sir Eyre Coote making for Wandewash, the French stayed behind.[10]

It was not only that they were too poor to march. Duchemin's fatal illness had at last assailed him and the dying man was comforted by Souillac's latest orders not to compromise his force before Bussy arrived. But when Haidar reached Gingee he decided that, after all, he did need the French before he committed himself to battle with Coote. A succession of couriers appealed to Duchemin to march, but the soldiers were at that moment short of both courage and goodwill. With the nawab's departure, the bazaars had suddenly closed down and the moneylenders gone. No one would raise a loan for the army—and there was no food to be bought, even if they had. Haidar refused to send anything more than rice, promising that he would look after it properly when it arrived at his camp. On 2 June Haidar and Coote met near Arni and the Mysoreans withdrew, discomfited. The nawab repeated his summons. When Duchemin refused to move, Haidar withdrew to Killenur and let it be known that he would talk once more to the agents of Fort St George.

Coote, however, having relieved Wandewash, could not take advantage of the rift in the alliance. He retreated wearily to Madras.

'Had I possessed the means of subsistence, I could not only have driven Hyder up the Ghauts, but most probably have got hold of his grand magasine at Arni.'[11] 'Hyder is such a fly-away bird,' Macartney commented drily, 'that he never waits till we throw salt on his tail or we should have caught him many a day ago. These victories almost ruin us in powder.'[12]

Nevertheless Duchemin's pathetic expedition *had* so far kept Haidar Ali in the Carnatic and he had not turned west to deal with a threat from that quarter. For on 8 January 1782 the Bombay army had broken out of Tellicherry and inflicted a crushing defeat on the investing Mysorean army. Then, on 18 February, Colonel Humberstone, who had sailed on to India after Commodore Johnstone's coup at Saldanha Bay, landed 1000 men from the 9th and 100th Regiments of Foot at Anjengo. His orders had been to join Medows in Madras but, hearing that Suffren might be waiting for him off Ceylon, he judged it more prudent to put ashore on the Malabar coast, where on 7 April he vanquished a large force under Mukhdum Ali. Fear of a second front from Bombay had caused the nawab seriously to think of leaving the Carnatic, but when Duchemin went ashore at Porto Novo he changed his mind. His son Tipu and a French mercenary, Henri de Lallée, went instead to deal with Humberstone. Three months had now passed since that decision and Haidar was beginning to wonder whether he had done the right thing.

On arrival at Cuddalore, Suffren saw with dazzling clarity that his squadron now provided the only hope for French survival in India. Unless he could put some life into the French effort, Haidar would bend before the war-weariness of his people and come to terms with the British. Somehow he must persuade the nawab to wait for Bussy, even though nothing would happen before he came. Duchemin's health had almost wholly collapsed and his mind was wandering, the safety of his money uppermost in his more lucid thoughts. His second in command, the Comte d'Hoffelize, was depressed by rumours of a concentration of 200 Europeans and 500 sepoys assembling in Tanjore for a descent on Ceylon. His men were prostrated by dysentery and erysipelas and his doctors puzzled and incoherent before the suddenness of tropical death. Action alone could clear the air of its torpid miasma of Mysorean suspicion, and Suffren alone could take it. Haidar Ali had, he was told, greedily devoured every detail of the Battle of Provedien and

was offering to sign the vexed treaty with him alone. He was eager
to provide whatever he could for the fleet, which was more than
he had ever done for the army. To keep him in this frame of mind,
Suffren decided to seize Negapatam.

It would be but a poor substitute for Trincomali, but it would
give him an anchorage across the sea route between Madras and
the harbour he coveted. Success, moreover, would both foil any
expedition against Ceylon and convince Haidar that the French
meant business. He sent Moissac to the nawab's darbar to beg his
permission to embark 400 French troops and a battalion of sepoys
from Cuddalore. Haidar, who had been irritated by Duchemin's
arrogant insistence on taking all decisions that involved the French
troops, was flattered. He ordered one of his generals, Sayyid Sahib,
to approach Negapatam with 2000 horse and 4000 foot while his
vakil, Banaji Pant, was to see that Suffren was provided with
everything he wanted. The contrast to the slippery indifference
with which Haidar had treated Duchemin was pointed.[13]

The 400 troopers were taken on board at once to bring his
crews up to strength, and another 300 Europeans and 800 sepoys
stood by for the actual assault. The *Vengeur* and *Artésien* were
sent to ship biscuit from Pondicherry while d'Hoffelize planned a
diversion by land. On 23 June the *Bellone* burst into the roadstead
of Negapatam, scattering and burning the rice-boats and skiffs he
found there. Two days later she flew back to Cuddalore to report
the English squadron at anchor south of the threatened port. For
Sir Edward had resolved to sail as soon as he saw Suffren pass
Trincomali. He was not as ready as he would have wished. Most
of the supplies Macartney had sent him had failed to arrive and,
though the *Monmouth* was remasted by 2 June, his sick were very
slow to recover. And they were little better by 24 June when,
packing every able-bodied man he could muster on board, he
sailed after the French. When he learned they were off Cuddalore,
he anchored off Negapatam, resolved neither to seek nor to shun
an engagement 'until I am reinforced . . . when I doubt not I shall
be able to drive them from the seas'.[14]

His appearance was unexpected. Suffren hastily recalled the
Vengeur and *Artésien* and ordered the assault troops on board.
If Hughes's coming indicated, as the military men feared, that
an invasion of Ceylon was imminent, he must be smashed into
uselessness without delay. On 29 June *La Fine* brought in a

welcome prize, the East Indiaman *Fortitude*, last encountered at Porto Praya, with a cargo of fresh fruit and vegetables, doubly welcome in a land as dry and devastated as a desert. There was only one thing left to do before sailing to meet his rival, and on 30 June, in the haste of the moment, the Commander de Suffren made a decision which was to cast an indelible shadow over his reputation and to tarnish a career that was otherwise in the finest traditions of the Knights Hospitaller of St John of Jerusalem.

18. Suffren's Shame

Nelson at Naples, 16 years later, made a worse decision when he ordered the republican rebel, Prince Caracciolo, to be hanged summarily from the foremast yard of the *Minerva*, but the glow of his maimed body, tortured by love and doubt, soon recovered its wraith-like brightness. No sentimental fuddlement impaired the conscience of the French admiral when on 30 June he decided to hand over his British prisoners of war to the capricious mercies of Haidar Ali. It was an act for which the British never forgave him and which even his humanity lived to regret. But at the time no other course seemed open to him.

He had already proposed a cartel of exchange to Sir Edward Hughes for the 60 officers and 400 men in his hands, but the British admiral had referred Suffren to Lord Macartney. The governor of Madras, suddenly afflicted by a deference to his commander-in-chief when for once deference was not called for, referred the matter to Sir Eyre Coote who, to the credit of his heart, insisted that the exchange should be effected for those who had been longest in the hands of Haidar Ali. Suffren rejected this proposal as impractical. He had, at this stage, no influence over the nawab. Macartney appears then to have let the matter rest.

Suffren, several months later and troubled in his conscience, confided to William Hickey that while Hughes had behaved in a manner 'that did honour to his feelings as a man', Macartney, 'that arrogant lord', had insulted him by 'his insolent and rude silence'. He wrote twice, he claimed, but in vain, to the governor, warning him the second time that he would be forced to hand over his prisoners to Haidar. 'Having been twice treated with contumely by Lord Macartney, I particularly desired no further reference might be made to him whom I considered deficient in common good manners and who had behaved towards me with a rudeness and impertinence unprecedented between gentlemen.' At Suffren's third application to Sir Edward, Hughes professed his powerlessness to do anything 'in the most pathetic terms', but begged the Frenchman not to send his prisoners to Mysore which 'would be worse than condemning the unfortunate men to death'. 'I have been stigmatized,' Suffren exploded to the Calcutta lawyer, 'abused in the grossest terms as void of humanity or feeling, as a savage wretch that ought to be scouted from society ... But what could I do?' Short of provisions, without a port, unable to send them to Île de France for lack of ships, 'it would have been unreasonable in the extreme to suppose that I was to set at liberty near 500, the greater part able seamen. Common justice to my sovereign forbade such a measure.'[1]

Common justice, however, was not all that was at issue. Suffren was also governed by another overriding concern: to improve relations with Haidar Ali. 'It is rather to increase his confidence in me,' he wrote to Souillac on 2 June, 'than to reply to the proceedings of Macartney, Hughes and Coote that I confided my English prisoners to the Nawab.'[2] And another letter, to the minister, also suggested that his conscience was not so clear in July 1782 as it had become by the time he was talking to William Hickey in January 1783. 'I receive letters from prisoners enough to make humanity groan but it is less a reply to the way the English have responded to my overtures than as a means of gaining the Nawab's confidence, that I have sent him all my prisoners.'[3]

Macartney, in his turn, denied that he had ever received any proposal for a cartel. Unwilling to write to Suffren after the prisoners had been handed over to Haidar's gaolers, he wrote instead to the man who had led him away captive after the surrender of Grenada, Captain du Chilleau of the Sphinx. Affecting to know him a man of honour and good sense, he proposed another cartel on Coote's terms in his most genial turn of phrase, the sweet reason of a man of honour ashamed to have such harsh things to say of the other's chief, and looking forward to the pleasure of returning the compliment of 1779. He was thrice insistent that he had never received a formal proposal from Suffren.[4]

The intendant of Pondicherry, it was said, together with the principals of the city begged Suffren not to consign Europeans to 'a barbarian notorious for his contempt for the laws of war',[5] and Suffren tried to ensure that they were treated like prisoners taken in a war between civilized people, appointing an officer to look after them and agreeing with Haidar's officers a generous rate of subsistence. But Suffren's commissar was soon ignored and helpless, and the miseries of Haidar's captives became a catalogue of inconsequential ill-treatment, capricious gaolers, brutal marches in the broiling sun, infested dungeons, a litany of horrors punctuated by moments of unexpected relief, generosity and consideration soon to be obscured again by indifferent cruelty.

There were no deliberate atrocities, rather a profound ignorance of how to look after prisoners who were less useful than coolies. And the Mysoreans could not be expected to treat their prisoners better than their own soldiery. From these doleful sagas come stories of the uncomplaining devotion of sepoy captives to their European companions in misery, whose loads they carried in the burning heat of the noon-day march and with whom they shared the rations which Haidar had increased in order to seduce them to desert and join his service. The tales began when Baillie and his broken ranks were marched away from Perambakam; they were told of Suffren's prisoners as they were driven, chained in pairs, to the stinking pits of Chidambran, and they concluded only when Seringapatam was stormed and the dungeons released their occupants in 1799.

The act is comparable to the return of Soviet deserters after the end of the 1939–45 war when Stalin's allies wished to make a gesture of goodwill to the then Nawab of Moscow. But it is difficult to know how much the British, too, were at fault. Macartney, for all his professions to du Chilleau, could not have been ignorant of the proposals for a cartel and could have accepted one on Suffren's and not on Coote's terms. Warren Hastings implicitly recognized that Macartney was wrong. 'The squadron wants men more than the French do, and we are more embarrassed by the charge of prisoners taken from them than they are by our own,' he told Sir John Macpherson. 'We must not allow a People of Frenchmen to grow in these provinces and a stop must be put to it or they will ruin us.'[6] Bussy, who knew his Indian princes, was horrified to hear what had happened and deplored a decision 'which has revolted all

Asia, Europeans and others alike and which could have unhappy consequences'.[7] (What seemed to upset Bussy most was that the British prisoners were chained in pairs without distinction of rank, and both officers and men forced to march barefoot. He was a true child of his time.) But he understood that Suffren's only reply from Macartney was a statement that to consign the British prisoners to Haidar would be contrary both to the law of nations and to humanity and that the British would treat their French prisoners of war as Haidar treated his British.

This was not quite the silence with which, Suffren told Hickey, his approaches had been met. Hickey's prodigious memory is almost too prodigious at times and it is possible that he heard Suffren wrongly. But it is more likely that on this occasion he recorded Suffren accurately, since the point Suffren was making was that Macartney had ignored him. Whether he was telling the truth is harder to determine, since his real reasons for handing over the prisoners were no secret to himself and others, and the stain of what he did was indelible.

The disagreeable transaction completed, Suffren dashed off a note to Souillac on 2 July. He was leaving 300 sick ashore, and without men he could do nothing. He was also very short of cash. There was nothing to be hoped for from the Dutch in Ceylon. Only Batavia had parted with any money, most of that unwillingly since he had taken it off Dutch ships before they got there. Even so, of the 200,000 florins he had 'received', half had gone to serve the needs of the army, and half of what remained to the Dutch. No one would accept a bill of change. 'See to what a state I am reduced. The captain's tables are a source of desolation to me; they want a quarter of a million *livres* to maintain them, and I must pay for skiffs, lascars and the rest of it. It is little short of miraculous that with so little money the squadron can subsist at all. I sail tomorrow to attack the English. If I am successful I shall assault Negapatam.'[8]

To the minister in Paris he was less querulous. Between the Dutch and the sale of prizes he had enough money to survive for six more months, and he was certain of his rations of wheat and rice for a year, thanks to Haidar. He was, however, so short of frigates that he had to rely on his faster battleships for privateering, but he could no longer expect to take prizes with powder and shot on board now that the British knew that nothing was safe in the

Bay of Bengal. His continued survival would become progressively harder but it was all in the finest tradition of his hero, Michael de Ruyter. It was certainly something no one had attempted in these waters before.

On 23 March his provisions and stores had nearly all been consumed and he had only 6000 dollars and what was left in his convoy to keep him going. After Provedien he had scarcely enough powder and shot for another engagement. Now, three months later, he was proposing to fight a third battle, to vanquish his sturdy opponent and, if possible, capture a base. Yet, writes the admiring Captain Mahan, 'he lived in the epoch of d'Estaing, Guichen and de Grasse, before the days of the French Revolution when the uprising of a people had taught men how often impossibilities are not impossible; before Napoleon and Nelson had made a mock of the word'.[9] On 3 July, with all the men he could muster on board and only 600 European troops fit enough to guard the hospital and depot, Suffren sailed from Cuddalore for his third 'impossible' encounter with Sir Edward Hughes.

The *Eagle* sighted the French at 10.30 hours on 5 July, sailing from the north-east quarter. Hughes was sure the French had troops on board and were making for Trincomali. Its loss would be very bad for, having spent one winter off the Coromandel coast, he could certainly not pass another at sea and would have to return to Bombay before the monsoon broke. With so much at stake, he felt he must be absolutely certain of Suffren's intentions, so he stayed where he was, anchored in line of battle between Negapatam and Nagore. The *Eagle* had counted 12 ships of the line, five frigates (in fact only three, the others being a corvette and a sloop) and a brig.

Against Suffren's 770 guns Hughes could, with his 11 line ships and the *Seahorse* frigate, pit only 732, but when the French came in sight at 13.00 hours he had one weapon which had not been his at either of their last two encounters: the wind. And this struck with a shrewd blow for him at 15.00 when it freshened from the land and fell in a sudden squall on the French line. It caught the *Ajax* lying along with the ports of her lowest tier of guns open and the sea, suddenly whipped into a froth, began to pour through them so quickly that within a few minutes the great ship began to keel over. Bouvet, in terror of being overset, ordered her main topmast and mizzen topgallant yard to be cut down over her side but, as she slowly righted herself, the ship, temporarily crippled, was forced back to the rear of the line. Nevertheless, though Suffren was now to the leeward with a wounded ship, Hughes judged the hour 'too late to do the business properly'.[10] Determined to take his chance on the morrow, he ordered his squadron to stand to the southward all that night in order to keep the wind. Suffren, unexpectedly reprieved, ordered the *Bellone* and *Sylphide* to succour the *Ajax* and brought to on the starboard tack, anchoring for the night at 18.45. He supposed from the activity on board the *Ajax* that repairs were well under way.

At dawn on 6 July the French were still at anchor seven or eight miles to the north-north-east of the British but when, at 06.00 hours, Hughes saw them getting under way and standing to the westward, he ordered his ships into line of battle at two cables' distance and at 07.10, with his line well-formed, made signal to bear down on the enemy for a parallel action, ship against ship. The wind was still blowing freshly in his favour from the south-south-west and he looked forward to a neat and tidy engagement on the classical model, his heaviest metal massed in the centre for a concentration there, and the *Monarca*, his next ahead, under orders to attack the same ship as he.

Suffren's first unpleasant surprise came at 05.45 when, ordering his ships into line of battle, he received a request from Bouvet to remain at anchor. The tardy veteran had succeeded in repairing only his mizzen topgallant yard and felt unable, without a topmast, to take his place in the line. Suffren and Hughes were for once unexpectedly equal, and for the only time during the campaign the French were without possession of the wind. The French admiral brusquely ordered the *Ajax* into line and sent the *Orient* down to take the end of the line in case Hughes chose to repeat his own tactic at Sadras and double on the French rear. Such tactical subtlety was, in fact, no part of the admiral's design, but by taking one of his heavier ships out of the centre Suffren had unwittingly strengthened Hughes's attacking dispositions.

For over an hour the two squadrons sailed north-west by north, Suffren content to trail his coat until an opportunity offered to shake the English off his tail. He thought it had come at 07.35 when the wind shifted to the west and he saw a chance to cut across Hughes's rear and gain the wind of him by tacking, 'countermarching' and then tacking again, once he was landward of the English line. The manoeuvre, which had at best only a slim chance of success, failed because Landelle in the lead did not understand the order and, by the time it had been repeated and explained, 25 minutes had been lost. It was to be another three-quarters of an hour before his line was sailing on the opposite tack, and by that time the *Ajax* had fallen out. Bouvet, frightened of being left behind, lost his head, cut his cable and without an anchor drifted helplessly to the rear. Hughes watched the enemy's ships turning for an hour without response, realizing that something had gone wrong when he saw Landelle's *Bizarre* put between the *Vengeur* and the *Orient* in the French rear.

At 09.30, when the two squadrons were almost abreast sailing in opposite directions, but with Hughes still to landward, Sir Edward, alarmed at the speed with which the French were sailing, ordered his ships to tack all together. For the next hour the two lines sailed in parallel, only a few miles apart on a bearing south-south-east, until at 10.00 Hughes, unwilling to postpone the action any longer in case Suffren's object was to race him to Trincomali, decided to bear up and attack, even though four of his ships in the rear were far astern and splayed out at a sharp angle to his centre and van. At 10.40 his leading ships, the *Hero* and *Exeter*, exchanged their first shots with the *Flamand*, now at the head of the French line.

19. The Battle of Negapatam, 6 July 1782

The Battle of Negapatam began, for Hughes, with one of those mishaps that had hitherto dogged his rival. The 50-gun *Flamand* was too tempting a victim for her two 74-gun assailants; in their enthusiasm to close upon her, the *Exeter* ran into the *Hero* and in the confusion neither ship was able to lay herself alongside. Cuverville meanwhile kept up a brisk and effective cannonade which disconcerted them both, while the *Isis*, holding back in order not to run into the *Exeter*, found herself uncomfortably poised between the *Sévère* and *Annibal*. Tromelin, instead of pressing forward to relieve the *Flamand*, accepted Lumley's *Isis* for a partner—and for this inglorious decision, though 24 guns heavier, he was to lose 28 dead and 80 wounded. Cuverville, meanwhile, was left to the mercies of Hawker and King.

As the rest of the English van and centre closed, the two 64s, *Sévère* and *Brillant*, were engaged respectively by the 70-gun *Burford* and the 74-gun *Sultan*. Greek once more met Greek in the centre where the two flagships met for the second time, and the *Monarca*, under orders to assist her admiral in his work, lay slightly astern of the *Héros* and worked on her with her forward guns and on the *Sphinx* with her aft. The remaining five French ships—the *Ajax* was *hors de combat*-—and four English were too far apart to engage closely, but they exchanged a furious though largely ineffectual fire, so that the battle raged fiercely in the van and centre only.

By a curious irony, the French failure at Provedien was now repeated by the English. On 12 April the French rear had failed to press home the advantage. Now the *Worcester, Monmouth, Eagle* and *Magnanime* were content to let the heavy ships in the centre bear the brunt of the fighting, leaving the *Orient* and *Bizarre* mere spectators, while the *Vengeur, Artésien* and *Hannibal* fired as fiercely as they could across the gap into their masts and rigging. Though Suffren tried to bring the *Artésien* and *Vengeur* into action, both Maurville and Forbin merely increased the rate of their distant broadsides, while the failure of the wind prevented La Pallière in the *Orient* from closing up.

In the van and centre the duel continued with terrible ferocity for over 90 minutes until, shortly after noon, the *Brillant*, shorn of her mainmast and mizzen topgallant yard, and with 200 casualties on board, was beaten out of the line, and the *Flamand*, victim of some 100 guns, with 13 dead and 56 wounded, her sails and rigging shot to ribbons but with her spars still standing, was forced to edge away. Tromelin was still busily locked with the *Isis* and Cuverville expected to be followed, but his guns had put the *Hero* to such distress that she was already making inshore for Negapatam, while the *Exeter* was too stunned to make any move either to pursue the *Flamand* or to go to Lumley's assistance. The retreat of the two French ships, however, allowed the four ships of Hughes's centre to press home their attack on the *Héros, Sévère* and *Annibal*, causing frightful casualties.

At 12.35 the wind took a hand in the battle, shifting suddenly from the south-west to the south-south-east, catching both squadrons unprepared. Hughes's line was wildly disordered and most of his ships paid off to landward, but the *Burford* and *Sultan* in the van and the *Worcester* and *Eagle* in the rear, which had suffered less in their rigging, had seen the change coming and turned their heads towards the French. Of the French line, all but the *Sévère* and *Brillant* turned their heads to the east; but these two vessels, both of which had been badly cut about aloft, were spun bows foremost towards the scattering English. Facing each other in the gap between the two squadrons there were now six ships, of which the *Brillant* was almost totally incapacitated. The *Sultan* was quick to lay herself alongside the *Sévère*, with the *Burford* in support, while the *Eagle* and *Worcester* bore down upon the helpless Saint-Félix in the *Brillant*.

There followed an incident at once bizarre and confused, in which for the first and only time in five battles the English came

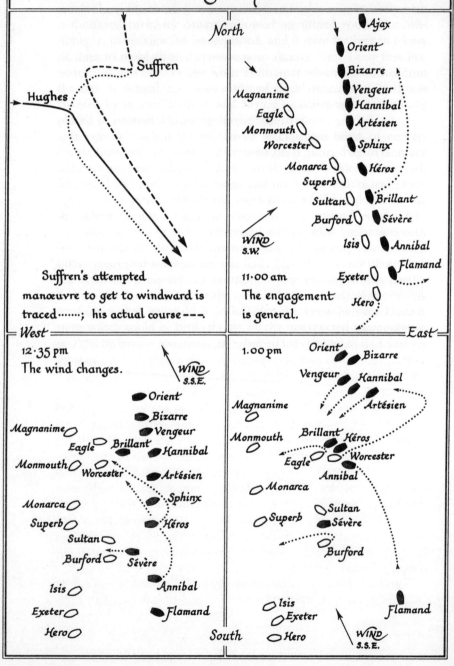

The Battle of Negapatam
6 July 1782

North

Suffren

Hughes

Suffren's attempted
manœuvre to get to windward is
traced ·······; his actual course ---.

West

East

South

near to making a prize. Cillart from the quarter-deck of the *Sévère*, ten guns lighter than the *Sultan* and already savagely mauled, seeing the *Burford* closing in on her larboard bow was seized by panic. A ball had shattered the leg of his second officer and his third was also wounded. The *Héros, Annibal* and *Sphinx* nearest to him appeared to be in no position to come to his help and, as the *Sultan*'s shot began to crash into his side, he lost his nerve and gave the order to strike his colours. The officer who received the order was an auxiliary called Bonvallet and he refused point-blank to obey, running from the quarter-deck. Cillart, now alone, began, according to Captain Watt in the *Sultan*, to run up and down, waving and dropping his hat and shouting at the top of his voice that he wished to surrender. At last, finding a sailor ready to execute his order, Cillart made him lower the flag, but two other auxiliary officers, Dieu and Rosbo, who had heard of their captain's intentions from Bonvallet, ran up on to the deck and shouted at Cillart to run the flag up again.

'You can lower the flag,' Dieu shouted above the din, white with fury, 'since it's only a rag in your hands. But we shall never accept the shame you wish to lay on us. The crew is with us and we shall carry on firing.' Cillart then pulled himself together and Rosbo himself hauled the white flag of the Bourbons again to the masthead to shouts of 'Vive le Roi!' It was bravely done, but Watt had already ordered his guns to hold their fire and his boat to be lowered to take possession. At that moment his second officer reported a signal from the admiral summoning him to join the line at once—the *Burford* had already obeyed and turned her head west—so the boat was never lowered.

By then Dieu and Rosbo had taken command of the lower tier of guns on the *Sévère*, the only ones fully manned, and in their enthusiasm fired a shattering broadside at the silent *Sultan*. Watt's sense of propriety, as well as his timbers, was rudely hurt. In the etiquette of war the two auxiliaries had acted with greater attention to zeal than to manners. Suffren was later to jest that 'Cillart voulait perdre le Sévère, mais Dieu le sauva', but the two officers had done wrong to fire when they did, knowing that the *Sultan* was holding her fire out of respect for their captain's untimely surrender. Their broadside, while it symbolized the recovery of the *Sévère*'s honour, to the English smacked of a *ruse de guerre* and that was how Hughes was to see it.

Sir Edward, meanwhile, seeing the *Burford, Worcester* and *Eagle* on their former tack and closing on the French with great speed, and assuming that the shift of the wind had seriously shattered the cohesion of the enemy, wanted to hoist signal for a general chase, but Captain Gell in the *Monarca* reported his rigging shot away and his vessel ungovernable, while the *Hero* could be seen hauling in towards land with a distress signal out. Suffren, ordering his ships to wear and form line in any position they could, had also managed to drive the *Héros* between the *Brillant* and the *Worcester* and *Eagle*, while Tromelin, rising to the occasion for the first time, sailed up in close support and raked the *Worcester* with such a murderous broadside that when Suffren subsequently blasted her as well his broadsides were received in deathly silence. Suffren then bore down upon the *Eagle*, summoning the *Vengeur* and *Artésien* to his support, and at 13.20 Hughes, realizing that a general chase was out of the question, changed his signal for one to wear and stand to westward, following it ten minutes later with a second to re-form in line of battle ahead, and to renew the engagement as soon as Gell had the *Monarca* once more under control.

The *Eagle*, granted a moment's respite by an explosion on the *Artésien*, fought her way back to the admiral. The French ship was soon ablaze from stern to bows and Suffren, noting irritably that it was once again Maurville's ship that had muffed its chances of reducing a vessel already much damaged aloft, abruptly ordered him to lay to. At 14.00 the wind dropped and for the next half-hour Hughes concentrated on gathering his disabled and ungovernable ships into some sort of order. By 14.30 they were all tolerably close, except the *Hero* making south and the *Worcester* describing an arc seawards to escape her two powerful opponents. Both squadrons were sailing towards the shore in rough and ready formation with ungovernable ships to protect and, the wind starting up from different quarters every few minutes, any hope of renewing the combat disappeared. To the French, Hughes seemed to acknowledge the worst of it by standing south-westward with his ten ships, while to the British, Suffren's little huddle in the north-north-west looked sadly chastened. At 16.30 Hughes lowered the signal for close action and an hour later anchored where he had started from the day before. Suffren anchored shortly after 18.00 hours off Karikal, about 12 miles to the north, and both admirals licked their wounds.

They were the most savage so far. Throughout the night the English ships were closely employed in securing their lower masts, almost all their standing rigging being shot away, splicing the old and reeving new rigging and getting serviceable sails to their yards. Hughes counted 77 dead, including his own flag-captain, and 233 wounded. The worst sufferer was the *Sultan* with 16 dead and 24 wounded, an eloquent testimony to the valour and efficiency of the gunners in the *Flamand*. Despite the horrible broadsides of both the *Annibal* and *Héros*, however, only one lascar had died in the *Worcester*, and though Gell had described his *Monarca* as ungovernable he had lost only 8 dead. Suffren's losses, on the other hand, were dreadful. The squadron had 178 dead and 602 wounded, mainly in the *Brillant* (47 dead; 187 wounded), *Annibal* (28;80), *Héros* (25;72), *Sévère* (20;77), *Sphinx* (19;85) and *Artésien* (12;38). If the French claimed the victory, it had cost them dear, for how were they, desperately short of men before the battle began, now to replace losses like these?

Hughes had had the wind for the first time in conflict with Suffren and, through Bouvet's imbecility, an unexpected equality of numbers. He concentrated his metal on ships of lighter power and with five 74s, a 64 and a 50 he had engaged two 74s, two 64s and a 50. By bearing down upon his enemy in the light but lively south-wester he had shattered the hulls of his opponents and done terrible execution on their crews, while the French, swung on to their heels by the same wind, had torn him to shreds aloft.

The carnage read more like a combat between giant fleets of 20 to 30 ships each, not a minor action in a secondary theatre of war. On 17 April 1781, when Rodney with 19 ships of the line and a 50, engaged de Guichen with 23 line-of-battle ships off Martinique, the British lost 120 killed and 354 wounded, the French 222 dead and 537 wounded. At the Saints, a battle between 36 line ships and 33, Rodney's casualties were 243 killed and 816 wounded.

Sir Edward claimed the victory. 'In this engagement His Majesty's squadron under my command gained a decided superiority over that of the enemy and had not the wind shifted and thrown HM Squadron out of action at the very time that some of the enemy's ships had broken their line and were running away, and others of them greatly disabled, I have good reason to believe it would have ended in the capture of seven of their line-of-battle ships.'[1] His casualties were certainly lighter. His losses could be replaced and he would shortly be reinforced by Bickerton. Negapatam was saved and Suffren should be—indeed must be—at the end of his resources.

Yet Hughes had not won the battle. He might have been nearer the victory he claimed had he followed Suffren's tactic at Sadras and concentrated on the French rear, but by persisting in his choice of a parallel action he had allowed Suffren to change tack and then not been able to bring his rear into close action. The *Brillant* and *Flamand* were not so near capture, the *Sévère* could not have been held, to justify his claim that seven prizes were snatched from him by the wind. He suffered grievously, too, in sails and rigging, and would have suffered more had his sailors not been among the finest in the fleet. The *Monarca* and *Hero* were too seriously wounded for him to contemplate renewal of the action, had the wind permitted it, in the four hours of daylight left to him. He knew by now that Suffren would waste no time in making all shipshape again, and when he returned to the roadstead of Negapatam he lost Trincomali.

He made an attempt, however, to claim the *Sévère*. On 7 July, when Suffren sailed his battered squadron into the lee of Tranquebar, Captain Watt came in the *Rodney* brig under flag of truce to claim his prize, which he mistakenly believed to be the *Ajax*. Suffren refused to receive him. Unable to believe that an officer of La Grande Marine could have acted so cravenly, he had accepted Cillart's first report that a shot had severed the halyard of his flag, which he had never intended to lower, and the admiral was deeply offended that Hughes should base his claim on an accident of battle. He was also bitterly angry at Watt's reference to Dieu's broadside as 'the after conduct of the captain or officer commanding the *Ajax* [which] was such as would disgrace a Turk'. Watt was kept waiting while Suffren dictated his reply. Admiral Hughes must be mistaken. If Captain Watt's claim were well-founded, the king would attend to it. 'As for me, who do not see things with the same eye, I think that I neither can nor ought.' Even if the *Sévère* had struck her colours—which he did not admit for a moment—Suffren himself in the *Héros* was on his way to her relief and she would soon have been retaken. The *Rodney* brig went back empty-handed.[2]

'Activité, activité, vitesse, vitesse': Napoleon's famous order to Masséna was now Suffren's unspoken command to his squadron as soon as it had anchored at Cuddalore on 8 July. If it was ever to capture Trincomali it must be at sea again before Bickerton arrived—and he might arrive at any moment. The lethargic garrison was startled by the requisitions and the bustle. Suffren needed 19 topmasts and they did not exist. So the *Pourvoyeuse* frigate surrendered her mainmast, topmasts, yards and sails to the *Brillant* and replaced them from the captured *Fortitude* East Indiaman. Another topmast was improvised from the mainmast of the *Sylphide* corvette, two more from the lower spars of the *Pulvériseur* fire-ship. Another East Indiaman prize, the *Yarmouth*, was stripped of all her spars, which were shared out between the corvette and the fire-ship, and the *Pulvériseur* was despatched to Malacca to purchase a new mainmast and other spars from the Dutch. The *Fortitude* was to go to Pegu to replace her mainmast there and Cook's *Resolution* was sent back to the Pacific to find spars, biscuit, rigging and Filipino seamen in Manila. The hull of the *Yarmouth* was sold. The *Sylphide* was sent with despatches to Île de France, with a jury mast specially fitted for the journey.

As Hughes was still at sea no time could be lost. In the sweltering heat of noon and the clammy reaches of the night, clad in vest and breeches without stockings, Suffren hauled his sweating bulk with prehensile vigour from ship to ship, shinning down ropes with an ease and speed that were to astonish William Hickey some months later in Trincomali, supervising everything, encouraging the carpenters with oaths, padding bear-like and bare-footed among the yards and rigging laid out on the decks and delighting the men with Provençal asides which his officers, trailing behind him in full dress uniform, could not understand.

He sent carpenters ashore to tear the timbers from the houses of Cuddalore and by 18 July, incredibly, his squadron was fit to go to sea. The *Orient* and *Vengeur*, true, leaked badly and the sheaths of his coppered ships were working loose. The timbered hulls were green and bearded with algae and rotted with teredo worm. The flotilla was beginning to look more like a pack of sea-beggars than a squadron of His Most Christian Majesty's navy. And on the 18th, to stop the mouths of those that hoped the squadron was now, at last, on its way back to Île de France, Suffren made public the changes among his captains that were to electrify everyone, officers and men alike.

20. Suffren Meets Haidar Ali

The truth of what had happened on the *Sévère* during the battle of Negapatam could not be hidden for long, and when Suffren heard it he resolved on fierce and salutary retribution. In three battles now, he had had cause to complain of several of his captains, and he could afford to overlook their shortcomings no longer. A sharp example was needed and, with the great prize still to be gained, he could wait no more.

Cillart was placed under arrest and ordered to France to stand court-martial. With him would sail the two least satisfactory of his captains, his cousin Forbin commanding the *Vengeur* and Maurville the *Artésien*. As captains of his two fastest ships they had consistently mishandled their vessels. Forbin had behaved stupidly at Porto Praya and had failed to show any spark of ability at Sadras, Provedien or Negapatam. Bidé de Maurville had been factious from the moment Suffren had arrived at Port Louis. He was too preoccupied by his losses in a trader at Batavia and by his desire to get his wife's fortune safely to France to relish being on this endless campaign; he had caballed against the appointment of Morard de Galles to the *Annibal*; he had allowed the small flotilla of Company ships bound for Trincomali to escape. At Sadras he had done nothing and at Negapatam he had allowed his ship to be incapacitated as she bore down on the *Eagle*. Both must go.

'You will be annoyed, perhaps,' he wrote to Castries on 22 July, 'that I have not made an example of them sooner. But I must ask you to take into consideration that the *Ordonnances* do not give this right to general officers—and I do not hold that rank—and no general has done it yet. I am only doing it now because I am convinced that the service absolutely demands it and that it is the surest means I have to make the best use of my squadron.'[1]

The minister did not hesitate. On arrival Maurville was confined to the prison of Île de Ré and his name struck from the lists. Forbin languished in the Château du Pont St Esprit. Both were released only in September 1784, when Forbin, because his conduct had shown more incapacity than malice, was allowed to resign his commission. Cillart was too shattered to face the music. He disappeared at Île de France and fled to Europe in a neutral ship, never to return to his homeland. Later rumours were to associate his name with Suffren's death, what was actually a fatal apoplectic haemorrhage being attributed to a vicious attack from the demented Cillart in the gardens of Versailles. There is no truth in the tale. Cillart was not malicious, but in four battles he had behaved cravenly, and of that Suffren was unpitying.

Saint-Félix, on the other hand, who had wanted so violently to return to Île de France, had fought as brilliantly at Negapatam as he had at Sadras and Provedien, and this should be recognized. To those who had behaved well, Suffren was generous. The minister was urged to reward them handsomely, more handsomely than was customary for action in seas nearer home, for news travelled slowly to the Indies and it would be a long time before a man could enjoy his reward. It was a pity no commanding officer had the power to confer the Cross of St Louis on the spot 'for the distant expectation of receiving it after two or three years is unlikely to excite emulation in others'.[2] Even Tromelin had redeemed his poor performance in earlier battles. Du Chilleau, badly burned and wounded, had never forsaken the quarter-deck of the *Sphinx* and his behaviour in all three battles had expunged the memories of Porto Praya. He deserved a pension. Cuverville, 'the heroic Cuverville, has conducted himself as perfectly as he always has and always will'.[3] He also asked for promotion of those auxiliary officers whose spirit had touched his imagination. Dieu and Rosbo both deserved the rank of captain of a fire-ship (the most a *bleu* could expect, so rigid was the caste system of Le Grand Corps) and Bonvallet should be given the brevet of a *bleu*.

Suffren could now promote those lieutenants who had shown something of the spirit he required. Cuverville took command of the *Vengeur* and Perrier de Salvert replaced him in the *Flamand*.

Saint-Félix left the *Brillant* for the *Artésien* and Pas de Beaulieu the *Pourvoyeuse* to take command of the *Brillant*. Another Maurville, Maurville de Langle, a cadet member of the family, replaced Cillart in the *Sévère* and Suffren's own nephew, Pierrevert, now commanded the *Bellone*. There was one other command to give. Bouvet, 'old, and attacked by a languorous sickness, had lost the energy and military skill he had shown so gloriously in the last war'.[4] He came to resign command of the *Ajax*. Out of respect to his grey hairs Suffren accepted his resignation. Beaumont de Maître took over his ship, while the broken veteran waited for the first opportunity to return to Île de France. He never saw France again, as he died of scurvy in Port Louis.

Sir Edward Hughes meanwhile returned to Madras on 20 July. He had found it impossible to repair the loss of topmasts and the other damage without a supply of spars, fishes and cordage, and he had virtually exhausted both his ammunition and ships' stores. His actual needs were 16 lower and 17 top masts, 18 lower and topsail yards and four bowsprits, as well as anchors and cable, and it was soon clear that he was not going to find them at Madras. No naval supplies had reached the presidency since the arrival of the *York* storeship in July 1780, and the East Indiamen which had sailed with Johnstone loaded with salt provisions and the accessories he now desperately needed had put them ashore at Bombay, 'which mismanagement on their part now reduces His Majesty's squadron to great straights [sic] and all the salt provisions at this place furnishes only three months allowance'.[5]

His habitual phlegm, too, was also subjected to the corrosion of a blistering row. Macartney's claims to the Negapatam prize-money in the name of the Company seemed little short of base ingratitude. 'Consider, my lord, who the men are you mean to injure! The very individuals who are sacrificing their lives for you and the Company's protection, and to whom you look up, my lord, and sometimes call aloud for their protection.'[6] His Majesty's grant by proclamation reserved all prizes made by His Majesty's forces as their lawful perquisites, and his lordship's was 'a very poor performance in a bad cause'.

Macartney in turn was at odds with Sir Eyre Coote, and the admiral's angry buzzing now made Government House sound like a beehive. It was bad enough with two queen bees, let alone three, and the cause of his row with the commander-in-chief was his discovery of secret correspondence with Haidar Ali. Conducted through a Maratha agent at Haidar's darbar, the results were no more than the governor would have expected. Haidar declared at last that he would stay in the Carnatic for another two years if necessary to ensure the destruction of the proud and arrogant English. This style of private politicking irked his noble lordship. No general—not Condé, not Turenne, not Eugene, not Marlborough himself—had the sole and exclusive conduct and control of all military operations. Was it the constitutional system of this government that implicit discretion should be given to the commander-in-chief to conciliate the dependent chiefs of the Carnatic? If so, he told Macpherson on 26 July, he must go to school to learn a new catechism.[7]

There was small comfort to be had in those drab and sweltering days, but a crumb fell unexpectedly when the first of Bickerton's squadron arrived. Captain Samuel Graves, in the 64-gun *Sceptre*, had lost the commodore en route to Brazil, and sailed into Madras roads on 13 July while Hughes was still off Negapatam. The *Medea*, which had strayed with him, was still escorting the prize they had taken together from Peynier's convoy off St Helena.

Graves decided at once to find Sir Edward and set off with the *San Carlos* and *Mercury* brig to look for him. He fell in with the *Bellone* which, under Suffren's nephew, Pierrevert, led him a sprightly chase until the *Artésien* appeared to help her, and together they became the pursuers. Graves prudently decided to return and found Hughes at Madras on the 28th. There he joined in the makeshift refit on which Sir Edward was assiduously engaged until they could learn where Suffren would strike next. Never in their careers had Hughes's captains encountered an enemy so resilient or so dangerously resourceful, and as the admiral paced the empty arsenal of Fort St George he was consumed by a gnawing anxiety for the safety of his tiny garrison at Trincomali.

In Haidar's camp all this time, the French agent, Piveron de Morlat, was distracted by the presence of Coote's Brahmin agents. Respect for the French had never been lower but, if Haidar had publicly shown what he felt about Duchemin's expeditionary force, he had just as publicly expressed his admiration for the indomitable squadron and its commander. 'At last the English have found their master! Here is the man who will help me to exterminate them.'[8] Even before Negapatam he had declared his wish to see this 'extraordinary man, to embrace him and testify my complete admiration for his heroic valour'. When on 19 July Suffren's letter came with the news that Bussy with a mighty force had left the Cape for Île de France on 30 April, Haidar insisted on a meeting. 'The interests of our nation,' wrote Piveron in his agitation, 'are absolutely and entirely in his hands at this moment and it is above all essential to convince him of the imminent arrival of our reinforcements.'⁹ Tormented as he was by his desire to capture Trincomali before Hughes threw in his own reinforcements, Suffren recognized the greater need and agreed to wait for the nawab to move his camp nearer the coast.

There was some piquancy in the thought that there were few precedents for a powerful Muslim leader to travel 120 miles to meet a Knight of Malta—in fact, Piveron added in order to spice the compliment, it was said in darbar that Haidar would not go so far to meet the Grand Mughal. Suffren's only previous encounters with Islam had been as a *muchacho* in the embassy to the Emperor of Morocco and a conversation he had once had with the Pasha of the Dardanelles during a Levantine cruise. He would have relished the encounter more, had this 'cavaliero de San Juan, demonio en la guerra', known that Grand Master de Rohan in sacred council on 19 February 1781 had made him a Knight Grand Cross, one of the two dozen senior dignitaries of the Order, which gave him his title of Bailli, or Bailiff, by which he is customarily known in France. News travelled slowly from Valletta to Paris to India, but the Nawab of Sera and the Bailli de Suffren were to meet as equals.¹⁰

On 25 July, 100,000 men encamped two leagues north of Cuddalore. The next day, towards sundown, Suffren in full dress uniform, set off for Manjikuppam with Cuverville, Pallière, Saint-Félix, Beaulieu and Moissac. He was met by the sepoys of the French mercenary Bouthenet, and by Ghulam Ali Khan, Haidar's chief general. At 21.00 hours, a company of Austrasian grenadiers on either side, his palanquin set off for Haidar's camp. The painted casques and white belts of the French infantry gleamed in the torchlight as they tramped through the evening heat, swallowed up from time to time in the whirl of turbaned horsemen, armed cap-à-pie, who pressed in to look at the nawab's guest of honour. Haidar had arranged his army and court to achieve an impressive effect. Miles of pavilions and tents were all bedecked with lamps, the burning fuses of the artillery spluttered like fireflies, his infantry and horses stood massed in serried ranks, apparently as limitless as the sand in the darkness. Suffren had come face to face with an army that was little different in appearance from the huge force that Suleiman the Magnificent had landed, 217 years before, on the rocky shores of Malta.

The nawab received him at the entrance of his pavilion of cloth of green, dressed in white silk frosted with gems and girdled with a belt of gold thread embossed with amethysts. Upon the arrival of the palanquin the nawab saluted Suffren as a fellow prince by stepping down to greet him. The Bailli was then led to a raised platform and seated on an embroidered cushion at the nawab's right hand. Encased in his tight uniform and fanning himself with his tricorne, Suffren tried to ease his enormous bulk gracefully onto the proffered seat, but as the eager Mautort recorded, 'the extreme grossness of his body . . . his gallic vivacity, the continuous heat of the tent made him very uncomfortable. Several more cushions were brought with which to prop him up at the sides when he threatened to keel over, but these mountains of stuff made him sweat more and more until the nawab, noticing his embarrassment, called for a divan, remarking that while it was always better to sit than to stand, it was still better to lie down.'[11] That first meeting, in the oriental way, lasted three hours and consisted of an elaborate duet of praises, uttered in counterpoint, while the Bailli guzzled *pan* and sweetmeats.

There followed an exchange of gifts. When Indian princes received allied generals it was the custom to present the visitor with an elephant, but as this would only have been an encumbrance on board the *Héros* Suffren received its value — the sum of 10,000 rupees, in silver. Haidar added to it an aigrette feather set in a diamond clasp which he plucked from his own turban and pinned to the Bailli's tricorne, and he thrust two jewelled rings on the tips of his fat fingers. Each officer in Suffren's entourage received the traditional *serpeau* or cloak of honour woven of gold thread and muslin and was also given, besides diamonds set in silver rings, cash worth nearly 300 francs in place of the fine stallion that was his due. The elephant was consigned to Duchemin and marched at the head of the troops for the rest of the war, though, presumably because it did so little marching, it grew bored and towards the end of the campaign ran amok. Perhaps it was an unstable animal that Haidar was glad to be rid of.

Suffren's gifts cost him nothing for they had all been taken off English prizes and had been intended for the Emperor of China: a clock in the shape of a pagoda with a chime of bells in every storey and a pendulum suspended from two clusters of polished stone on which stood an emerald dragon with a ruby tongue, two crystal lustres and one of Josiah Wedgwood's Etrurian vases on an ormolu stand. The cash they had all just received, moreover, was instantly redistributed in the court among those thought to be wavering towards a peace with the British.

The first encounter was a dreadful ordeal for Suffren, who suffered indescribably from the heat and the interminable ceremonial, which only ended after midnight when the admiral was allowed to retire to his bed in the nawab's camp. The following day there was a ceremonial banquet when the nawab dined with the Bailli personally, 'an honour that he did not accord to his own son, nor to his chief minister'.[12] Suffren did full justice to the richly spiced pilaus and curries, to the astonishment of the Indians who watched them so dexterously handled and impenitently swallowed, and on the 28th there was a tactical meeting with the nawab, at which Piveron de Morlat assisted.

This time the oriental courtesies proved not to be without substance. Despite his complaints about the army, Haidar agreed that he would wait in the Carnatic for Bussy and send only sufficient forces to the Malabar coast to keep Humberstone in check. The garrison at Cuddalore would be plentifully supplied. When the nawab wished that Suffren would take command of the French expeditionary force, he had to explain that Duchemin was senior in rank and there were no orders Suffren could give him. The valour of the Mysoreans themselves had more than made up for his deficiencies. 'When you put yourself at the head of your troops, they march from victory to victory.' They would continue to win, Haidar replied wryly, if only they did not have to fight in so many places. One reverse and he would have the Marathas about his ears. 'You will not suffer a reverse,' Suffren assured him, with Bussy on his way with reinforcements for them both. Haidar just hoped that the general would show more spirit than Duchemin; as for Suffren, he knew that he would make good use of more ships.

The admiral took his cue: 'As my squadron cannot survive without a base, I am going to take Trincomali. Then as soon as my reinforcements have arrived I shall attack Admiral Hughes for a fourth time and, God willing, I shall destroy him.' 'May your God hear your acts of thunder and words of lightning. Your courage and skill will give victory. The English have never had to fight an adversary of your valour.' This gave Suffren his chance to rise. 'The minutes are precious and I ask your permission to rejoin my combat post, while it is still daylight. The welcome you have given me has been the greatest honour of my life.' Would the nawab care to grace his ship with his presence before he sailed? Haidar declined the invitation gracefully, rising in his turn. 'Suffren, now that I have seen you, I have seen all.'[13]

It was a diplomatic triumph that had an unexpectedly well-timed sequel, for that very evening Bussy's Intendant des Affaires, Launay, arrived looking for Suffren. He brought with him a portrait of Louis XVI for the nawab and news for Suffren more welcome still. The *Illustre*, *Saint-Michel* and *Consolante* frigate were already at Galle with six transports and 600 men. They had left Île de France with d'Aymar on 25 June. When the Bailli went to take leave of his host the following day, he was able to announce the precursors of the legendary marquis. Haidar Ali was moved to superlatives: 'Happy the sovereign with a subject as precious as you. May God protect you for your sake and for mine and bring you back soon covered in new laurels. I cannot tell you how much I desire it nor the high esteem and confidence with which you have inspired me!'[14]

Suffren was glad that he had agreed to see the nawab. 'He treats me like a brother and takes my advice . . . If we had known how to deal with him from the start we could have had him do anything we wanted. My only cunning in dealing with him was to use none and to tell him always what was strictly true.'[15] But now he was furious to be off, for the *Bellone* reported Trincomali wide open. If d'Aymar could join him quickly, the port might be attempted for, despite Dutch reluctance to give him anything like what he asked for, he had enough ammunition for an attack. It was now or never. Hughes might still be at Negapatam—he did not know that the English had actually returned to Madras—but he was sure he had been worse cut about aloft and that he would be slower in putting it right. If he was wrong he must take the consequences, for his own ships now sailed so badly after their long campaign that they could never, if hard pressed, hope to gain the weather-gauge. Besides he had 600 wounded and 1400 sick ashore. But the risk must be taken. Trincomali, and the haven it offered his baseless squadron, was a prize worth high stakes.

He had to waste another day entertaining those of Haidar's officers who were prepared to trust themselves to the surf and visit his ships. Then, on 30 July, he dashed off a welcome to Bussy. Haidar was waiting for him in the Carnatic, but the Carnatic was a desert and an army could never subsist for long in a province where the roads were full of walking skeletons. If he came soon, they could attempt a landing in the Northern Sarkars. But Launay did not think that Bussy could arrive before the monsoon. If he was off the coast of India after 15 October—the date by which the monsoon was expected to break off the coast of Coromandel—he might do better to stick to the original plan of a landing on the western seaboard. There was no point in landing in Ceylon, even though, *Deo volente*, Suffren might by then have captured Trincomali.

Bussy received the letter on 14 September and read it with gloom. How on earth could Duchemin's pitiful force, even reinforced by his own pitifully inadequate expedition, decimated as it was by sickness, hope to besiege Madras? What would happen if Suffren ran into Hughes a fourth time and this time was defeated? What would be the fate of Cuddalore if Haidar failed to keep his word? How could it be evacuated in the face of hazards by sea and in the sight of a vengeful Hughes? But he noted hopefully in his journal: 'L'activité de mer de M de Suffren peut-elle vaincre tous évènements de la guerre et de la mer?'[16] He was inclined to doubt it. He did not know his man.

On 1 August Suffren sailed to meet d'Aymar at Batticaloa and during the night missed by only a margin of darkness the *Sceptre* and *Monmouth*, which had left Madras earlier in the day with 200 men and 3000 bags of rice for the garrison at Trincomali. Macartney would have given one of his fingers for Hughes and his entire squadron to have sailed with them, for, he wrote to Macpherson on 26 July, 'it runs strongly in my head that Suffrein will attempt it'.[17]

21. Trincomali Taken

It was rather late for Macartney to be worrying about Trincomali, and indeed the loss of one of his fingers would have been a poor sacrifice for the loss of a port, the defences of which Hughes had never ceased to remind him were dangerously undermanned. If the French were in possession they could winter off the coast and prey on the Bengal trade during his absence in Bombay. 'This is a point of view in which I fear you never saw the possession of Trincomali, else more attention would have been paid to its being well garrisoned in case of accidents.'[1]

The *Sceptre* and *Monmouth* returned to Madras on 10 August with the news that Suffren had sailed past the port on 7 August. That put Sir Edward in fear for Bickerton, but there was nothing he could do at that moment to protect either his reinforcements or Trincomali. It had taken him 12 days off Negapatam to repair the mainmast of the *Superb* sufficiently to sail her back to Madras, and when he arrived there at last on 20 July he had 'not a liner that had not to stop shot-holes, to fish her lower masts, many of them to shift and all to provide, not spare topmasts only but even the topmasts and lower masts wanted for immediate service'.[2] Even the *Superb*'s rudder had to be unhung to replace the ironwork, which had been destroyed by shot.

It was a critical moment in Sir Edward's career and many, the governor and select committee among them, believed that he failed the test. For by 18 July, when the British admiral prepared to limp home to Madras, Suffren had completed his remasting at Cuddalore and was ready to put to sea. Hughes was then to spend another 31 days at Madras before he was in a state to follow. When on 7 August Suffren appeared off Trincomali Hughes was still immobilized, 300 miles to the north. If it is impossible not to conclude that his fractional caution was to be his undoing, his difficulties were nevertheless formidable.

He was desperately short of experienced artificers, for Madras had never been considered a refitting station because of the hazards of the rolling surf, and there was no power in the country to compel Governor Hornby in Bombay to spare any from the dockyards there. Hughes reckoned that for his 68 artificers, or not quite six to every ship, Suffren had 2–300, since it had always been French policy to see that Île de France was properly provided for. Improvisation, however, was never the Admiral's strong suit and, while every allowance is made for the appalling difficulties he encountered at Madras, where the boatmen were fickle and lazy and everything was slow and laborious, he was culpably slow in making his squadron ready. If his phlegm had seen him honourably through three dreadful encounters, it was a disservice to him now. 'I believe no officer or seaman could expect that the repairs of 11 ships of the line in the state they came into Madras road could be effected in 23 days.'[3]

The select committee thought otherwise. When he announced that he would not be ready on 11 August, it summoned him to its presence. Suffren, it had every reason to believe, had left Cuddalore on the 7th, 'however extraordinary it may appear that a fleet over which a decided superiority has certainly been so lately gained and some of its ships greatly disabled, should under many disadvantages be able to refit and proceed to sea. Your desire, so often instanced in overtaking and engaging the enemy wherever the public safety required it, leaves us only to observe on this occasion to you, as our duty binds us, that we consider the public safety never more concerned than it is at present.'[4] Hughes declined to be goaded. He would 'proceed to sea with HM squadron so soon as it is in a condition for service' and not before.[5] But the rebuke rankled and his feelings for Macartney, whose hand he discerned in its framing, were not sweetened.

On 16 August the *Coventry* frigate arrived from the west coast with a company of troops from Bombay. Trincomali appeared to be in no immediate danger. Captain Mitchell had had a sharp encounter with the *Bellone* off Friar's Hood and his first volley had carried off her newly appointed captain, Suffren's much-loved nephew, and subsequent volleys killed the second officer and wounded the third. For two hours the two ships had slugged it out, each suffering over 40 casualties, until at last the *Bellone* broke off and slipped back to Batticaloa. Hughes had also been joined by the *Medea* so that he now had three frigates at his command. He made ready to leave on the 18th. Every hour was important.

Suffren wasted no tears on Pierrevert. As the wounded third officer tried to break the news gently the Bailli brushed sympathy aside brusquely. 'Give me a straight answer,' he snapped. 'Did you take the frigate? No? Then you have not done your duty. You may leave.'[6] To his cousin he wrote almost as coldly: 'If I have lost a nephew dear to me for reasons of heart and sentiment, the King has also lost a brave and excellent officer.'[7] Beaulieu was posted from the *Brillant* to take Pierrevert's place. The *Bellone* was Suffren's best frigate, absolutely indispensable to him; Beaulieu had just been promoted to a 64 and now was back in charge of a frigate. It cannot have been pleasant for him to see another frigate captain promoted to the *Brillant* but the transfer was a tribute to his active intelligence, sang-froid, intrepidity and skill. He had the qualities Suffren wished were more widely shared among his officers.

And on 18 August the *Lézard* cutter, which had brought Launay to Galle, brought Suffren two full measures of contentment. The first was news of his elevation to Knight Grand Cross of Malta. The second was His Most Christian Majesty's approval of what he had done at Porto Praya. The squadron celebrated that night and even Suffren's sanguine temperament felt a tremor of expectant hope. On 21 August the *Saint-Michel* and *Illustre* anchored in the roads of Batticaloa with the *Fortune*, an East Indiaman prize of 50 guns, seven merchantmen, two Dutch East Indiamen and 600 men of the Regiment of Île de France. He spent a couple of days to take stock of his convoy, land the sick, take on board a battalion of Malay troops and cast off.

On 25 August he was outside Trincomali harbour, which the *Lézard* reported empty. But as the narrow entrance was too heavily guarded, he decided to sail into Back Bay, land troops and storm Fort Trincomali from the rear. In the early afternoon the *Saint-Michel* sailed in close to the land batteries, engaged and silenced them, and by 17.30 his squadron was at anchor in the lee of the promontory. The first troops went ashore at 03.00 hours on the

26th, three miles to the north of the fort, and though Colonel des Roys was in nominal charge he was too slow so Suffren went ashore at 05.00 and took command. In high glee 300 troops of the Regiments of Austrasie and Île de France and the Légion de Lauzun, and 600 sepoys, most of whom had been embarked to capture Negapatam, took up their positions with the smell of action in the torpid air. Only a few mortar bombs disturbed them and at 10.00 the artillery went ashore; over the next three days Suffren himself helped to supervise the raising of batteries and opening of trenches, personally exhorting the men to greater efforts and rewarding the gunners who scored direct hits from his purse. Enfilade parties stormed into Trincomali town to find it deserted.

Lieutenant Hay MacDowell knew that the game was up but made one sortie on the 27th to fire the brushwood over the forward trenches, but on the 29th when the batteries opened fire he had nothing with which to fire back. Suffren ordered the batteries forward and at 08.00 hours on the 30th they began a fierce cannonade. MacDowell, only 26 years old, tried to bargain. He could not agree to include the neighbouring Fort Ostemburg in any capitulation but, when his envoys returned with Suffren's promise to reopen the bombardment, he concluded that Hughes must have been worsted in battle and that there was no point in prolonging resistance. He satisfied honour by complaining that the French had not played the game by forcing a breach without first summoning him, to which the Bailli replied that he would not have insulted a British garrison by expecting it to throw in the towel before a shot was fired. He was granted the honours of war.[8]

Fort Ostemburg was set on a wooded hill along which alone it could be approached. Its commander, Quelso, refused to acknowledge that MacDowell had any power to include him in the capitulation and Suffren decided on assault. It took only a short exchange of fire on the 31st for the business to be done. The walls of the fort were crumbling away and there was no water. Quelso too accepted the honours of war. Suffren had no time to waste and wanted no prisoners, certainly not 300 Europeans and 400 sepoys who would return to Madras at the first opportunity. The loot in the fort, on the other hand, was very welcome: 50,000 piastres, 20,000 lb. of gunpowder, 30 cannon, ten mortars, four field pieces, 1650 bullets, 1200 rifles and six months' victuals. Trincomali town added 40 cannon, 20 cast in bronze and pretty old, and a plentiful supply of ammunition. It had all cost him 25 casualties—a small price to pay for a base in the Bay of Bengal.

Trincomali was his, but Suffren could not afford to rest on his laurels. Its loss would be such a blow to the British that they must surely make an instant attempt to recapture it. Men were set to patching the walls of the forts and a garrison was installed. Suffren personally supervised everything, for he knew he could not trust others to work at the speed he required. Sure enough, at 15.00 hours on 2 September, the guns of the *Héros* announced sails to the east-south-east. Suffren was on board at 17.30, ordering his squadron to prepare for action, and when at nightfall Hughes was anchored nine miles east-north-east, the French ships were in turmoil. But Suffren insisted on following his dessert of mangoes by broaching a bottle of the sweet Constantia wine which d'Aymar had brought him from the Cape. Sir Edward could not be allowed to interrupt him at dinner.

Sir Edward Hughes had expected MacDowell to hold off an attack for longer than he did and when he hove in sight, Back Bay being invisible, he believed he was in time to save his base. If so, it would have been little short of a miracle, for in the first week of his leaving Madras he had covered only 16 miles. Suffren could have lured him in by flying the British jack from the point but he rejected such a ruse. The way to defend Trincomali was to fight Hughes off, and now that he had the *Saint-Michel* and the *Illustre* he reckoned he had three more ships than his rival. He did not know yet about the *Sceptre*. With Hughes defeated, Commodore Bickerton could be dealt with at leisure, but to defeat Hughes he needed more than a scrimmage round the mouth of Back Bay. When on the morning of 3 September the English saw the fleur de lys flying from Forts Trincomali and Ostemburg, 'such was the general indignation spread throughout the whole squadron that no superiority of force could stand in the way of vengeance nor induce a sufficient consideration of the consequences of pursuit'.[9] Hughes could see that the French were preparing to sail out against him. The two champions stripped for action.

In three battles now Suffren had learnt that neither his captains nor his crews were the equals of the English in the prompt and efficient handling of their ships or in preserving the cohesion of their line. If some of his officers conceded nothing to their opponents in courage, tenacity and skill, as fighting teams the two squadrons were vastly different. Only the energetic, imaginative and daring versatility of their chief had given the French the advantage in two battles and enabled them to fight the third to a bitter draw, and now there was to be a fourth confrontation without preparation. There was no time to brief his captains or lay down a plan of action. The ships must make for open water at once, and in driving rather than leading his men Suffren showed his most serious shortcomings as a commander. The battle of Trincomali was to be a scarifying experience.

Despite the bustle, the French were not ready when Hughes's sails were sighted. The yards of some were not across, others were even then bending sails, and when the squadron began to move at 05.45 there was terrible confusion. The wind blew freshly from the south-west, then west-south-west, sufficient to carry Hughes gently before it as he ordered line of battle ahead at two cables' length distance and shortened sail to allow his van to get into position. He would continue like this until he had lured the French a long way out of port, for if he could defer combat until noon, night would cover his retreat if he had the worst of it; and if he were successful, his enemy would be far from base.

The French came out slowly. Suffren's plan was to put two fast, copper-bottomed vessels in the van, one in the rear and the other in the centre so that the sailing speed of the whole line would be consistent. But at 07.30 the *Hannibal* entwined her shrouds round the bowsprit of the *Héros* and, though Morard de Galles endured the frenzied abuse of his admiral, the two ships were extricated only after a chafing delay. While they were locked together, the other captains took advantage of the respite to come on board the *Héros* to advise Suffren against battle. But the *Bellone* had reported that the English had only 12 ships. The Bailli dismissed them with a ringing sentence: 'If the enemy were our equal in numbers it would hurt me not to attack them. Against an inferior force there can be no question. We shall fight!'[10]

All this time Hughes, his line well locked up, sailed further and further from Ceylon, with his biggest ships in the centre, hoping to catch the wind if it changed out to sea and complete the deadly work they had begun at Negapatam. It was all the more infuriating to the impatient Bailli, wrestling with his own erratic ships, to see the enemy almost casually giving way before him, steering from 08.20 to 11.30 smoothly under topsails east-south-east, and occasionally bearing up and luffing to prevent the distance between individual ships from widening. By contrast his own line was a thing of fits and starts and by 11.30, when only four miles from the English, it was still not properly formed. His van was led by the *Artésien* under Saint-Félix, with the *Sévère* and *Saint-Michel* in close support. But it soon outstripped his centre while the rear, brought up by the *Vengeur*, lagged far behind.

Despite repeated signals to close up, his line was never better than ragged. There was certainly incompetence and there may also have been ill-will at work, for every captain could have kept his place in the line and, when the action began, the three ships which came first to grips with the enemy were one very good sailer (the *Héros*), one only passable sailer (the *Illustre*), and one rank bad sailer (the *Ajax*). The pace was not too fast nor the manoeuvres impossible for ships of very different speeds.

From noon to 13.55 the shadow chase continued, until Hughes had lured Suffren 25 miles from base and the French could wait no longer. Though his line was not locked up, the *Artésien* was only half a cannon-shot from the head of the English line, and he made the signal for her to close, hoping that the rest of the line would close with her. But Saint-Félix made his first major mistake in the campaign, luffed too soon and was borne too far forward to bear down on the *Exeter*. Like sheep the five ships astern followed his course and, as they all converged on the van, a parallel action was out of the question. In despair Suffren ordered every ship to bear down, choose an opponent and then do as he did; only the *Vengeur* and *Consolante* frigate were to double to leeward. In order to draw attention to the new signal he fired a gun. It was now 14.30. The example he proposed to set was engagement at very short range, but as he made straight for the heart of the enemy the suspense was too great for his gunners, watching their admiral's huge, shambling figure pacing the quarter-deck, impatient to get close enough to open fire. As soon as they heard the gun drawing attention to his signal, they took it for the signal to open fire.

Before the *Héros* was in pistol-shot range her broadsides opened up. By the accepted rules, the action of the flagship was followed by the rest of the squadron, and when they saw the *Héros* blazing away at comparatively long range they did the same and assumed that close action was not Suffren's plan for the afternoon. The rear ships, moreover, were not even within range. Seeing what had happened, Suffren made a new signal for engagement at close range and worked his ship towards the *Superb*, but as the smoke of their guns rolled across and obscured the English line, nearly every ship failed to turn with the wind along the sterns of their opposite numbers and in the muddle that ensued the *Saint-Michel*, *Orient* and *Brillant* bore down all together on the *Exeter*, which the *Artésien* and *Sévère* had already passed. In the rear the *Vengeur* and *Consolante* tried to double so clumsily that they were quickly forestalled, the *Worcester* threw her main topsail back and blocked their way, followed by the *Monmouth*, and the quartet started a little action of their own quite separate from the rest. In the fore-centre, the *Sphinx* and *Hannibal* stretched ahead and failed to get into the action at all. Only three ships—the *Héros*, *Illustre* and *Ajax*—were to engage at all effectively, and that fact was to burn an indelible scar on the memory of the Bailli de Suffren.[11]

22. The Battle of Trincomali, 3 September 1782

The Battle of Trincomali was a battle of absurdities. In the van seven French ships were either too far ahead to fire usefully at all or able to fire only into the *Exeter*, and they represented half the squadron. The rest of the centre and rear, the *Annibal*, *Bizarre* and the *Flamand*, were not near enough to be of any help to their admiral and had placed themselves too badly to change their positions quickly.

In the centre a conflict of hideous intensity had begun. The *Héros* was now broadside on to the *Superb*. Bruyères in the *Illustre* had driven for a position between the *Sultan* and *Burford* and the two 74s were joined shortly after 15.00 hours by the *Ajax*, whose new captain, Beaumont, was resolved to redeem her loss of face at Negapatam. Beaumont took his position behind the *Héros* and opposite the *Monarca*. Against these three ships was ranged the metal of four 74s and the 64-gun *Eagle*, firing into the bow quarter of the *Ajax*. Folly and sheer bad seamanship seemed to have delivered them to their enemies and, with the English closing into a minatory semicircle, this gallant trio was to bear the brunt of the battle for over two and a half hours.

Suffren tried desperately to call his ships to him, but the wind had dropped and it was almost impossible to move. D'Aymar, trying to pull the bow of his *Saint-Michel* round from taking pot-shots at the *Exeter*, opened his lower gun-ports inadvertently and, since the ship was inclining steeply, they were promptly swamped. The second agony of the *Exeter* came to an end at 15.30 when the French ships which had crippled her mainmast and fore topmasts and cut her rigging to ribbons allowed her to drift away as they hauled their heads round with the aid of their boats to go to the help of their admiral. The *Vengeur* in the rear, after an unequal battle with the *Worcester* and *Monmouth*, sailed out of the battle shortly after 16.00 hours with her mizzen topsail ablaze. Tromelin's superb *Annibal* was stationary throughout until, either stung by remorse or finding his seamanship again, he tried to force her up to Suffren's support towards the end of the second hour, but there was no wind to help him and, with the *Bizarre* and *Flamand* similarly motionless, Suffren was ready to believe that he had been sacrificed by his enemies.

By 16.30 the *Héros* had become unmanageable, but the frigates were too far off to come to her assistance and the agony continued until 17.30 when the wind began to blow stiffly, this time from the east-south-east. Hughes quickly gave the signal to wear, 'which was instantly obeyed in good order, the ships of the enemy's squadron either wearing or staying at the same time and the engagement was renewed on the other tack, close and vigorously on our part'.[1] But he missed his opportunity. 'If they had tacked,' Moissac wrote later in the state-cabin of the *Héros*, 'all three of us would have been cut off and no doubt been destroyed.'[2] But the *Illustre* and *Ajax* redoubled their fire to hinder this manoeuvre and the *Héros* still flew the signal to bear up. As the 12 English ships veered down upon them, the ordeal was renewed on the opposite tack. Shortly after 18.00 hours the mainmast of the *Héros*, riddled with shot and with no rigging left, crashed to the deck and had to be cut overboard. The *Illustre* had lost her main topmast and mizzen and the two ships had to endure another 45 minutes of raking fire before relief led by the *Artésien* closed up and the English bore away. Suffren shifted his flag to the *Orient* and the *Héros* was taken in tow by the *Sphinx*.

Many stories were told afterwards about that dreadful afternoon. Suffren at one point seized his speaking trumpet and shouted across to Bruyères that 'since he had been betrayed and abandoned he would rather perish alone than bring the *Illustre* to destruction with him'.[3] But the gallant captain replied that he would rather sink than desert him. 'And,' wrote the envious Bancenel, a soldier doomed to serve in the lethargic army of Duchemin, 'in spite of the *jean-foutres* and traitors they were able to do so much damage to the English that they had to abandon the struggle and flee with all

The Battle of Trincomali
3 SEPTEMBER 1782

North

WIND

WIND

12·00 noon
Suffren's line is ragged and it bears down on Hughes in natural order.

2·30–3·30 pm
The French van have gone on too far: Suffren's three centre ships are heavily engaged and the *Vengeur* and *Consolante* have failed to double.

— West ===

=== East —

5·00–6·00 pm

WIND
E.S.E

The wind has changed and both fleets have turned about.

Suffren's van (now rear) come up to screen the *Ajax*, *Héros* and *Illustre*.

FRENCH ●	ENGLISH ○
Vengeur (64)	*Worcester* (64)
Consolante (40)	*Monmouth* (64)
Bizarre (64)	*Magnanime* (64)
Annibal (64)	*Eagle* (64)
Ajax (64)	*Monarca* (74)
Flamand (50)	*Superb* (74)
Illustre (74)	*Sultan* (74)
Héros (74)	*Burford* (74)
Sphinx (64)	*Sceptre* (64)
Hannibal (50)	*Hero* (74)
Brillant (64)	*Isis* (50)
Orient (74)	*Exeter* (64)
Saint Michel (64)	
Sévère (64)	
Artésien (64)	

South

sails spread.'[4] When the mainmast of the *Héros* fell to the hurrahs of the English, bringing down his flag with its topgallant yard, the Bailli's mighty voice could be heard above the din shouting for 'flags, more flags. Bring me every white flag aboard and hang them all over the ship'.[5] In a few moments a tablecloth had been nailed to the stump of the mainmast as the proud banner of the Bourbons and dinner napkins fluttered from every spar. In the volleys that the crew, cheering lustily, poured into the *Sultan*, Captain Watt fell, mortally wounded, in a hail of grapeshot.

The noblest tribute came from Sir Edward Hughes himself to William Hickey six months later. 'Mr Suffren is as gallant a man as ever lived. After fighting his ship in a manner bordering on desperation and performing wonders the superior fire of the *Superb* and *Sultan* completely silenced that of the *Héros*. These two British ships continued pouring their broadsides into her without her being able to return a single gun. My ship being within pistol shot, I could distinctly see all that occurred. Her upper deck was more than once completely cleared, scarce a man remaining on it except Mr Suffren himself who ran up and down like a lunatic, crying out most earnestly for some fortunate shot to take him off. I have never thought of the scene but with astonishment and how the *Héros* sustained such a tremendous galling fire is still incomprehensible to me.'[6]

About 19.00 hours the body of the French squadron hauled their wind to the southward, and the British fire continued for another 20 minutes, when the engagement ceased. Admiral Hughes had to admit that 'the ships of our squadron had apparently suffered so much as to be in no condition to pursue them'.[7] The rapid fall of tropical night now obscured the ocean and the van and centres drew away, Hughes keeping his line running south-west before the wind, while the French limped into some sort of order to the south-east. The *Hannibal* passed a line to the *Illustre*, whose mainmast fell at last at 20.00. Suffren now had only one thought and that was for Trincomali. Without a pause for taking stock he made all speed for the port. It was not much. With a topmast serving the *Héros* as a mainmast, they did not make it until the next day. On 6 September the *Lézard* reported the English off Point Pedro.

Sir Edward Hughes had once again to admit that he was in no position to follow the French. First reports from the *Eagle*,

Monmouth and *Burford* suggested that they were in danger of foundering, while his own *Superb* was leaking badly. The French having the wind had fired ceaselessly into the timbers of their opponents. The *Burford* had received, in addition to the fire of the *Illustre*, such a series of raking broadsides from the *Artésien* and *Orient* when they tacked and passed under her stern as she was attempting to wear that she was making water at four feet an hour. From the hull of the *Monarca* 55 pieces of shot were later extracted, most of them very near the waterline, and she was also badly cut about aloft. The *Eagle*, all of whose seams had opened, was leaking at two or three feet an hour. The *Worcester* had lost a topmast and the *Magnanime*'s standing rigging was in shreds. The *Exeter* for the second time was reduced to such a state that no mast could bear sail. The north-easters begin to blow strongly at this time of year, and it was too dangerous to stay off the coast of Ceylon. There was nothing for it but to make for Madras. With the monsoon only a month away any hope of recapturing Trincomali had to be abandoned. This time the gallant admiral made no reference to victory.

But for the French, the bread of Trincomali was bitter to the taste. On 3 September Suffren had believed that with his 14 ships to Hughes's 12 he could be 'master of India'.[8] Instead, 'it is frightful now to have had four chances to destroy the English squadron and to see it in existence still'.[9] The three ships which had borne the brunt of the battle had suffered cripplingly not only in masts and rigging but in men. Sixty-four of the 82 dead were in the *Héros* (30), the *Illustre* (24) and *Ajax* (10); of the 255 wounded, 82 were in the *Illustre*, 72 in the *Héros* and 24 in the *Ajax*, 178 in all. If they were not quite what the *Annual Register* in its first flush of enthusiasm called 'a slaughter seldom equalled except in cases of burning or blowing up', they were horrible enough.[10] No other ship suffered more than five casualties, and in the *Orient, Sévère, Hannibal* and *Annibal* there was none.

The stunned and sobered Bailli felt no exultation from the superb performance of his ship. He tried to be objective when he wrote to the minister, but it was difficult. 'I can only attribute this horror to a desire to have done with the campaign, to ill will and to ignorance, for I dare not suspect worse. The result has been terrible. The damage we have suffered would have been appalling in Europe. Judge how much worse it is in India where we have no resources.'[11]

He could not rid himself of the impression that at the back of this horror lay a nostalgia for the uxorious comforts of Île de France. 'Those officers who have been there a long time are neither sailors nor soldiers. They are not sailors because they never do any sailing, and not soldiers because the spirit of merchandise, independence and insubordination are absolutely opposed to the spirit of fighting. The masters there have contracted the spirit of avarice which it is impossible to eradicate. You cannot imagine what little ruses they have got up to to persuade me to return.'[12] He could only see in their most recent action 'une défection aussi lâche que générale et incroyable'.[13] As he scribbled notes in the margins of the list he sent back to Castries, he noted sadly that some of those who had hitherto fought well had failed him on this occasion: Saint-Félix had fought badly; Langle in the *Sévère*, Galles in the *Hannibal*, du Chilleau in the *Sphinx*, Salvert in the *Flamand*, 'very badly'. Of Tromelin he wrote briefly. 'No one could have done worse. He was never within range.' And of Landelle in the *Bizarre* this damning comment: 'Badly in all four battles, but without doing anything sufficient to have him sent home.'[14]

Île de France had to be the scapegoat, for palpable intrigue had to be ruled out. It was not in character for Saint-Félix to connive at defection of this kind, and on Perrier de Salvert and Morard de Galles no suspicion of intrigue could fall. Ignorance, pusillanimity and lack of skill were partly to blame, but so was the Bailli himself. He was so eager to sail into action that he pressed on when his line was irregular and he did not help it find its cohesion by making signals with confusing rapidity. He had learnt enough of the capacity of his own and Hughes's men to know that the British were too good to take liberties with and must not be attacked in anything but good order. His escape could be attributed less to his own valour than to Sir Edward's decision to wear and not to tack, thus failing to take the indomitable trio from both sides.

An unsigned account of the action written on board the *Héros* is scornful of what Admiral Mahan called Hughes's lack of enterprise and *coup d'oeil*.[15] 'The English admiral, having always avoided the earlier combats our sailors called him Madame Hewz, but the faulty manoeuvre that saved us has now demoted him to Mademoiselle.'[16] It was unjust to a gallant officer who never shirked battle, but on this occasion Suffren owed his survival to one of his few 'Miss-isms'.

It was soon clear from the brooding silence on the stricken *Héros* that Suffren was contemplating drastic action. Tromelin, fearful of the fate of Forbin and Maurville, decided to forestall the trouble he had seen gathering when he had gone on board to explain how his *Annibal* had failed to support the admiral. 'I know, Monsieur,' the Bailli replied shortly. 'It is quite true that your manoeuvre failed for I was not taken, nor killed nor sunk!'[17]

On 23 September, Tromelin came to the Bailli with Saint-Félix, Landelle and Morard de Galles to ask permission to quit their ships. They were kept waiting for an hour while the crew studiously ignored them, and when at last they were admitted Suffren was too angry to remonstrate. Both Tromelin's parents had died and the news reaching him just before the battle, he said, had knocked him up badly, particularly as he was suffering the first onset of scurvy. Saint-Félix also claimed to be ill and reminded Suffren that he had promised to send him back to Île de France after the next battle.[18] He would return as soon as he was well again. Landelle gave no reasons but he knew he had failed. Morard de Galles, from being the hero of Porto Praya, was reduced to a sick and nervous shadow of himself. His going alone Suffren regretted. But he was glad to see the back of Tromelin. He had been unco-operative from the start and had fought as a good officer should only at Provedien. His *Annibal* had been little more than a 'benevolent spectator' in the last action and, as the self-appointed leader of the Île de France faction, he had been a constant source of unrest among junior officers. His reception at Île de France showed that his superiors were under no illusions about him. Souillac refused to accept his reasons for returning and reminded him that his letters had constantly referred to divisions in the squadron of which he was the instigator. The Marquis de Bussy refused to see him and in July 1784 he was dismissed the service.

Though Saint-Félix had been difficult, he was a good fighter. When Suffren refused to guarantee him a command upon his return, he took this as tantamount to dismissal. But to his credit he swallowed his pride and returned to fight with his usual vigour as flag-captain of the *Fendant* at Suffren's last battle. William Hickey recorded a highly coloured version of Saint-Félix's interview with Suffren. His health, he averred, was not so bad that he must resign his command, and he felt quite competent to do the duties of it. 'The Admiral, astonished at his effrontery, coolly replied: "You are grossly mistaken. You are every way unfit to retain the command you have held and have a more fatal complaint than you are disposed to admit, though you must be conscious of it. You are a rank and infamous coward, so away, sir, join your dastardly colleagues and meet the fate that awaits you in France." '[19]

But Saint-Félix was no coward and had in fact been recommended by Suffren for a pension. After the war he received the Cross of St Louis and a pension of 1200 francs. In 1793 he was vice-admiral of the Levant but, his loyalty suspected, he was arrested, imprisoned and transported to Île de France. He died in 1819. Hickey's tale is in character but it is fiction. Suffren may have said something of this sort to Landelle.

With their departure the Île de France faction was broken, but by whom were they to be replaced? D'Aymar? He had not distinguished himself at Trincomali. Peynier? An excellent officer but he could have no conception of the type of campaign Suffren was committed to fight. Why could Castries not fetch d'Albert de Rions back from America and send him out by frigate? Had he been allowed to come in the first place, he would have a very different story to tell and the French might be masters of India. He himself was not immortal. Another Trincomali and there could be no one to command. Let d'Albert come at once![20]

D'Aymar took command of the *Annibal* and Lieutenant Dupas the *Saint-Michel*. Beaulieu could no longer be left in command of the *Bellone* and replaced de Galles in the *Hannibal*. Another lieutenant, Tréhouret, took over the *Bizarre* from Landelle and the *Bellone* was given to Villaret-Joyeuse, then 32 years old, until then commander of the fire-ship *Pulvériseur*.

But there was also to be another change, both disastrous and unexpected. Though Suffren reached Trincomali on 5 February, it was 12 days before a choppy sea and seaward wind calmed enough for his ships to enter Back Bay, and at dawn on the 7th distress guns were heard off Foul Point at the southernmost tip of the bay. La Pallière's son, a junior officer in the *Orient*, had contrived to ground the 74-gun battleship on a reef. In the rough swell she sank deeper and deeper on to its cruel coral and defied all efforts to refloat her. There was just time in the nine days that followed, as her timbers were slowly prised apart by the razored teeth, for the carpenters to salvage her fore- and mizzenmasts. La Pallière accepted full responsibility for his son's fatal error and, now without a command and in disgrace, he joined the other four captains waiting for a ship back to Île de France.

The loss of one of his most powerful vessels through a futile mistake after four bitter battles was a blow harder to bear than the failure of 3 September. But Suffren had no time to be downcast. His squadron was only gathered safely into Back Bay by the 17th and once more he had to complete extensive repairs. Most of them on the *Ajax* had been completed at sea by 5 September, and now he ordered the *Héros* to be rigged with a new mainmast made up of the *Orient*'s foremast spliced to the stump of her old mast by her topgallant yards. Splints were also fixed to her fore- and mizzenmasts. The *Bizarre* parted with her mainmast to the *Illustre*, which replaced it by that of the *Consolante* frigate, which in her turn made do with the truncated mainmast of the *Orient*.

All this was completed at top speed between 18 and 29 September, when the Trincomali garrison was sent back to Madras. After the traumatic experience of the 3rd, Suffren could have been forgiven had he rested awhile in the safe reaches of his new base; but rest was alien to his temper and he had no intention of passing the monsoon in Ceylon. There was much to be done before the winds broke upon the coast. As Lieutenant Bancenel of the Regiment d'Austrasie wrote later: 'He could not be a month out of sight of the enemy without feeling wretched.'[21]

23. Waiting for Bussy

The news from India brought Suffren a small crumb of comfort as he was waiting to enter Back Bay. Sir Eyre Coote had retreated from Pondicherry, so the Battle of Trincomali had saved not only Trincomali but also the army at Cuddalore. No one could reproach him now for attacking Sir Edward Hughes when he did. It had been strongly rumoured that the commander-in-chief wanted to crush Duchemin's starveling garrison upon his return from Arni in June, but Hughes insisted on priority being given to the defence of Trincomali and refused to co-operate unless Suffren was first driven from the coast.

As Suffren refused to go and Bussy's forerunners began to arrive, Coote insisted that he must wipe out the French beach-head without delay. When Hughes sailed for Trincomali on 20 August, he promised on his return to give the general all the support he needed. Unwilling to wait any longer, Coote decided to take advantage of Tipu's absence from Tanjore, where Colonel Nixon was steadily clearing the land south of the Coleroon, to march on Cuddalore. Haidar was a fortnight's march away and, with the *Medea* to carry the military stores and siege train down the coast, Coote hoped for a rapid success.

On 6 September, when he reached the high ground outside Pondicherry, only a day's march from his goal, there was no sign of the British squadron. His scouts, too, reported that Haidar was on the move and when on the 10th he learned what had happened at sea seven days earlier, he knew that he must call off the attack. Uncertain of the true strength of the French and unwilling to attack without support from the sea, he decided upon retreat. Racked by fever, hollow-eyed from exhaustion, Coote's indomitable will faltered. He struck camp and set off towards Madras. With the worst famine in its recorded history depopulating the Carnatic, with Fort St George reduced to iron rations and 2000 of the 2290 villages in the neighbourhood devastated by Haidar's marauders, with French cruisers now based in Trincomali and Bussy expected hourly, with four of Hughes's battleships in no shape to fight another battle, Madras was too vulnerable to leave undefended. Everyone's spirits sagged to their lowest pitch since the onset of the war.

Suffren was mightily relieved at the news. With three of his ships in no state to sail to the rescue of Cuddalore and with only one 74 fit to put to sea, he knew it would be madness to challenge Sir Edward Hughes again. The uncoppered *Vengeur* was so eaten by worm she could hardly sail. If coppering was ever necessary it was here in India and he was still being sent ships from France that had not been sheathed in copper. 'I left Île de France with six months' supplies on board and about 4000 piastres,' he reported to the Ministry. 'I have now been in India for eight months, made ten cruises, fought four major battles and taken one port.' Happy his colleagues who got promoted for less, but that was not what afflicted him; it was the lack of support. 'If I am not sent some other captains for my ships I can do nothing.'[1] To Souillac he urged the early arrival of Bussy with his reinforcements. 'With them, we can undertake great things, but until then there will be terrible moments to endure.'[2]

It was nearly October and Bussy had been in Île de France since 31 May. Suffren supposed him already at sea. Haidar's patience was not endless. The portrait of Louis XVI had been received in full darbar on 31 July with a salute of 21 guns, but the nawab was not interested in the oil painting of a non-combatant. When was the great marquis himself coming? He had been promised a date in October but that was too late. He had been asking for an expeditionary force for three years and the governor of Île de France had sent him Duchemin! 'What can be done when your thousand or so Europeans in Cuddalore are not fit to undertake a long march?' he asked Bussy's ADC petulantly. 'As soon as they have covered two *cosses* [about two and a half miles] they can go no further and lose all marching order. How can troops like these be matched against the English, who always keep excellent order and can cover in one day distances that you can scarcely cover in three?'[3]

Launay had found his stay in Haidar's camp distinctly uncomfortable. He was required repeatedly to explain Bussy's orders while the nawab checked every word to see that they had not changed since he had last heard them. He was tired of hearing what Haidar Ali had given up to wait for Bussy: the chance to make peace, the opportunity to extend his power in the west. He understood only too well that Haidar did not really trust his allies. He knew that Bussy would have preferred an alliance with practically any other country power than Mysore, but Launay did well to persuade the nawab to stay within easy reach of Cuddalore. 'Let Bussy come quickly, but let him come quickly!' Thus, he wrote to the marquis, 'you are awaited here like the exterminating angel'.[4]

The exterminating angel, however, was at work in another place. Bussy, dismayed by the ravages of disease on his already inadequate force, was himself to fall seriously ill. For a week he hovered between life and death, and for three months he was convalescent. Not that Bussy in the prime of life and pink of health could have moved his expeditionary force from Île de France before Peynier arrived; and Peynier, who reached the Cape on 19 May, was kept there until the end of July by sickness and the neurotic van Plattemberg, who would let him sail only if he replaced the troops Bussy had left behind with another 1300 men.

Souillac first tried to persuade the old warrior to let some of his troops go ahead of him, but the marquis refused, less from vanity than from a sensible understanding that Haidar expected, not a further supply of broken men who could not march, but the great general himself. He refused to sail with d'Aymar on 25 June, this time holding that the arrival of the great general himself without his full muster of troops would be interpreted as meaning that there were, after all, no troops to come. With a quickening sense of apprehension as the weeks passed, Suffren waited for Bussy and Bussy waited for Peynier.

The first 12 ships of the convoy that was expected to change the history of India sailed into Port Louis on 29 July, escorted by the *Cléopâtre* frigate. They carried 1500 men and at once 1032 of them had to be admitted to hospital. Peynier himself followed on 15 September with the other men-of-war and the rest of the convoy, but laid out on the decks gasping for land and relief were another 1200 sick. The hospitals at one point were so overwhelmed by 1800 cases of scurvy, dysentery and malnutrition that standing cases were not admitted. One of Peynier's ships was in no better case. Indeed she should never have been sent to sea. The *Alexandre* was rotten to the core of her timbers, a floating hot-house of disease, rat-infested and thought to be a contagious source of the scurvy. Throughout the squadron service on board was considered a death sentence. She had to be burned.

'A ship intended for India,' Suffren wrote in his exasperation, 'should be examined more stringently than if she were just going for a cruise off Ushant.'[5] Peynier's own *Fendant* was Rochefort-built and in good condition and her sister 74, the *Argonaute*, was a powerful vessel only three years old. But the 64, the *Hardi*, was 32 years old and very slow. The two frigates, *Cléopâtre* and *Naiade*, had already arrived.

With Peynier came the news that there were no immediate reinforcements to be expected from France, while Hughes was to be reinforced by Bickerton. Bussy, depressed by the aftermath of sickness and worry, pored over the maps and wrote up his journal, painfully, day by day, but he knew that there would be no action to record until his men were fit to sail. From July to September he counted 369 European troops to their graves. The burying parties were so enfeebled by sickness that, to the horror of the fit and convalescent, wild pigs disinterred the badly buried corpses and scattered half-chewed limbs round the streets of Port Louis.[6]

On the other side of the Indian Ocean the exterminating angel had at last summoned Duchemin. There was no one to mourn him, for he was widely detested by both officers and men. Unduly under the influence of his younger brother, who was in charge of the commissariat, he was far more interested in making money than in waging war and his troops, enervated by scab and dysentery, were unpaid while the general's close entourage salted away fortunes. The final insult came when Major de Boissieux of the Regiment of Austrasie went to beg money from the nawab. He was contemptuously handed a sack of rupees. 'M du Chemin is dead,' wrote one of his junior officers, 'but unhappily for our reputation in India, he has lived.'[7]

The Comte d'Hoffelize now assumed command. No one envied him. Since the expeditionary force had arrived, Haidar had allowed it only five *lakh*s of rupees and the men's pay was five months in arrears. 'I fear he will finally refuse us even provisions,' the new commander wrote gloomily to Souillac on 17 October. 'He finds what we spend on administration and hospitals very extraordinary and does not understand why white men eat more than black!'[8] What was more, the Poona envoys at Haidar's camp were assiduously telling the nawab that Bussy's imminent arrival was a fiction and that the British reinforcements on their way were overwhelming.

Haidar too, in a moment of exasperation, had made an alarming confession to the French agent. 'Two and a half years ago I descended on this province and have lost 20,000 horses, many elephants, camels, bullocks and men. I have spent immense sums of money. My army compared to what it was is now reduced to nothing. I dare risk nothing till Bussy comes. If he does not arrive before the English reinforcements what shall I gain by remaining your ally?'[9] Because Cuddalore was so weakly held, he could not go off to plunder the Northern Sarkars and recover some of his losses. Nor could he deal with the growing threat to his power in the west.

Suffren had no comfort to offer. He did not know where Bussy was and he must start making plans for the winter. Trincomali was not the place to recover his weary and sickly crews. Fresh fruit and vegetables were scarce and the climate was lowering. His men needed a complete rest and change of air. If Hughes went back to Bombay—as everyone confidently expected he must—then he would seek more salubrious waters to rest his squadron. He chose the bay of Achin at the northern tip of Sumatra, whence in January he could sweep back into Indian waters on the tail of the north-east monsoon before Hughes was back from the west coast. If the marquis could not leave Port Louis before 10 September, he should rendezvous with the Bailli there. He would leave a small garrison and a frigate at Trincomali to welcome all the naval supplies he could send.

He had a fortnight before the monsoon broke to put reinforcements into Cuddalore and inform the nawab of his movements. An appearance off the coast in full rig was needed to refute the rumours that the recent battle had finally immobilized him. On

3 October the British watch on the ramparts of Negapatam saw the entire squadron parade before them. For a moment they thought an attack was to follow, but Suffren's target was the Company ship *Prince William*, loaded with ammunition and sheltering under the shore guns. Suffren's 'Maltese' colleague, the Chevalier de la Tour du Pin, who 16 years later was to be present at the surrender of Malta to Napoleon, was sent to board her, but when she ran herself ashore he assumed she was lost and set her alight. The explosion of hundreds of casks of powder which he desperately needed was a sound Suffren wished he had been spared. But the next day he was to hear worse: the rough grind of ships' timbers on gravelly sand as the *Bizarre*, sailing into the river mouth off Cuddalore, drove herself on to a bank, split and filled rapidly with water. She was a total wreck.

Her loss, so soon after that of the *Orient*, was stupefying, part of the heavy price Suffren paid for the promotion of untried officers, for Lieutenant Tréhouret had sailed too close to the shore and when the *Sphinx* bore down on him he failed to tack in time. The weather was perfect, the sea as smooth as glass. By two strokes of idiocy the advantage of d'Aymar's arrival had been wiped out, the odds were once more evened, and when Bickerton arrived they would be lengthened to 17 against 12. Once again the only consolation lay in the *Bizarre*'s salvaged masts, and to make matters worse the *Lézard* cutter was taken by the *Sultan* off Tranquebar.

Ten days remained before the monsoon was due to break and already the sea was turbid with the presage of its arrival. Despatches from Bussy confirmed that he would meet Suffren at Achin, but the admiral was galled by the accompanying information that only one of Peynier's squadron was copper-bottomed. To the best of his knowledge every one of Bickerton's was, and if Hughes went back to Bombay the English would have had all the advantage of a winter in a well-stocked base. His only hope, then, was for a quick and sudden coup against Madras with Bussy's men and Peynier's ships before Sir Edward returned. That could end the war.

Everything depended on Haidar remaining in the Carnatic until Suffren returned, and to this end he wrote to the nawab to tell him that he was off to meet Bussy at a secret rendezvous. He could not tell him where, as all darbars were like leaking sieves and the news must be kept from the English. And his information from Poona was that the peshwa did not really intend to pursue a policy of peace with the British. 'Soyez tranquille,' he ended hopefully, 'rapportez-vous en à M de Bussy!'[10] But to Piveron de Morlat he could say what he could not say to Haidar Ali. No operations with Bussy could begin before the end of January. The French agent must do what he could to nourish the dream of an irresistible coalition of Haidar, Bussy and Suffren, of Madras invested by Colonel d'Hoffelize from the south, by Haidar from the west and by Bussy from the north, while Suffren cut off all supplies from the sea. The presidency must fall in 25 days. The same winds that were to blow him to his secret destination, he reminded the nervous agent, must also blow Sir Edward Hughes off the coast.

But an inspection of the defences of Cuddalore alarmed him. Though he had been able to put 600 men ashore after the loss of the *Orient* and *Bizarre*, he did not think d'Hoffelize could hold it in the event of an attack. So he dashed off another note to Haidar, reminding him that he had suffered 1000 casualties in his last four battles and had 1400 more sick ashore in the hospitals of Trincomali and Cuddalore. He did not think it unreasonable to ask the nawab for the loan of 500 horse and 3000 sepoys. But, he confessed to Piveron, he did not feel able to ask for money. 'I understand the full force of the Nawab's reasoning. We render him scarcely any service but we never stop importuning him for funds.'[11] The last *lakh*, paid to Piveron on 16 September, had barely paid the interest on the loans raised in Tranquebar, and d'Hoffelize needed two more to put Cuddalore into any state to defend itself. But while Haidar was ready to be generous with a fighting ally, he was just not disposed to support an idle army.

A sudden gale from the north-east burst upon the Coromandel coast on 15 October and Suffren, who had bruited it about assiduously that he was bound for Trincomali, ordered his ships to cut their cables and fly triumphantly before the wind. He had done all he could to keep the stage clear, but the *mis-en-scène* was profoundly unsatisfactory. Only the chorus was left to perform through the winter and, while the *basso profondo* retired into the wings, the *primo tenore* was still nursing his voice in Île de France. Piveron's letters followed him east.

Haidar had decided not to march into the Northern Sirkars and had therefore not detached any troops for Cuddalore. 'I have great confidence in everything M de Suffren says,' he told the French agent, 'and what you have told me on his behalf has given me the deepest satisfaction and I believe it. Please God the moment has already arrived and that nothing will happen to upset our splendid projects, for I desire the glory of your nation as much as my own.'[12] The magic of Suffren's name was still potent in the camp. 'Let him leave promptly, let him go and join M de Bussy, let them return as soon as possible and we shall do great things. This will console me for the inaction in which I am forced to remain.'[13]

24. Winter, 1782–3

Job's Satan might go to and fro in the earth and walk up and down in it. Admiral Satan on his way to Sumatra left enough of his restless spirit off the coast of Coromandel to bring Admiral Hughes and Lord Macartney to a quarrel. Trincomali had been a savage defeat. Captain Watt had died in the *Sultan*, his right arm smashed to pulp, and Captain Lumley in the *Isis*. For their deaths Hughes had nothing to show but gaping shot-holes low down in the hulls of the *Hero, Eagle* and *Monmouth*, only kept afloat by the constant action of their pumps, and a tangled lace-work of snapped spars and shattered rigging. 'The short time the squadron can with safety remain on this coast will scarcely be sufficient to refit them for sea.'[1]

This laconic phrase stung both Macartney and Coote into sudden protest. The departure of the fleet at this moment in their fortunes was unthinkable. On 13 September the select committee agreed unanimously that the admiral must winter off the Coromandel coast. Haidar and the French must be shown that the loss of a mere port, so great were the resources of the English, was only a temporary setback. For his part the admiral had little opinion of Macartney's resources, and to remain on the coast for a second winter with his ships in their present state was mere madness.

Last October his six vessels had been 'well-found, each ship with four bower anchors and eight cables, clean out of the docks, no pumps going, masts unhurt and every way well-stored'.[2] Look at them now! To winter with this squadron 'is absolutely risking its further destruction ... If it be ruined, not the Carnatic only but every possession in India of the English will follow, and vain will be any effort to resist when the enemy become complete masters of the sea.'³ Coote might be pining for a conclusive victory somewhere, preferably at Cuddalore, before the end of the year and the total breakdown of his health, but Hughes would on no account expose his fleet to ruin in a wind which might cause half to founder and the rest to be dismasted and 'fall prey to the enemy rushing out on them from a secure port. This resolve is, my dear General, final with me, however odd it may appear to you.'⁴

This exchange was barely over when the select committee was informed that Suffren was attacking Negapatam. This was the filibuster on 3 October when La Tour du Pin fired the *Prince William*, but the select committee assumed it was a full-scale attack and ordered Hughes to sail to its rescue at once. When he refused, the governor turned his pen to elaborate irony. 'If the safety of His Majesty's ships were to be the sole or even primary object of His Majesty's commander-in-chief, they should never meet the enemy at sea or even go out of Bombay dock.'⁵ He had the right to demand in the king's name the admiral's assistance in the defence of territories and possessions of the East India Company. If Bickerton were not already on his way, he would have given him every European in the presidency to retake Trincomali before Suffren was back from Cuddalore.

The French admiral had boasted that he would make the ocean his harbour until he could find a better. 'It may be right to be taught even by a foe and not to mistake the means for the end you were never meant to answer—the defence of the British possessions which you seem willing to put to a great hazard rather than put your ships to hazard.'⁶ As soon as Hughes was on his way to Bombay, Suffren would burn every ship in the roads, intercept the grain convoy and, when he returned in the new year, the French flag would be flying from Fort St George. Could he explain how 'a squadron defeated on 6 July and some of its ships greatly disabled, yet proceeds to sea the 1st of August, while the victorious squadron, while acquainted with the movement of the enemy, remains in port until the 20th of that month?'⁷ Hughes had allowed Trincomali to fall. He must now recapture it.

This was too much for Sir Edward. By return of messenger he delivered a broadside which shook the very timbers of Government House. He started *piano*. His sense of duty was every bit as developed as the noble lord's, but his was a larger view, not just of the presidency of Fort St George, but of all India. He rose rapidly to *fortissimo*. Macartney threatened an enquiry? Then let him beware a public account of the folly which had starved Trincomali against his repeated reminders through the summer.

The select committee proposed a series of alternative anchorages, but they were all—the Hooghly, the Andamans, Mancourie in the Nicobars—quite inadequate for his needs, having no docks, no stores, no water, no carpenters, no provisions. Achin, which he had also considered, was in hostile hands. 'Insignificant as you are in the scale of the National and even the Company's interests, it will, I believe, be thought by all men highly unbecoming in you to attempt to hector or bully the commander-in-chief of His Majesty's forces by sea in this country into a compliance with your selfish measures for the preservation of yourselves from danger at the risk of destruction of that force on which the whole of the British dominions in India greatly depend for preservation.'[8]

'The compliments which the Select Committee are pleased to pay Mr Suffren,' he told the Admiralty, 'are far from unacceptable to me. I believe him all they say, able, active and sagacious, and, more, brave . . . yet they compliment Mr Suffren at my expense. That Mr Suffren expected to have effected a great deal more against His Majesty's squadron than he did is clear by his having dismissed and sent to France within these few months no less than eight of his captains.'[9]

Major-General Stuart and 85 merchants of Madras made a more conciliatory approach on 11 October. If the grain convoy from Bengal were intercepted, Stuart said, 'then the army he has now the honour to command and which is equal to any army by France and Hyder to be produced, in short the sheet anchor of India by land, must . . . be disbanded for want of rice only, and at the very time when the enemy will strike their stroke by land, he means the third week of December next'.[10] The date was sheer guesswork but in other respects he was right. There were not six weeks' provisions in the presidency. Hughes bowed to a good military argument, civilly expressed. He would stay until the grain and rice convoy arrived, but more than that he would not undertake.

Even that was not to be. The 68 artificers had worked as hard and as fast as their skill and the surf permitted to put the ships into the best condition for sea, but from 12 to 14 October the rollers began to run so high that no skiff with a load on board could ride them. Since his watering was far from completed, Hughes grew anxious about the punctuality of the wind. Sure enough, the monsoon broke on 15 October, and the same wind that had blown Suffren out of Cuddalore now unleashed its fury on the squadron in the roads of Madras. During the morning so many anchor cables had snapped that by 14.00 hours the admiral gave the signal for every ship to cut or slip. By 17.00 the squadron was all under sail and he stood out with it to seaward.

Throughout the night the wind rose to cyclonic force and as the sea was lashed into a boiling cauldron of foam and spray, the *Superb*, still feeling the wounds of 3 September, lost first her mizzen- then her mainmast within an hour. The great ship began to labour dreadfully and every hand was set to pumping and baling. Then at 03.00 hours on the 16th the gale abated. Had it continued, the gallant warship would certainly have foundered. There was no hope now of returning to Madras. The uncoppered ships would never make it against the wind and current, and Sir Edward, shifting his flag to the *Sultan*, ordered the squadron to make for Bombay. Having, for the most part, only one bower anchor to each ship, they were were all nearly driven on to the shoals off Point Pedro on 22 October and it was not until 20 November that the battered squadron, many of the ships without topmasts, crawled into the first safe anchorage, Anjengo, on the western coast.

The sea front of Fort St George on 16 October was a sad and stricken sight, but among the pulped wrecks of the 150 *praus*, sunk with their loads of rice in the roads, there was no vessel of His Majesty's squadron to be seen. As he surveyed the desolate prospect, Macartney believed that Hughes had intentionally broken his word and he sat down to write a bitter letter to the governor-general. Warren Hastings 'unfortunately read it before going to bed and slept ill'.[11] He made no serious comments on it but yet hoped that Sir Edward 'meant to deceive Lord Macartney and blind Suffrein, and take him at Trincomali by surprise'.[12] It was a very faint hope and the governor-general's main anxiety was that he would miss Bickerton.

He did indeed. Sir Richard sailed into Madras roads on 27 October. He had spent only four days in Bombay to water and sailed on the 19th, determined to join the admiral as soon as possible. Advised to give Ceylon a wide berth, he had missed Tom

Troubridge in the *Active* and now, to Macartney's chagrin, arrived too late to be of any use. The commodore realized that he would do no good by remaining where he was and, after putting ashore the men of Sir John Burgoyne's Regiment of Light Horse, 400 Hanoverians and 1000 raw Irish recruits, he prepared to return to Bombay. Macartney urged him to be brisk. If he caught up with Sir Edward there might be time for them to make a joint attempt on Trincomali for, despite the long and tedious voyage, Bickerton's crews were in fine fettle. In fact his squadron was in such good form that it beat Hughes back to Bombay—what a contrast to the lame wretchedness that Peynier had led only with difficulty into Port Louis!

After the sailor, the soldier. Coote's health was now broken and he demanded a return to Bengal. Macartney, 'for a great while imposed upon by his military reputation in this country till I found from persons of his own silly trade how little bottom there was to support it', was only too ready to see him go.[13] His successor, Major-General James Stuart, was still practising with his wooden leg, directing operations in Coote's absence from a two-wheeled horse carriage or 'Tin Whiskey'. The one-legged general was old, over-cautious and totally unenterprising, and much given to vexatious counteraction in select committee. He was brave, it was true, but also an object of derision to his troops because of his silly go-cart and foul temper.

But he had one definite quality: he had been on the half-pay list of the king's commissioned officers since 1775. He was on loan to the Company and, though he had been gazetted with the rank of major-general, he was not borne on the strength of any regiment. As far as the British army was concerned he was only a half-pay colonel, and as far as Macartney was concerned he was a Company general and there could be no nonsense about his being independent of the governor of the presidency of Fort St George. Stuart, then, would do.

The grip of famine meanwhile slowly and inexorably closed on Madras. The 'black town', or native quarter, was nearly depopulated by death and migration. The presidency had swallowed over two million rupees from Bengal and needed more and more, but the creditors of the Treasury in Calcutta were beginning to resent the constant drain on their resources. Macartney's letters to Warren Hastings grew shriller and shriller, complaining of everything and everyone. His friend John Macpherson gave him a timely caution. 'If much more public writing and political altercation between your government and . . . the supplying if not superior government is to take place, the soul of the public service will sink under such disputes and Madras will be literally—wrote off to Hyder and Suffrein.'[14]

But the governor was impervious to advice. Immured in his palace, his household subjected to a régime of total austerity which was not imitated by the rest of the community—William Hickey found not a single candle alight in government house when he called in April 1783—he continued to direct his barbed reports to Bengal. The bland diplomat had become as sour and as cranky as Coote. The silence of famine, interrupted by the jingle of harness as Haidar's flying squadrons of cavalry cantered up to the walls of the Mount, closed over all but the spluttering pen of Lord Macartney.

On 30 October, Suffren's ships, bright prisms of phosphorescence under metallic skies, were off the north-eastern tip of Sumatra. Just in case Hughes had decided on Achin rather than Bombay, *La Fine* reconnoitred the wide natural bay, sheltered from winds and tides, in which they proposed to rest. There were two ships there but they were soon identified as the *Bellone* and *Fortune*, which had beaten them across from Trincomali. Rest was something they all needed, none more than Suffren himself, rest, sweet water, fresh fruit and freedom, as far as possible, from anxiety. But the air of Achin was not as fresh as he had hoped; a marsh surrounded the stilted town and his convalescents took a long time to mend. Some, indeed, grew worse.

The sultan, moreover, had taken fright on seeing so large a force appear off the coast and left the town. He was convinced that they were the Dutch, with whom his relations were far from cordial, and his viceroy proved very suspicious and unhelpful. In the absence of the sultan, he would not permit hospital tents to be pitched ashore and, having no instructions to provision his overlord's allies, he referred the commissariat to the town's bazaars where they were royally fleeced. The beauty of the town was a great deal poorer than that of the women, but these were doubly dangerous as they nearly all had both gonorrhoea and a jealous Malay husband ready to satisfy honour with a knife. So Suffren kept his men on board ship. While he sprawled in his chaise-longue, a straw hat on his head,

his feet on the taffrail and the perpetual cheroot in his mouth, his
sailors swam, sunbathed, carried out their exercises and overhauled
their ships.[15]
The frigates and corvettes were kept busy. The *Fortune* was
sent to make quite sure that Hughes had not selected another
anchorage in the archipelago. *La Fine* went to Kedah for rice,
the *Bellone* and *Pulvériseur* to Malacca for spars and rice. The
latter under Lieutenant Lanuguy-Tromelin fell in with five British
East Indiamen bound for China. Lanuguy decided that a fire-ship
loaded with so valuable a cargo of masts was not expected to
attack stray merchantmen and let them sail on unmolested. Suffren
was not pleased. 'I have read your log, M de Lanuguy, and I have
to say that you have stained your flag.'[16] There could be no excuse
for timidity. On 27 November *La Fine* returned, her holds bulging
with rice, and on 3 December the *Pourvoyeuse* was fitted out with
a ready-made mainmast to replace the one which had passed to the
Brillant.
It was now a matter of waiting for Bussy. But the marquis by
himself was not going to dismay the tough, trained soldiers of
the presidency and the arrival of Peynier was not going to make
Suffren so strong that Hughes would skulk from fear in the safety
of Bombay. Suffren continued to lament the lack of good officers
and money. And coppered frigates. If the *Bellone* and *La Fine*
could be reinforced by six 50-gun ships and 12 good frigates,
the commerce of the Honourable East India Company would be
at an end and, even if success by land were to elude the French,
the British must soon sue for peace. As it was, Suffren's position
was far from strong and he was still undecided about his next
move. The squadron was almost totally in the dark about what
was happening in France, at the Cape, in Île de France. 'We never
know what is afoot except by chance, no one writes to us and . . .
Peynier has not thought fit to send me despatches by frigate.'[17]
On 24 November news came at last and it was not to his
liking. The corvette, *Duc de Chartres*, brought the long-awaited
despatches from Bussy. The great marquis was not yet on his way
to Achin! Instead Suffren read a catalogue of woes from a modern
Book of Job. Bussy had been close to death, his men were still
prostrated by sickness, Soulanges' convoy had been dispersed, the
Alexandre had had to be burned. To crown all, Suffren learned of
his comrade de Grasse's terrible defeat at the Saints on the day

he had fought the Battle of Provedien. 'It is too many disasters at once,' he wrote dejectedly to his widowed cousin in Provence. 'If I am able to return from India with honour it will only be by the greatest good fortune!'[18]

The whole conduct of the war was now back in the cauldron of speculation. If Peynier failed to arrive soon, Suffren would find himself matched with 12 battle-scarred and sea-stained ships against 12 coppered and five new-fitted vessels in an English squadron of 17. A coup against Madras was now out of the question and he had no more assurances to give Haidar Ali. 'But I shall tell him you are coming soon,' he wrote dutifully to Bussy on 26 November, 'and that I have no doubt you put off your departure until you knew we had captured Trincomali. I shall explain to him that this was to make our union more sure, though it has had the effect of delaying your arrival off the coast. These little subterfuges are, I must say, all so alien to my nature that I fear I lie very badly.'[19]

For himself he must make the most of Hughes's absence in Bombay and sweep back into the Bay of Bengal in an unremitting *guerre de course* which would hit the merchants of Calcutta where it hurt them most. Then, when Peynier at last arrived, he would do battle again with Sir Edward. If he sailed quickly he might catch the rice convoy to Madras.

The *Duc de Chartres* was turned around at once and sent back with despatches to Île de France. The rendezvous with Bussy was changed to Galle. If on arrival Bussy found Suffren blockaded in Trincomali, he should land on the western coast and march across land to Cuddalore. If he could not hope to reach India before the end of March, he should land on the Malabar coast anyhow for, with 17 ships against him, Suffren would be able to give him little support. Three weeks later, on 16 December, he sent the *Vengeur* and *Pourvoyeuse* to Trincomali; they were so badly in need of careening that they were of little use to him in a daring war of speed. Announcing his imminent return to Ceylon, he begged Governor Falck in Colombo to send caulkers and carpenters to the port, and on the 20th he set sail for the coast of Orissa.

25. Bussy in India

In January Sir Edward Hughes learnt from a China merchant arriving in Bombay, that Suffren was in Achin, and from the garrison of Trincomali, returning under the terms of the surrender, he learnt that Bussy had buried 1000 men in Île de France and was seriously ill himself.[1] He thought it safe, therefore, to assume that Suffren would wait off Sumatra until Bussy was ready to sail, which could not be for some time.

But with Suffren there could be no safe assumptions; when Hughes received the news of his rival's wintering in Achin he had already left and Bussy was even then at sea. The soldiers, fit and convalescent, under his command were not the 10,000 he had first demanded. His motley expedition numbered 2200, most of whom had been sick and many of whom were still feeble. At Cuddalore he might, he calculated, join another 1000. Despite the sad reality after the triumphant vision he could delay his departure no longer. On 18 December, two days before Suffren left Achin, they were on board Peynier's transports, but he was forced to dawdle at Bourbon to pick up more convalescents. The marquis had no great expectations left. He had left good troops behind at the Cape to hold the hand of the Dutch governor. But at last the great Bussy was on his way: in poor voice and in danger of missing his cue, the *primo tenore* was returning to the stage of his greatest triumphs.

Another month passed before Hughes learned that both Suffren and Bussy were on the move, but he was in no position to imitate them. His journey to Bombay had been a torment. At Tellicherry he had been obliged to put 450 men ashore in the last stages of scurvy and leave the *Isis* to bring them on if and when they recovered. His squadron then split. The *Superb*, towed by the *Magnanime*, and the remainder of his uncoppered ships were sent to Bombay. The rest were to go to Goa for new masts and careening in the Portuguese dockyard. From 11 to 17 December he struggled up the coast alone in the *Sultan* to meet Sir Richard Bickerton at last.

Then began a long struggle with Governor Hornby and the select committee, both of whom became as difficult as Macartney and his committee in Fort St George. The governor needed two reminders that the United Company of Merchants Trading to and from the East Indies was obliged under Sections 18 and 22 of the Act of Parliament in the 21st year of the reign of His Majesty George III to supply and victual His Majesty's ships as necessary. The select committee held that it was out of their power. There was nothing with which to victual and supply them, and no money to buy anything. Laboriously keeping his temper, Hughes was able to coax the dockyard to copper-bottom the *Eagle*, *Exeter* and *Superb*. As soon as he had 15 ships copper-sheathed, he would return to the Coromandel coast to disappoint both Suffren and Haidar Ali in their designs against Madras. That might in fact not be before Vice-Admiral Hyde Parker arrived in the *Cato* to take over his command.[2]

Hughes knew that another inconclusive encounter with Suffren would achieve nothing. He did not know that Suffren had lost the *Bizarre* or that Peynier had burned the *Alexandre* and therefore assumed that the combined French squadron would be 17 ships strong. He was ready to sail with only 15 in the hope that careened, watered and victualled they would be superior to 17 which had spent a winter at sea and of which only eight were copper-bottomed. But he would not sail with fewer, and it was to be 20 March before he was ready to leave Bombay. On 8 January the *Annibal* and *Bellone* had appeared suddenly at the mouth of the Hooghly and the rest of the squadron anchored in the roads of Ganjam on the coast of Orissa. Once more Suffren had beaten time and among the country sailors the arrival of Admiral Satan was a token of gloom.

Suffren hoped to mark his return from Achin by the sack of the British factory at Visakhapatnam, but the surf ran too high

and he had to content himself with taking rice-boats. Then on
11 January he had the stroke of luck his energy and resource
deserved. At 22.30 in the lustrous gloom of an Indian night, the
Coventry frigate sailed calmly into the midst of what she took to
be Bengal merchantmen sheltering from a French frigate reported
in the vicinity. Captain William Wolseley sent an officer to enquire
whether anyone had seen the marauder. He clambered on board
the *Ajax*. At almost the same time Suffren sent a boat to the
Illustre but the officer in charge was so drunk that he climbed
on board the *Coventry*. Cursing roundly in French he stumbled up
the rope ladder while the astonished watch, noting his condition
and presuming that he had mistaken the *Coventry* for his own
ship, also anchored secretly like a wolf in the fold awaiting its
moment to pounce, arrested him and the boat's crew at once.
At 22.00 hours a savage burst of cannon-fire tumbled Wolseley
out of bed and, when the captured officer was hustled in to his
presence, the sight of British uniforms sobered him sufficiently to
tell his captors that they were surrounded by the French squadron.
The captain, seeing the looming shapes ranged round him in a dark
and threatening circle, bowed to the inevitable. Suffren, learning
that Wolseley had commanded the *Coventry* in her action with
the *Bellone* when his favourite nephew, Pierrevert, had been killed,
forbade his officers to mention the subject and received the nervous
and crestfallen officer graciously.[3]

The *Coventry* was a god-send: a coppered frigate, taken
undamaged. Over the following week there were daily prizes,
praus and country ships loaded with rice, sometimes with powder,
one with valuable ordnance, until every ship in the squadron was a
floating granary. But they were three weeks too late for the great
Bengal convoy which saved Fort St George from starvation. On
the 18th the *Coventry* took her first prize under new colours—an
18-gun grab—and followed it on 31 January with a merchantman
from Pegu. But all these prizes were taken as the squadron sailed
south with all speed, for William Wolseley had brought Suffren a
piece of alarming news. Haidar Ali was dead.

The nawab had died of the 'royal sore' on 7 December. A huge
abscess on his neck had swelled to the size of a coconut. The
French surgeon in the camp advised lancing and sent for Noël,
the chief surgeon at Cuddalore. When he saw it, he wanted to
operate at once. The pandits consulted the stars and affirmed that

the auspicious moment would fall 72 hours later. 'Is it possible,' Noël exclaimed with astonishment 'that a great man like you can submit to such a superstition?'[4] He could and did. The endless applications of his Hindu doctors had given the abscess a tough rind so that the knife, even at the auspicious moment, could not deal with the whole of it at once. The nawab supported the operation with a fortitude worthy of his rank, but the wound was infected and four days later, at eight o'clock in the morning, the scourge of the Carnatic was dead.

His son, Tipu, was 'enlightening the environs of Coimbatore and Palghat by his presence' at the time but wasted no time in striking camp. The French were surprised and gratified by the smoothness of the succession. D'Hoffelize sent a detachment of troops to stand by in case he needed them, but Tipu took over the government without bloodshed. In no time his camp 'from the splendour of his standard became the envy of the starry heaven'.[5]

The son was in many ways more terrible than the father and his implacable ferocity was to burn itself on to the folk memories of British India. He lacked the humanity of his father, who could never have had constructed the mechanical tiger which roared with terrible realism in the act of mauling a British soldier. With Tipu were to crumble at last into the blood and slaughter of Seringapatam the brilliance and wealth that were the kingdom of Mysore, but that was not to be until 1799. If Piveron de Morlat did not think he had the tactical ingenuity or the diplomatic finesse of his father, 'the most astonishing prince who has ever appeared in Asia', he had no doubts about his hatred of the common enemy. The resources of a formidable state were now in the hands of a man whose skill was still untried. 'Tipu Sultan knows how the late Nawab, his father, treated me, but in the direction of affairs—what a difference of spirit, of inspiration, of action, of governing, between him and the great man who is no more!'[6]

Colonel d'Hoffelize was even more disenchanted. One-legged Stuart, who was far from agile in mind as well as body, was on his way to destroy the walls of the Carnatic towns before they could be of any use to Bussy, and as he did so at his leisure through February and early March he invited the Mysoreans to battle. Tipu did not accept. 'The Nawab is less than useless,' the Colonel spluttered. 'He has not the least idea of military science and it was all I could do to stop him fleeing at the approach of the enemy . . . He counts it a victory to have camped once in his life only three miles from the English.'[7]

But Tipu had other priorities. He had had to hurry back to the east to secure his throne when his father died, leaving the Bombay army in possession of the field in the west. Now that army under General Matthews was approaching Haidarnagar, the newly named but ancient capital of the Cannarese and the depository of the nawab's private treasure. Its presence, so near the vital heart and jewel of his dominions, decided the new ruler to leave the Carnatic as soon as possible. Suffren had been afraid of something like this happening when he abandoned his fine projects against the Bengal commerce and hurried south. He was off Cuddalore on 6 February.

His *guerre de course* had been short but successful. Prizes included the *Coventry*, an East Indiaman loaded with cloth, a 20-gun sloop, a brig carrying field guns, another with a cargo of pepper and alum, five rice-ships and other *praus* disgorging a total of 500 tons of grain. 'I could have done better still,' he told Piveron de Morlat, 'but, but, but—I have many sick in the squadron, many of them sailors, and we need rest. Yet it is time for action. Our disasters in America [the defeat of his old shipmate Admiral de Grasse at the Saints] do not mean that India must be abandoned.' Perhaps Tipu could give him fresh meat and butter, but he did not like to ask for too much. 'I am a little embarrassed about M de Bussy. I think we must expect him very soon.'[8]

It was while he was watering at Porto Novo that Piveron came post haste to tell him of Tipu's decision to march west. On 20 February half the army set off for the Malabar coast, accompanied by 600 reluctant Frenchmen under Major Cossigny. Tipu had hinted that if the French lent him these men he might personally wait in the Carnatic, but Piveron did not believe him. He had been sent to find Suffren but he was confident that it was only a ruse so that Tipu could move off the rest of the army while he was out of the camp. But without Bussy there was nothing Suffren could do or say to change Tipu's mind. What influence he had had over the Mysorean ruler had vanished with Haidar's death. On 23 February he returned disconsolately to Trincomali. There was very little to cheer him there, though the first of Peynier's convoy had arrived and the *Fortitude* was back from Pegu with her cargo of spars.

Then, three days later, the *Naiade* frigate returned from looking for Suffren at Achin. Bussy was on his way at last. But if Tipu were to be stopped from marching west, Bussy must be landed at Cuddalore without delay, whatever the state of his troops. All ships were ordered to prepare for sea, Moissac was sent to the Mysorean camp to use all his persuasion to keep Tipu in the Carnatic, while every hour of the day the lookout in Fort Trincomali scanned the horizon for the wings of the 'exterminating angel'.

At last, at 15.00 hours on 10 March 1783, to everyone's undisguised relief, the legendary marquis sailed into Trincomali harbour, saluted by every gun. Three ships of the line, the *Cléopâtre* frigate, 32 transports and 2500 men was the final total of the great enterprise. The marquis had arrived 'better late than never, better alive than dead. It took three months to make the *Hardi* shipshape and this held up my reinforcements and made everything miscarry ... Here is your expedition, costing a hundred million and designed to secure a general peace, spoiled by the ineptitude of ignorant cheese-parers who were content to let ships in such a deplorable state leave harbour.'9 Bussy would have done better not to have waited for the *Hardi*, as two months of good weather for landing on the Madras coast were more essential than the addition of one ship; and it would have been better if Castries had ensured that all Peynier's squadron was copper-bottomed.

The arrival of Bussy also affected the destinies of two very humble persons caught up in these great affairs, for when Suffren had returned to Trincomali he found a battered Portuguese ship which had limped into the port after a terrible storm. On board were two disconsolate passengers, the Calcutta lawyer William Hickey and the adorable Charlotte Barry, who with Suffren's arrival became prisoners of war. Hickey had stolen the wanton and irresistible beauty from the morose son of the Earl of Peterborough and would have made her his wife had she let him. Now, after their terrible experience on board the *Rainha do Portugal*, the consuming sickness that had made her decline his name had begun to ravage her delicate constitution. The surgeon of the *Illustre* was able to prescribe a glow back into her wan features and soon the attractive couple were on easy terms with their captors.

But William was depressed by the talk of the fleet. Sir Edward Hughes had been four times fought and four times beaten, Madras was closely invested by land and swept by famine and disease, a brave and experienced general was on his way to deliver the *coup de grâce*. 'This was a melancholy history for me, and from the fall of Trincomalay as well as Suffren's fleet appearing to ride triumphant and unopposed in these seas, I really feared it was but too true and the British sun was near setting in the east.'[10]

Suffren soon came to hear of the unusual couple who were the toast of dinners on board the *Flamand* and picnics ashore arranged by Perrier de Salvert. Hickey came in person to plead that his 'wife's' weakness might recommend their release from a port so generally admitted unhealthy. Suffren agreed to put it to Bussy on arrival and asked the couple to dinner. Women, apart from the faithful widow in Provence, had figured little in Suffren's life, but after the bedraggled winter he was ready to be another willing victim to her charm. He even dressed in their honour in a 'blue jacket of thin coast cloth, his shirt collar buttoned, with a black stock on. He had also pulled up his stockings, buttoned his breeches knees and put on shoes instead of slippers,' very different from the 'English butcher' William had met when he first called on him.[11]

The *Héros* could provide, however, none of the graces of Perrier's little supper parties. The table was tolerably supplied but served on a dirty cloth, with 'knives, forks and etceteras rough in the extreme'. The Bailli ate with his usual Olympian appetite and after coffee he took them over his ship. The Hickeys were suitable shocked by 'the scene of filth and dirt as I could not have believed had I not seen; it had more the appearance of an abominable pig-sty than the inside of a ship of the line bearing an Admiral's flag!'[12] (The French were not as punctilious as their enemy over the cleanliness of their ships. Hickey's sharp eye found only the *Vengeur* and *Flamand* 'as neat and clean as any British man of war', and he was soon to remark the contrast with Sir Edward's spruce and shining vessels.)[13]

Suffren finally announced his intention of taking a constitutional on shore, at which point a savage fellow appeared, covered with pitch and tar, to inform him that the boat was ready. After taking his polite farewells, he went down the ship's side by a single common rope as quick and as light as any midshipman. The apparition in pitch and tar turned out to be the boatswain, to whom and to no one else Suffren applied for anything he wanted for himself, and it seemed that Suffren never left his ship by any other way unless on ceremonial occasions. Such an occasion was imminent when Hickey went on board to remind the admiral of his promise while he was dressing to call on Bussy. He found him sweltering under a heavy laced uniform suit of clothes, facetiously observing that he 'felt like a hog in armour, for so long a period had elapsed since he had been obliged to dress otherways than in the lightest and thinnest clothing that he was really uncomfortable. But etiquette required his waiting upon the Commander-in-chief properly equipped, even at the expense of his feelings.'[14]

Dressing for the arrival of the new commander-in-chief was not the only expenditure to which his feelings were to be put, for the moment Bussy reached India Suffren would have to subordinate his squadron to his overall command. To ignore Bussy's orders if he did not like them would be less easy than when they came either from the governor of Île de France or from Castries in Paris, and the marquis had a reputation for harshness and arrogance. He would not be an easy chief and Suffren had made no secret of his distaste for Bussy's absolute command. 'I am vexed because I cannot see any good coming from it, but I shall . . . do all I can to see that there comes no harm. Either the commander at sea knows his job or he does not. If he does, why put him under the orders of one who will not know it? If he does not, why clip his wings and leave him there at all? Orders from someone more ignorant than he, who is actually on land while the other is at sea, cannot be expected to lead to the right results.'[15]

With thoughts like these, the 'hog in armour' was on board the *Fendant* within minutes of her arrival. Bussy must go at once to Cuddalore, escorted by all Suffren's coppered ships, before Hughes was back, before, with luck, Tipu actually left the Carnatic. Bussy, who recognized that he was talking to a man of authority, agreed. In fact he scarcely had the strength to resist. The Bailli was appalled to see the drawn and tetchy features of a very sick man, another Duchemin. Could this be the hero who must achieve a miracle?

26. The Siege of Cuddalore

Bussy's pride crumbled before the demonic energy of his comrade at arms. Suffren could only go to sea in his copper-bottomed ships since they were the only ones ready. The *Vengeur* was still being careened and he was 1,800 men below strength. But if he waited until he was ready, he could be at Trincomali until October. The violent decisiveness of the sailor masked foreboding of disaster, but in the frantic bustle of the port Suffren had time to remember the Hickeys.

They were to be allowed berths in the *Blake*, a small English prize, and a gallant leave-taking of Charlotte punctuated the more strident preparations for action. Captain du Chilleau hoped William would give his respects to Lord Macartney whom he looked forward to escorting from his government in the east as he had from his government in the west. Perrier de Salvert gave Charlotte his pet mynah bird, a prodigious specimen that could not only call out the different instructions for putting a ship about but could also sing: 'Connaissez-vous Amiral Anson, ce général de grand renom?'

Even the admiral joined in the lamentation at their going. When William climbed on board the *Héros* to say goodbye, he apologized for not bringing Charlotte with him, but she was in the jolly boat below. 'Is she so? I now heartily lament that my ship has not been accustomed to receive the honours of visits from the fair sex and therefore we are without the means of getting Mrs Hickey on board which I should have been happy to have done. But this being the case, I must go to her and offer my compliments and my adieux.' As he was in his usual state of undress he hastily called his servants, with whom he retired for a few minutes, reappearing in full uniform. Though the ship was rolling rather deep, he nevertheless stepped nimbly down the side and wished Charlotte joy at the approaching end to her most unfortunate voyage. With surprising gallantry he added that, as his present visit must needs be his last, he would make it as long as possible.

The reason for this became clear in half an hour when his steward appeared down the side with a choice collection of provisions for the journey, which Suffren pressed with great gallantry on his amiable prisoner. He kissed Charlotte's hand, shook William's and jumped up the side of his ship as nimbly as he had descended, and the jolly boat pushed off. In a few seconds the crew of the *Héros* suddenly gave the departing couple three hearty cheers, repeated by the *Sphinx* and *Cléopâtre*. The 'few articles of refreshment' were all stolen goods, being papers of chocolate, a variety of preserves, confectionery, fruits, savoury cakes, liqueurs, a beautiful pair of shawls, six pieces of very fine worked muslin, four pieces of Visakhapatnam long cloth, four rich kincobs [cloth of gold brocade] and six pieces of handkerchiefs, all taken off a prize in the Bay of Bengal![1]

Suffren had also filched the copper sheathing off the *Rainha do Portugal* which had provided him with his ebullient and invaluably garrulous guest. This was now beaten on to the timbers of the *Illustre*. On the morning of 15 March the convoy of seven ships of the line, three frigates and 12 transports set off for Cuddalore. Throughout the night of 16–17 March, the Regiment of Marck, battalions of the Regiments of Aquitaine and the Royal Roussillon, all at far from full strength, together with 300 gunners from Besançon, went ashore unceremoniously in the estuary of Porto Novo. On the 18th the *Naiade* frigate captured a Danish merchantman with two English officers on board. Suffren, who might need the goodwill of the Danes, released both the ship and its passengers and transferred the Hickeys to it as being more comfortable.

William was mightily relieved. He had not enjoyed his brief sojourn in Cuddalore, where he had been lodged in a house bereft of doors and window frames, all torn out to provide fuel for the cooking pots of Tipu's soldiery whose ferocious appearance he found unnerving. But the company of the two English officers cheered him up. The British were not done for yet. Madras was strongly garrisoned and in good heart. The Bengal Treasury was full and, best of all, Sir Eyre Coote was now well again. When Admiral Hughes and Commodore Bickerton arrived, the French sun would set for ever.

It was not quite true that Coote was well again, but he was fit enough to leave Bengal on 2 April just as Suffren sailed from Cuddalore for Trincomali. When he had left Madras on 28 September, pursued by a swarm of recriminations and reproaches, Warren Hastings had been almost at his wits' end. He could not help remarking drily to Macartney on 23 October that 'under the alarms which the contents of your preceding despatches had left us ... it was some relief to find that you had both time and inclination to labour through a discussion of 29 close-filled pages without a reference to the dangers which surround you'.[2] But with Trincomali lost, Hughes in Bombay, Bussy arriving at any moment and Hastings himself under threat of recall, now more than ever Britain's resolve must not be seen to be weakening. The supreme council went on bended knee to Sir Eyre: 'We see no possible salvation to the country unless you shall be able to return there and assume the immediate command of the army.'[3] Infirm as Coote was, Hastings still believed that his presence would yet retrieve the miserable state of the Carnatic, 'even though he should be deprived of the power of motion'![4]

What comforted Hickey depressed Suffren. He could no longer feel that events were moving his way. He could make no plans. The only thing of which he had sufficiency were spare topmasts, but all his other needs would be met by three things, he had told Castries repeatedly, 'good ships, COPPERED FRIGATES [he wrote in large capital letters] and men. With these we have everything.'[5] He left Cuddalore with what he had on 2 April. Peynier and the *Fendant*, *Saint-Michel*, *Cléopâtre* and *Coventry* were to cruise off Madras to intercept Hughes's expected convoy, while the rest inched painfully south against adverse currents and idle winds. Then in the late afternoon of 10 April, within 20 miles of Trincomali, the *Bellone* signalled 17 men-of-war approaching from the south. Sir Edward Hughes was back.

Strictly in character, the admiral had sailed as soon as he was ready, not before. His military friends in Bombay failed to convince him that Suffren's sudden reappearance in the Bay of Bengal was a feint, that Bussy would land on the west coast, ally himself with the Marathas and attack Bombay. His duty was clear: it was to seek the French squadron off the Coromandel coast. He was 2000 men short through sickness, but those on board were in good spirits. And, by his ill-fortune, he missed Suffren off Ceylon. The indefatigable Tom Troubridge had cruised off Ceylon in the *Active* throughout the winter, but he did not know that Suffren had ever been out of Trincomali when he met Hughes off Friar's Hood on 8 April. A passing grab, however, reported four ships of war off Madras. Without reconnoitring further, Hughes steered north at once and Suffren, crowding on all sail through the watches of the night, was safely back in harbour on the 11th.

Peynier must be warned at once. Summoning Villaret-Joyeuse, now in command of the *Naiade* frigate, coppered, swift but lightly armed, he gave him his instructions. 'Since you have singled me out for this honour,' the future admiral replied, 'perhaps you could give me letters of introduction to both Lord Macartney and Admiral Hughes.'[6] Suffren shrugged. The *Bellone* was too valuable to hazard, the *Naiade* the only vessel of any speed he could spare. 'But if anyone can succeed in a venture like this, it is you.' Thus Lord Jupiter knew how to sugar the pill. And the young officer's worst presentiments were fulfilled.

That very night in the light of a full moon he fell in with the 64-gun *Sceptre*. The wind was too slight for escape and at 22.00 hours the cannonade began. An hour later Captain Graves invited the little ship to surrender, but Villaret-Joyeuse replied with a broadside; and for the next three and a half hours, their yards touching, Goliath subdued David until, her masts and rigging shorn away and her guns dismounted, the *Naiade* surrendered. 'You have given us a very fine ship, Monsieur,' Graves told his captive wryly, 'but you have sold her very dear.'[7] The casualties, none fatal, were 24 on the *Sceptre*, 34 on the *Naiade*.

Despite this, Peynier's luck was in. The citizens of Madras had been painfully aware of his presence when they watched the *Coventry* destroy a Dutch prize under the very guns of Fort St George, which could not fire a single shot of protest since the keys to the arsenal had been mislaid.[8] He raised the blockade on 13 March when word flashed up the coast that Hughes was back. He was just in time, for later on the same day the English squadron anchored in the roads. Nevertheless, tantalized by the suspected presence of the convoy he had been sent to intercept, he hung off the coast. Sir Edward in his anxiety detached five ships to look for it, and three days later Peynier was cheated when the *Bristol* and her 20 transports came in under escort of Hughes's men of war.

But if the *Fendant* had missed her quarry, she was to strike a doughty blow for the cause, if only by accident, within very few days. Sailing north-east from Madras at midnight on 14 March, Peynier sighted the Company ships *Resolution* and *Royal Charlotte* with gold on board and, more valuable than gold, Sir Eyre Coote. For four days the *Royal Charlotte* and her passenger, prostrate with anxiety, fled before her trackers and at last, only 15 miles from Trincomali, Captain Mercer threw them off the scent. But without firing a shot Peynier had contrived to remove his country's most formidable enemy. To Coote's disordered mind, French ships cruising off Madras could only mean that Hughes had been defeated and when, in the darkness of the third night, the *Royal Charlotte*'s tiller rope snapped and she flew around, seeming to fall on board the *Resolution*, Sir Eyre, waking to the alarm that the *Fendant* was upon them, fell into an apoplexy.

When his numbed and motionless frame was taken ashore at Madras on 24 March, the end was near. Three days later, with a letter 'holding him amenable to our orders' from the select committee by his bedside still unopened, the commander-in-chief expired.[9] Death now solved the bitter dispute and the grave yawned between the governor and the general. It was dug near the pulpit of St Mary's in a space specially cleared among the bags of rice which now composed its permanent congregation. His corpse was accompanied to its last rest by persecutors and colleagues alike to the Dead March from *Saul*, and when the prayers were concluded the dragoons marched briskly away to the air of 'Nancy Dawson' and fired the last salute in a less congested area.

Worse was to follow 'Nancy Dawson', for the governor and admiral fell to squabbling over the money the old general had brought from Bengal—the admiral claiming it as payment for loans made on the general's personal guarantee and threatening to sue his widow, the governor attempting to appropriate it for the needs of the presidency. The times were sadly out of joint when an admiral so phlegmatic was reduced to abusive bickering with a diplomat so bland, while the defence of Madras fell on the uncertain shoulders and wooden leg of James Stuart.

Further south, the paladin of France, in blissful ignorance that fate had rid him of the only foe worthy of his steel, was taking stock of his situation among the ruined orchards of Manjikuppam. It was not reassuring. The walls of Cuddalore were low, with 14 crumbling bastions set at great distance from one another and each at the moment so stocked with powder that a careless flame could blow a breach wide open. Tipu was even now marching westwards and, between what he had brought with him and what he found, Bussy now commanded 3500 Europeans, 3–400 *Coffres* or native troops from the Cape, 4000 French-trained sepoys and 8–10,000 Mysoreans, believed to be the scourings of Tipu's soldiery, led by the shifty Sayyid Sahib. The nawab had promised another 35,000 men as soon as he had eliminated General Matthews, but Bussy knew from old what promises like that were worth. The five million *livres* he had carefully husbanded might last him five months, but it had to pay Suffren for the rice he had put ashore from his prizes so that he could pay his restive crews some prize money. He also had to pay the arrears of his sepoys. Frenchmen would have to take letters of credit on Paris. The Dutch had been quick to warn him not to count on the other five million they had promised, since Falck had to pay his own Malays. 'Our actual position on the Coromandel coast,' he noted despondently in his diary, 'is such that I should not care to establish it even in time of peace.'[10]

In his prime Bussy had overcome odds greater than these, but that was 30 years ago. He had returned in the winter of his years, 'a painted caricature covered with decorations,' wrote one of his junior officers, the future Director of France and patron of Napoleon, the Comte de Barras. He spent his time posturing in his finery and displaying 'a mechanical contrivance which, drawing the skin to the back of his head, diminished the wrinkles in his forehead'.[11] The 'veterans' of the Regiments of Île de France and of Austrasie were not reassured when they were presented with the legend face to face.

For a start he was so racked with gout that he had been put ashore only with the greatest difficulty and his fingers were so swollen that he could not hold the reins of a horse and had to be carried everywhere in a litter. Their access to the recumbent general was blocked by a close ring of familiars who formed his general staff, grossly out of proportion in size to the unexpectedly small army he commanded. Thirty years before the marquis had been the uncrowned ruler of the princes of the Deccan and the richest of them all, but now all they saw was Duchemin reincarnated in a more lordly avatar than that rapacious and incompetent officer. Indian servants issued from his headquarters in resplendent uniforms, and officers who were obliged to see their chief could gain access only with a bribe. And, like so many new arrivals, Bussy set about finding fault with everything that had been done before his arrival, undoing it and then having to call in d'Hoffelize to put it right again.

A deserter put Stuart's army at 3000 Europeans and 20,000 sepoys, and there was no sign of the troops and provisions Tipu had promised. Sayyid Sahib refused to move closer to the coast than Arni, claiming that he must cover Trichinopoly, but, Bussy feared, meaning that he too intended to follow his master west. The marquis could take little comfort from the fact that he had never wanted the Mysorean alliance. All he could do was make the best of a bad job, and if men and money came from France he would throw off the thralldom of Mysore and engineer the alliance he had always wanted with the Marathas and Hyderabad.

He wrote secretly to Montigny in Poona asking him to announce his arrival to the peshwa and to the nizam, even to the Grand Mughal himself in Delhi. His enemies might accuse him of foolish vanity, but the magic of his name was for the moment virtually the only important weapon he had. His most pressing letters, however, went to Tipu. His small army, he assured the nawab, would soon be doubled by reinforcements from France and in the meantime he needed every soldier Tipu could spare. But the appeal had been made so often that it caused not a ripple of attention in the court of the nawab, accompanied as it was, even, by the news that Stuart was at last ready to march on Cuddalore.

Suffren had always reckoned that this would coincide with Hughes's return so he had refused a request from Tipu to blockade Mangalore on the west coast. If Cuddalore was invested, then he would disarm the frigates, impress every man he could and risk a battle. He could sail in 20 days and with luck the monsoon wind would have turned about and he would have the weather-gauge. Rumour had it that seven line-of-battle ships had left France in October for the Indies. How much he would like to think—and how little he could—that they would arrive any day now.

For the first time in his life, the prospect of a battle was unwelcome. Bussy must inevitably summon him, with five of his ships commanded by promoted lieutenants, only seven of them copper-bottomed and the rest worse sailers than cargo ships, none of them, apart from the *Vengeur*, having spent more than three weeks in port since they left Île de France 12 months ago. With these he would have to battle against 17 or 18 ships recently refitted and nearly all copper-bottomed. And there was no way he could refuse to go. What was worse, while waiting for the summons he could not even mount a *guerre de course*. He had plenty of ships, prizes for the most part, but how was he to get them to sea? 'If I had men and strips of copper I could cover the sea with cruisers.'[12] As it was, the *Naiade* was lost, so he was worse off than before. Survival had become as important and as difficult to achieve as success.

By 22 April all Peynier's ships were back in Trincomali harbour. Hughes had appeared off Tranquebar on the 12th, clearly spying out the coast for the forthcoming attack on Cuddalore, and Suffren knew that he would be allowed to stay in Trincomali no longer than it would take the *Vengeur* and *Illustre* to complete re-masting. They both leaked badly, as did the *Sphinx*, *Artésien* and *Saint-Michel*, but that summons might come at any minute. On 4 May he sent the *Coventry* up the coast to see what was happening. She returned on the 12th with a letter from Bussy. It was the summons he had been expecting.

Short of food, powder and shot, Bussy felt above all 'the pernicious effect your continued absence must have on the minds of the enemy, of our allies and of all Asiatics'.[13] And he could not undertake to find Suffren the 1500 men he needed for his squadron. At a pinch he could spare him 600 men from the garrison. After all those intemperate summons he had received from the Bailli in Île de France, it was now his turn to do the summoning! The crisis had come sooner than expected, but it was not physically possible for Suffren to sail before 26 May. He was not to know that on 15 May, when Sayyid Sahib moved unexpectedly closer to Cuddalore, Bussy had changed his mind. Less nervous of immediate disaster and increasingly conscious that he was inviting the squadron to destruction, he ordered Suffren to stay where he was. The order never reached Trincomali.

Peynier's unconscious victory over the iron constitution of Sir Eyre Coote was to prove greater than anyone had realized, for

General Stuart was no Coote and, when he at last set out for
Cuddalore on 21 April, it was not by the shortest march, due
south along the coast. Bussy's reputation in this respect was worth
a thousand men, for Stuart followed an inland route that was
unlikely, in his view, to be contested, and it gave the French plenty
of time to make their dispositions to receive him. Their first line
of resistance was to be the River Ponnaiyar which debouched into
the Bay of Bengal, six miles north of Cuddalore. Every ford was
covered by massed artillery and Sayyid's cavalry was strategically
placed to prevent a crossing further up-river.

It was reliance ill-placed. In an unexpected burst of energy,
Stuart marched up river and crossed on 6 June. The Mysoreans
fell back without a fight, and at a stroke Bussy's line was pierced.
The road to Cuddalore lay open and on 7 June Stuart had taken
up a strong position with his right flank reaching down to the
sea where Admiral Hughes, who had also arrived on the 6th,
was putting ashore the Hanoverian troops who had come with
Bickerton. In the desperate situation to which he was now exposed
Bussy recovered some of his old flair, turned his army about and
fell back upon his second position, a line of earthworks hastily
thrown up outside the walls of Cuddalore itself. Despite his
confidence that he could hold his own, he knew he now faced a
siege which could be broken only by the unexpected reappearance
of Tipu by land—too much to be hoped for—or by that of Suffren
by sea.

27. The Fleet to the Rescue

Bussy knew that if he repeated his summons to Suffren of 12 May it was tantamount to asking a gallant squadron to sacrifice itself in a lost cause. But General Stuart's rambling itinerary had allowed the French time to lay in stores from Pondicherry and they were short only of rice. If Suffren could send him two months' supply, Bussy reckoned he could hold out until the vengeful Tipu came storming back from the west. For the news from that quarter was good: General Matthews had allowed the nawab to slip through unguarded passes and himself to be cooped up in Bednore where, after 17 days, he surrendered with the honours of war.

The honours were not observed. The loot of Haidar's treasury which should have been returned as part of the terms of surrender was found secreted about the persons of the British officers, who were all packed off to join Suffren's prisoners in the hell-holes of Seringapatam. On 28 April, Matthews himself was dead, some said from boiling oil poured down his throat, others by his own hand.[1] All that was left of the Malabar front were the garrisons in Mangalore and Tellicherry. Madras had relied on Matthews and Humberstone between them to keep Tipu out of the Carnatic; but on 6 June, when Hughes appeared off Cuddalore to land supplies, he was greeted by the roar of 21 guns from the French garrison, celebrating the latest victory of the nawab.

The English squadron had already been at sea for over a month. Towards the end of April, Sir Edward had received information—denied to Suffren—that four French and six Dutch men-of-war had left the Cape and must even now be off Ceylon.

Though his watering was far from complete he knew he must sail to intercept them at once, for in conflict with a man like Suffren wasted time was a gift to the enemy. On 2 May, then, leaving the *Isis*, *San Carlos*, *Naiade* and *Chaser* to take the storeships down the coast to their rendezvous with Stuart, he set sail for Ceylon. On 15 May he spoke with two Portuguese vessels coming up from Trincomali who confirmed that Suffren was preparing to sail for Cuddalore, and from that moment Hughes continued to work to windward with the squadron alongshore in case the Bailli made a dash for it and fell on his unprotected storeships. As he did so, Suffren was assembling his squadron in Back Bay to emerge on the 26th. If ever the affronted gods of India proposed to have their sport, this was the moment.

By 23 May Suffren had stripped all his transports and frigates except the *Coventry* and *Cléopâtre* of their guns, he had loaded every available and seaworthy ship with food and ammunition, he had taken on board 250 European and 300 sepoy troops; but even when he had impressed every lascar in the port, he was still a quarter short of his full complement. Six of his ships of the line were in Back Bay on the 24th and the rest were to follow when the English squadron was sighted from Fort Trincomali. There was just time for the *Fendant* and *Hannibal* to slip round the point before Hughes's squadron was in full view filing past the bay. At this critical moment Sir Edward surveyed his opponents and decided that the squadron was not 'by any means eligible to attack at anchor under the cover of their guns and mortar batteries'.[2] He carried on south for a while, setting a close watch on Trincomali. If the ten warships from the Cape were in the offing, he had 17 ships with which to attack them.

The unexpected appearance of a squadron that should have been blockading Cuddalore caused Suffren serious anxiety. 'I cannot make out what Monsieur Hughes plans to do,' he wrote on 28 May to Souillac in Île de France. 'Is he waiting for his reinforcements or to intercept mine? Or is he waiting for the moment that I go to the rescue of Cuddalore when he will attack Trincomali which will fall very easily? For I have been obliged to take on all 500 men of the garrison in order that my ships shall be, I cannot say well-armed, but sufficiently manned to go to sea. So this is what I have done. I cannot with 15 ships, of which only eight are copper-bottomed, challenge 17, all coppered and stronger than mine. In view of their better sailing power I cannot get to the windward of them. But judging that his 18th ship is blockading Cuddalore, with the frigates, I have sent two transports laden with rice and artillery, under escort of the *Fendant*, *Cléopâtre* and *Coventry*. This seems to me the best way I have of succouring Cuddalore and not putting Trincomali at risk. For it is on Trincomali that our continued presence in Indian waters depends. I believe that in not obeying M de Bussy's orders, given when the situation was very different, I have in fact carried out his wishes.'[3] The loss of Trincomali would mean the loss of Cuddalore. By perverse logic, the loss of Cuddalore did not mean the end of the war in India. In the last analysis, Bussy was expendable. Peynier commanding the *Fendant* could not complain of lack of trust in his seamanship. Everything now depended on his getting through. Suffren's anxiety was painful as he paced the quarter-deck of the *Héros* like 'Admiral Satan on the threshold of hell'.[4]

In truth Hughes had miscalculated. There were no reinforcements near Ceylon at all, and by sailing before his watering was complete the admiral had reduced the time he could afford to remain at sea to little over a month. As early as 19 May this had become painfully clear but, when he informed Macartney that he must return to Madras to take on more water, he threw the select committee into a panic. How could he contemplate doing such a thing? How could he then give Stuart the support he was expecting? Why could he not take another lesson from his redoubtable rival? They no longer had any sympathy for the by now inflammable temper of old 'Hot and Hot'. 'We trust that you will be able to water the squadron at such places and in the same manner as M Suffren did before Trincomali fell into his hands. By your coming to Madras our operations to the southward would be exposed to imminent danger and the main object be defeated—as there is great reason to believe that so spirited and enterprising an officer as M Suffren would relieve Cuddalore the moment he knew that you returned from a station to the windward of that place.'[5]

If Hughes was enraged at the receipt of this insulting minute, it was largely because he now began to realize the extent of his blunder. Had he not appeared off Trincomali, Peynier would never have slipped out with Bussy's rice and Suffren would have emerged at last to engage a squadron superior in numbers and amply supplied with water. Hughes had played his ace too soon. Off Batticaloa the first signs of scurvy began to appear on Bickerton's ships. The intrusion of sickness and death before any sign of the expected enemy from the Cape turned him back. Suffren saw him off Trincomali again on 31 May where he 'manoeuvred and paraded before us three leagues out to sea'.[6] Suffren sniffed the wind and was momentarily tempted to try a battle to windward of the enemy, but on mature consideration, without the *Fendant* and his two frigates, he was 'forced to watch them without being able to sally forth—you can understand,' he told his correspondent in the Ministry of Marine, 'that I have never suffered so cruelly!'[7]

During the night two English prisoners were able to seize a rowing boat and escaped to tell Hughes that Peynier was at sea. It only needed the huge 74-gun battleship to pound Stuart's storeships to matchwood in contemptuous defiance of the *Isis* for Hughes's name to be indelibly insulted. He hurried north in high perturbation. On 3 June he sighted the *Fendant* but lost her at nightfall, and on the 6th he had resumed his station off Cuddalore. The water the select committee had urged him to find elsewhere was not to be had. At Porto Novo, Mysorean troops guarded every fresh-water creek in the estuary. In the ruins of Negapatam the wells were dry. At Tranquebar there was drought. All this time scurvy was spreading rapidly among the crews of the *Gibraltar*, *Inflexible*, *Defence* and *Africa*, lethally in the *Bristol*, so that by 8 June there were 1142 cases in the squadron to be transferred to the *San Carlos* for the hospitals in Madras. 'If Mr Suffren appears before the reduction of Cuddalore,' he wrote to Macartney in words very like those used by his rival to the minister in Paris, 'I must strip the frigates to man the ships of war.'[8]

General Stuart had not made the admiral's position any less critical by his one-legged speed. 'It required the utmost management,' he explained in justification, 'to be able in time to bring to this, our ultimate ground, rice and other articles, barely sufficient for our existence',[9] but the fact remained that he had consumed nearly everything he had and needed the squadron to cover his further supplies for at least seven weeks. 'If the fleet goes to Madras and Monsieur Suffren anchors off Cuddalore, with the means he will give Monsieur Bussy, in every respect, I fairly say to you, Sir Edward, I cannot succeed, speaking practically as a military man, and I leave to your good sense, judgment and experience to suggest the natural consequences to be apprehended from failure.'[10] Macartney, smarting from the impertinence of the *Fendant*, added his word too. If Hughes stayed where he was, he would do all he could to send water down from Madras.

Sir Edward's wild-goose chase now made his position very awkward. He had no choice but to stay where he was as long as his water lasted. This might be for a fortnight, for he was already pumping the ground tier which was pretty brackish, and his only hope was that, before he ran completely dry, Suffren might brave battle and force the issue. Another Portuguese ship reported that the Bailli was only waiting for the return of the *Fendant* before sailing, and Captain Drew in the *Seahorse* confirmed that on 11 June he had laid up the *Bellone*, *La Fine*, *Pourvoyeuse* and *Apollo* to man his ships. It was some comfort to know that his enemy's plight was every bit as bad as his own.

It was in fact worse. For Suffren had no means of knowing how Bussy fared. If he sailed prematurely he opened Trincomali to recapture, and he knew that if he received a summons from Bussy he must sail whatever the cost. 'My maxim is never to worry about myself . . . nor to balance my actions against the risk of causing displeasure or of being disgraced,' he wrote confidentially to Paris, 'but M de Bussy is very old and is led by very young men. He is in no state to do anything himself and in his thinking he is conditioned by the position in which he finds himself.'[11]

On 7 June the *Dromédaire* transport entered Back Bay with the news that the British and French armies had met at last. It also brought a letter from Bussy dated 30 May which forbade Suffren to take his squadron to sea unless he heard that Cuddalore was actually blockaded by land and sea. Like Suffren, the marquis had feared that Hughes had sailed south to lure the impetuous Bailli out of Trincomali into a disastrous combat. On 10 June Peynier and the two frigates returned to confirm that the siege had begun and that Hughes had taken up a position south of Cuddalore. Bussy's instructions were that he was to sail only if the trenches had been forced and the garrison had retreated within the walls. But how was Suffren to know this, with Hughes across the sea route?

In his perplexity he summoned his officers and read them Bussy's letter. Trublet de Villejégu, second in command of the *Flamand*, was not impressed by the equivocation of the aged warrior, who was cleverly establishing his alibi if things went wrong. If the citadel was forced to surrender, the commander-in-chief could claim that the squadron had abandoned him. If it sailed and was defeated, he could say that it should never have done so without his orders. Such thoughts may, indeed, have crossed the commander-in-chief's mind. War may be an option of difficulties, but an option of disasters calls for decisions which few men are equipped to take. Bussy undoubtedly hoped that the burden would be taken from him by his formidable colleague. The decision to sail or not to sail was one he could no longer force on the squadron, but the man who had fought five battles already was unlikely, if what his admirers had said of him was true, to shirk a sixth. Glory is dear to the French heart and if Suffren emerged from Back Bay no one could deny that it would be magnificent. Suffren only needed to know that, this time, all his men were with him.

'The critical state in which the King's affairs now find themselves demands that we all work together. Let us put far from us all misunderstanding that can prejudice success. Let us know that the honour of being Frenchmen can outweigh the advantages that the enemy has over us. The army under the walls of Cuddalore is lost unless we go to its rescue. Perhaps the glory of saving it is reserved for us. We ought at least to make the attempt.'[12] And since honour was all that was left, no one dared to disagree.

Immediately after the Battle of the Saints, a royal order had decreed that no general officer commanding more than nine ships in battle was to fight in future on board a ship of the line. In order to avoid a repetition of the fate of de Grasse, he must transfer to a frigate from which, so the theory went, he would have a better view of the engagement and could ensure that his signals were obeyed. By implication, too, he would the more easily avoid capture. 'I shall conform,' Suffren growled to the minister, 'as far as I judge this manoeuvre useful to the good of the service. It would be carrying out the spirit of this instruction wrongly if I used it as an excuse for not setting the example expected of a commanding officer, particularly on those occasions when he could fly his flag from his own ship just as effectively as from any other.'[13] To his officers he was more direct. 'Only an order from the King could prevent me from sharing the dangers of the action with you.'[14] If the Bailli, 'who could not be a month out of sight of the enemy without feeling wretched',[15] had ever seriously wondered if he should fight Sir Edward Hughes a fifth time, he had now recovered his instinctive knowledge that a fleet's purpose was to destroy its rival. At 08.30 on 11 June he sailed for Cuddalore.

He had 15 ships of the line—five 74s, eight 64s and two 50s—two frigates and the *Pulvériseur* fire-ship. Most of them had not been careened for two years, and the *Illustre* and *Saint-Michel* were so leaky that their pumps were at work night and day. Against him, sleek from the attentions of the dockyards of Bombay and Goa, were one 80-gun ship, five 74s, two 70s, eight 64s and two 50s, 15 of them coppered. He was not to know that Hughes was desperately short of water and that his men were falling like flies with sickness. It seemed instead as if the wheel had turned full circle since, over a year ago, Admiral Hughes had sailed out of the Madras roadstead with only nine ships of the line to challenge his 12.

But if the odds were against him, the wind was not. By the 13th he was off Tranquebar where Erasmus Gower in the *Medea* spotted him and scurried back to Hughes, covering the 30-odd transports still landing stores north of Cuddalore. At Tranquebar the wind became a fickle jade, blowing English, blowing French by turns, mostly but not invariably set from the south-south-east. The current, on the other hand ran north.

Sir Edward decided to move closer to Stuart's storeships. If he sailed down to meet Suffren, he might be blown unexpectedly off shore. But if he stayed where he was, nine miles to the south with the wind in its present torpid state, he risked being becalmed while the French could be carried up among them. By noon, however, it was clear that no action could be expected that afternoon and the Bailli dropped anchor at 14.15 off the mouth of the Coleroon. If he kept the wind he could soon make up the 23 miles that now separated the two squadrons.

When morning came, Suffren, in compliance with his instructions, shifted his flag from the *Héros* to the *Cléopâtre* frigate and made signal for the battle order which had been decided in the council of war at Trincomali. With both the wind and a measure of good luck it would reduce the advantage of the enemy for it massed his five 74s, the *Fendant*, *Héros*, *Argonaute*, *Illustre* and *Annibal*, with the *Saint-Michel*, *Hannibal* and *Cléopâtre* ordered to double, on the

five ships of Hughes's rear. The rest of the squadron, six 64s and
the 50, were to contain the 13 ships of the English centre and van,
where Hughes's heavy metal could be expected. In the first hours
of battle he could achieve the concentration he had always wanted.
At most he might destroy or capture three or four ships. At the
least he might beat the English squadron off its station near the
beleaguered fortress.

The wind on the 14th, however, blew very feebly from the
west-north-west, too strongly for Hughes to make any headway
against the current but not vigorously enough for Suffren to cover
more than 16 miles. In the afternoon the Bailli thought he might
scoop up some wind by turning slightly into it and Sir Edward
thought he was holding back. 'Mr Suffren,' he scribbled to Stuart,
'does not seem to like us in our position. He seems to be retreating
to the southward having come down *très cautement* this morning.
I shall turn the tables on him when I can prudently.'[16] Stuart,
meanwhile, should unload the transports as quickly as possible
and so relieve him of the need to give them protection. 'They
expect reinforcements and so do we, yet I think with you that this
is the finishing stroke of the French.'[17]

This access of confidence was the result of events on land. On
12 June the British had succeeded in dislodging Sayyid's Mysorean
infantry from their positions, and on the 13th there was a bloody
battle on the plain before Cuddalore. The British advanced in two
double columns and had soon overrun the outer trenches and the
first line of guns, capturing most of the French draught cattle.
Vigorous counter-attacks restored an equilibrium along the whole
front and at the end of the day, as the vultures began to settle in
the stunted trees, Bussy himself came down to embrace the officers
of the Regiment of Austrasie.

But the old general knew that he could not sustain a second
day like this. Stuart's casualties were 40 dead and 600 wounded,
the French about two-thirds that number, but their positions had
proved defensible only by strenuous and costly counterattack and
hand-to-hand fighting. While there was no limit to the resources
of the British, Bussy's men were wan and feeble with sickness
and hunger. He ordered the army to withdraw behind the walls.
The soldiers withdrew sullenly, for they thought Stuart was in
no state to mount another attack like the one they had so
bloodily repulsed. 'Yesterday the army won the battle in spite of

the general,' Mautort wrote sourly. 'Today he lost it in spite of the army.'[18] Throughout the night of the 14th, the sepoys dragged the field-pieces through the gates and abandoned the plain to the burial parties. Stuart was cock-a-hoop. If only Sir Edward could keep his position, the end was near.

28. The Battle of Cuddalore, 20 June 1783

Sir Edward, despite his jaunty air, was puzzled. Was Suffren looking for battle or for a chance to run troops and supplies into Cuddalore? If he could be sure the Frenchman wanted a fight, he would run before the wind out to sea and challenge his enemy to follow, but Stuart was expecting him to maintain the blockade. Yet while Hughes hung off the coast he was inviting attack in a lee berth, and, as he paced the steaming quarter-deck of the *Superb* and the hours crept by, the toll of sickness rose relentlessly. A brooding silence, too, had fallen on Cuddalore where the sweating men worked through day and night to plug the cracks in the bastions, waiting for the vice to close. Then towards noon a cry was raised from the sea walls. Far away on the horizon the first tips of white sails could be seen.

There was a sudden wave of excitement, followed by a roar of voices, like an explosion, which was wafted over the forward posts of Stuart's besieging army. At the sound of 'Voilà le Commandeur' echoing through the streets (the news of his elevation to Bailli Grand Cross was not yet widely known, so to most men he was still Le Commandeur de Suffren), Bussy hurried from the house where he had spent the last 24 hours poring over maps and asked for hourly reports of his progress. From the abyss of defeat the indomitable sailor was coming like a paladin. Unbidden, indefatigable, magnificent, the Bailli de Suffren had exorcized the ghosts of d'Aché and Tronjoly. From that moment the anxious watchers on the shore witnessed an epic.

But it was an epic with a long prologue. Throughout the whole of 15 June Suffren tried manfully to crawl up the coast, while

Hughes watched him cautiously, until in the afternoon the French weighed and stood, with their transports all together, out to sea. Towards dusk, with action again postponed, Suffren tacked and stood to the south-west. 'I believe M Suffren did not expect to find me here,' Sir Edward wrote to Stuart. 'He is seemingly at a loss what to do. I conclude he wishes to come into Cuddalore.'[1] He was wrong. Suffren was still hoping that the wind would freshen and give him the battle he wanted.

Dawn on the 16th found the two squadrons separated by many miles but there was a French wind. Suffren again moved to the *Cléopâtre* and by noon the gap had narrowed to nine miles. At 15.00 hours Hughes himself decided to weigh and formed line, whistling for the wind, and by 16.30 both squadrons were parallel on opposite tacks, the English taking an evasive course. Suffren ordered his line to tack and by 18.00 he was at last within range of the enemy, when night fell. By his manoeuvre, however, he had dislodged Hughes from his position off Cuddalore and the port was open. The east wind, which usually blew at this season, was late in coming. If it held off for another 24 hours he could slip in, put ashore his supplies and take on the men Bussy had promised him. Attack had once more proved the best defence. What Stuart had hoped Hughes would prevent, it was now in his power to achieve. The fickle wind, blowing mostly from his quarter, had favoured the brave.

Throughout 17 June Hughes waited for the wind from the east to bring him down for one last, decisive action before his butts ran dry and he was forced to consign his dead to the ocean. It was expected hourly but never came. Meanwhile Suffren had made contact with the Marquis de Bussy: if he ran in to pick them up, could the commander-in-chief lend him 1500 men? Bussy could promise only 1200, of whom 600 would be Europeans. If Suffren needed more, he must embark with his army and abandon India! Suffren settled for the 1200 and, at 20.00 that night, while the English hung helplessly out to sea, he was anchored in Cuddalore just beyond the bar. When the 18th dawned, the French ships, though slow and creaking in every joint, were fully manned, while the spectres of thirst and disease lurked in the rigging of the English line-of-battle ships, each of which had between 70 to 90 cases of scurvy.

For two days more the cautious sparring continued across the unruffled water while all action on shore was suspended. Sir

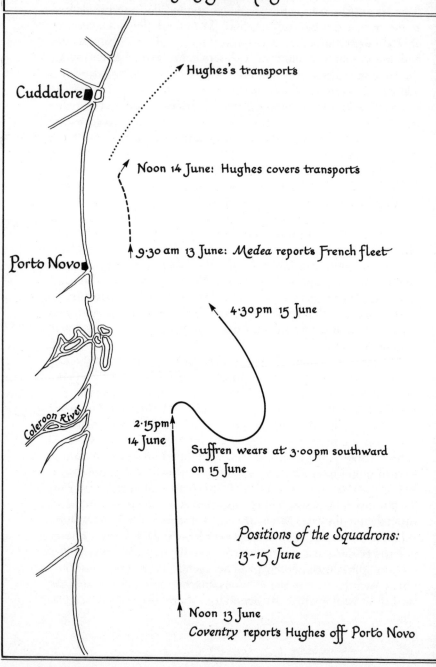

Cuddalore
13–15 June 1783

Cuddalore

Hughes's transports

Noon 14 June: Hughes covers transports

9·30 am 13 June: *Medea* reports French fleet

Porto Novo

4·30 pm 15 June

Coleroon River

2·15 pm
14 June

Suffren wears at 3·00 pm southward
on 15 June

Positions of the Squadrons:
13–15 June

Noon 13 June
Coventry reports Hughes off Porto Novo

Edward was now out to sea with Suffren inshore, and the wind was so mild that some ships could barely cover two sea-miles from dawn to dusk. The battle Hughes now desperately required could not be joined. Suffren, who had no inkling of Hughes's critical condition, could only pray for a good wind behind him and the courage of despair. The wind, however, flashed about the compass, never blowing from any one quarter to give either admiral the support he needed. If Hughes, with his superior weight of metal and numbers, seemed to avoid battle it could only be, to the Bailli's shrewd eye, because Sir Edward was a cautious admiral and could afford to wait for the wind before delivering his coup de grâce. It was inconceivable that a squadron so newly out of port could have any other reason for holding off. But if the strain was beginning to tell on the French commander, he refused to show it by altering his daily routine. He was as punctilious at his meals and as phlegmatic at his tobacco as old 'Hot and Hot'.

At last on 20 June the wind began to blow steadily, dimpling the placid waters of the Bay of Bengal, and contrary to expectation it blew from the west. The squadrons were now 20 miles apart and Hughes knew that he could wait no longer for the wind to change. By noon he had formed line on a north-east/south-west bearing and prepared for battle. But though the *Artésien* was just within cannon-shot range at 12.45 it was to be another four hours before the rest of the French squadron had reduced the 12 miles between it and the British. Suffren went on board the *Cléopâtre* again at 13.00 hours and at 14.00, 'the enemy showing a disposition to engage', Hughes brought to. Then at 15.15 Suffren abandoned the idea of concentrating on the British rear and decided on a conventional line battle. The tactic he had devised at the council of war depended on a strong, reliable wind, but the wind on the 20th was only light. Speed and surprise which were also necessary for its success were no longer his to command, and with Bussy's 1200 men aboard he felt he could better fight the parallel action, ship against ship, that his captains understood. Upon their willingness to engage closely he now staked his fortunes.

Hughes, superior by one 80-gun ship, one 74 and one 70, was sailing with the wind in perfect line when the *Sphinx* fired a ranging shot shortly after 16.00. A quarter of an hour later, the rest of the squadron opened fire, and nine minutes afterwards the English broadsides replied. This time there was no experiment and

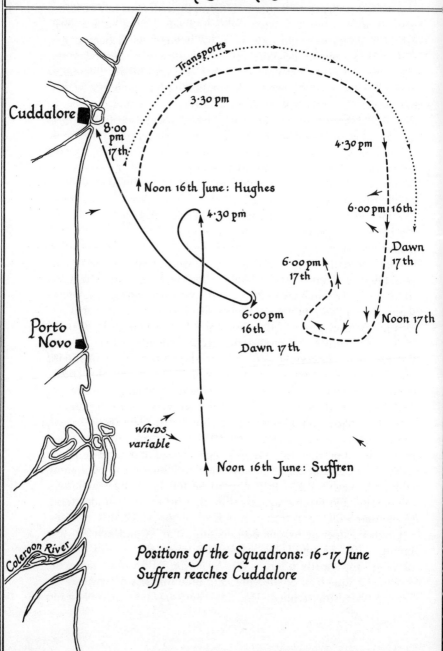

Cuddalore
16–17 June 1783

Transports

3·30 pm

Cuddalore

8·00
pm
17th.

4·30 pm

Noon 16th June: Hughes

4·30 pm

6·00 pm 16th.

Dawn
17th

6·00 pm
17th

6·00 pm
16th

Noon 17th

Dawn 17th

Porto
Novo

WINDS
variable

Noon 16th June: Suffren

Coleroon River

Positions of the Squadrons: 16–17 June
Suffren reaches Cuddalore

no folly. The ritual combat of the line, against which Suffren had four times rebelled, was begun. This time, too, there was no hope of victory, only of a short respite for the beleaguered garrison. After that anything could happen. Tipu might return to sweep Stuart back into Madras. Soulanges might arrive with reinforcements and once more give him superiority in numbers. The wind, what there was of it, was decisively French. He could force the action as he chose and his opponent could deploy his superiority only with difficulty.

Sir Edward was to dismiss the ensuing engagement with few words. 'A heavy cannonade ensued on both sides . . . and continued until 7.0 p.m. when the enemy hauled off.'[2] As a battle it was devoid of tactical interest, but for the first and only time on the campaign every one of Suffren's officers did his duty. Had they fought with the same order at Sadras, Provedien, Negapatam and Trincomali, there would have been no battle to fight. It cost the valiant Perrier de Salvert his life when he moved his 50-gun *Flamand* out of line between the *Fendant* and *Ajax* to engage two 64s, the *Inflexible* and *Exeter*; and when Trublet de Villejégu coolly disengaged under murderous fire, Suffren was so impressed that after the battle he pinned his own Cross of St Louis on the young lieutenant's chest. The *Héros*, now commanded by Moissac, was for the last time matched with the *Superb*. Peynier in the *Fendant*, supported by Saint-Félix, who had returned from Île de France to be his second in command, challenged the magnificent *Gibraltar*. Du Chilleau closed his 64-gun *Sphinx* with the 74-gun *Defence* to prove that his diffidence on 3 September had been an aberration.

Suffren himself was bitterly disappointed not to be in the thick of it and the *Cléopâtre* ran up and down the French line helplessly. She had no signals to make—for there was only one: to engage at pistol-shot range. At one moment she ventured so close that a shot severed the rope Suffren was clutching and deposited him with a crash upon the deck. The frigate captain, Rosily, ordered the helmsman to take the ship out of range, explaining to the explosive admiral that he was not going to be responsible for an English victory by sacrificing his general.

As daylight began to wane, the *Fendant*'s mizzen mainsail was set alight by the explosion of a barrel of grenades and she withdrew temporarily from the line. The *Gibraltar*, trying to edge in, was firmly repulsed by the *Flamand* and kept her place. In the dusk the cannonade continued as, exhausted and almost powder-spent, the two squadrons separated. Even in the rear, where the *Artésien* and the *Consolante* frigate had warily kept the 74-gun *Cumberland* at bay in case she tried to double, the battle had been well fought. It had been a match between heavyweights, devoid of science, a grinding, blinding battery which lasted until it was physically impossible to continue.

Counting the dead and wounded gave neither admiral much comfort. The British dead numbered 103, the French 102, the wounded 429 and 376. Hughes's complement had been short before the combat by 1100 men. The *Superb*'s main topmast was unserviceable, the *Gibraltar* and *Isis* had from seven to eight feet of water in their holds from shot-holes very low under water, and the *Defence* was unable to make sail. Sir Edward brought to in order to repair the damage with his ships' heads towards the land, and waited for the dawn. Moissac noted in his journal that the liveliness of the enemy fire had markedly declined towards the end of the day while that of the French had been sustained, and he presumed that the British had suffered worse. The *Héros* was badly cut about but she had not suffered in her timbers and no ship was incapacitated. Besides Salvert, Dupas, recently promoted to command the *Ajax*, was dead and Dieu, who had saved the *Sévère* at Negapatam, had also perished. That night the strong lee currents carried the French ships almost abreast of Pondicherry.

The next morning the two squadrons were still in sight of each other, the French at anchor in Pondicherry road, directly to windward of the British. Seeing some of Suffren's ships getting under weigh, Hughes made what sail he could and anchored that night off the ruined fort of Alemparve. Suffren watched him pass. His first inclination had been to cut his cables and give chase, but he was so short of anchors that he could not afford to sacrifice those he had. And he could not continue to deprive Bussy of his 1200 troops. The British ships, despite their hammering, could still sail faster than his, and Hughes could lead him far enough from the shore to make it difficult for him to work his way back against the strong current and shifting wind. At 20.00 hours that night he weighed and sailed down instead to Cuddalore.

Scurvy now continued with unnerving speed to complete the work on board the British squadron that the French guns had left undone. By 22 June so many of Hughes's men were dying every day, and so many were unable to come to quarters, that many of his ships were hardly 'able to weigh their anchors or to be navigated'.[3] Suffren had, in fact, been able to fight the battle with between 10 and 12 fit men for every gun, more than his opponent. Of the *Gibraltar*'s complement of 695, 169 were soon *hors de combat* and, indeed, throughout Bickerton's ships the proportions were similar: on the *Cumberland* 105 out of 600, on the *Defence* 122 out of 500 and on the *Inflexible* 103 out of 500. Why this should be so after a winter overhaul in Bombay is hard to explain—many of Bickerton's crews were pressed and may have been less hardy from the start. Certainly his ships had enjoyed a rotten health record from the moment they left Britain. The worst-afflicted vessel among Hughes's 'old faithfuls', the *Magnanime*, had only 87 sick out of 500. But even more seriously the squadron's water was now virtually exhausted. There was nothing for it to do but return to Madras. It was there on the 25th.

Suffren's welcome when he went ashore on the 23rd at Cuddalore was tumultuous. All action on shore had been suspended while besiegers and besieged alike watched their fate decided in a haze of smoke too far out to sea for the sound of guns to be heard. The 21st, with both squadrons out of sight, had been a day of tense anxiety, but when at last the *Héros* appeared flying Suffren's broad pennant, followed by her 14 companions, the soldiers deserted their posts to run cheering to the ramparts. Stuart, too stunned to act, listened disconsolately to the roar of voices which continued after the skiff bearing the Bailli had run ashore, and by the water's edge the soldiers fought for the privilege of carrying his palanquin. In the end, Suffren's own native servants bore him triumphantly through streets dressed for a carnival to the steps of Government House, where Bussy and his senior officers were waiting.

'Messieurs,' the old warrior announced in a voice shaken by emotion, 'voilà notre sauveur.'[4] He hobbled down the steps to meet the admiral; and the two men, one thin and gnarled by gout and age, the other vast, sprawling and glowing with sea health, as different from each other as the elements upon which they fought, embraced and disappeared into the council chamber. They reappeared from time to time to acknowledge the ovations of the crowd. The 1200 troops came back on shore, every man of them a hero, while Stuart skulked in his tent, bitterly convinced that Hughes had deserted him.

Suffren now began to blow some fire into the spirits of the garrison. His victory at sea must be followed by a sortie on land and, after he in his turn had lent Bussy 1200 men from the squadron, it was launched on 24 June. It was not a success. Badly planned if bravely executed, it failed to surprise the British outposts and achieved nothing. Disgusted by the performance, the Bailli returned to the *Héros*, intending to manoeuvre his ships as close as he dared to shore and bombard Stuart's positions from the sea. But before he could do so, the *Medea* was sighted under flag of truce. At 20.00 hours on the 29th Captain Erasmus Gower came ashore with the news that the war between France and Britain was over. Cuddalore was the last battle fought at sea by the pre-revolutionary navy, the last contest between Bourbon France and her traditional enemy.

When Hughes had reached Madras he found newspapers dated 23 January which contained an account of the preliminary articles of peace which had been signed on 20 January at Versailles. For several weeks the town had been abuzz with rumours of peace and Governor Macartney and General Stuart were both accused of mounting this unnecessary offensive against Cuddalore to recover face before the rumours proved true. The admiral at once disarmed the *Medea* and sent her to Cuddalore with proposals for a truce. Suffren, without waiting for any word of confirmation from Île de France, announced the news to his captains and crews. With loud huzzas the weary sailors cheered the end of their ordeal—for though the Battle of Cuddalore had, in the event, made no difference to the war, it had triumphantly vindicated the honour of French arms. To his men at least, as to the Bailli de Suffren, this was a greater salvation than that of the citadel itself. And with fêtes and acclamations, a duel unprecedented in the history of sea warfare came to an end.

It certainly seemed odd to Captain Gower that the French had had no more official intimation that peace was in the air than had the British. 'It is somewhat strange', he reflected to his friend, Philip Carteret, after the first official accounts had reached Madras on 30 August, 'that the saving of many thousands of lives of ours was literally owing to one private gentleman sending a newspaper to another!'[5]

29. The War Is Over

It did not take much to dissipate the élan of Cuddalore. Bussy, though he accepted the authenticity of Captain Gower's letters, was still Tipu's ally, and the nawab had no intention of making peace before he had consolidated his position in the west. The processes of peace were, accordingly, slow. In deference to Tipu, Bussy was obliged to make conditions before disengaging the French army from the war and General Stuart, annoyed that victory had been denied him at the last moment, became resentful and difficult. Negotiations were protracted for eight months and commanded all Bussy's failing powers of tact and diplomacy. There were disputes over the exchange of prisoners, charges of treachery and desertion from Tipu and reluctance on the part of Macartney to admit the French to *pourparlers* between the presidency and Mysore. The Treaty of Mangalore was signed at last on 11 March 1784, but for another 18 months the wrangle continued over the possession of Trincomali, which the British insisted should be returned to the Dutch.

Before the matter was finally settled, Bussy was dead. On 7 January 1785, the old warrior had a stroke. His last campaign had cast a shadow over his fame. His motives had been impugned and his generalship had been a thing of pessimism and languor. But his task had been impossible from the start and, when his gouty bones were laid at last in the soil of the land to which he owed his fame and fortune, the final French bid for India was over.

Suffren greeted the news of the end of hostilities with undisguised relief. 'Thank God for the peace,' he wrote in one of his informal despatches to the Ministry on 23 July. 'The fate of M de Grasse made me tremble.'[1] The Battle of Cuddalore had been a desperate gamble at best and when his reinforcements reached him shortly afterwards they consisted only of the frigate *Hermione* with a few troops of the Régiment de Meuron, followed by the 50-gun *Fier*. A sixth engagement with a watered and revivified Hughes could only have been fatal. 'I wait your orders with impatience. I hope they will allow me to leave. Certain things have so disgusted me that only war has made them bearable.'[2] A sense of listlessness and anticlimax grated on his disillusioned temper as he waited for his future to be decided.

He wrote again in September. 'I have no doubt the peace will bring about many changes but I hope they will be effected and consolidated before I return, for those who have been consulted up to now have ideas so different from mine that I should not wish to be associated with them. There have been some very stupid adventures, but if the general officers had been good and well-supported this war would not have lasted two years, we should have saved 500 millions and 50,000 men, and secured an honourable peace.'[3] To the Comte de Vergennes in the Foreign Ministry he was blunt. 'If everything sent from France had arrived in time we should now be masters of India.'[4] Bussy had been a sad disappointment. But the English had a huge country to watch. Tipu could put 100,000 men in the field against them. The Marathas would fight if supported. Even the Nizam of Hyderabad could be suborned. If war broke out again, 'we should need real warriors who combine talent with a desire for military glory and who, having a military fortune to make, will have enough ability and vigour to pursue it with the ardour that ensures success. For war in this country you need strong spirits and vigorous bodies—no more politicians, but fighters.'[5]

Castries in Paris bitterly regretted that news of Suffren's latest successes had not been known at the time the preliminaries of peace were signed. France might then have plucked some advantage from what had been another ignominious war against the old enemy. The proud hopes with which it had been launched had proved vain. France's revivified navy had challenged Britain's but not defeated it, and France went to the peace table without a winning card. Suffren, for his part, no longer believed the remedy lay with him. The gulf of hatred and fear which had yawned between himself and at least six of his officers was unbridgeable, and it was with precarious diffidence that he enjoyed the applause that was now his due. 'The consideration in which I am held in India is almost incredible: verses, songs, letters, the lot. But it could have been otherwise. The smallest thing can turn handclaps into hisses.'[6] The arrival of the *Hermione* in August brought the despatches that promoted him to the substantive rank of *lieutenant-général*, roughly equivalent to vice-admiral in the Royal Navy.

He left Trincomali at last for his triumphant return on 6 October. The despatches that recalled him had been delivered by curious chance to Madras and were brought on by Lieutenant Troubridge in HMS *Active*. The commissioners of the peace had decided to recall both admirals, leaving in Indian waters two squadrons of equal strength. Peynier remained to command the *Fendant*, *Argonaute, Brillant, Saint-Michel, Coventry* (now commanded by Villaret-Joyeuse) and *Bellone*. The *Vengeur, Flamand* and *Sévère* were to stay at Île de France, and Suffren was to return to Toulon with the *Héros, Annibal, Ajax, Artésien, Hardi, Illustre* and *Sphinx*.

To his ageing cousin in Provence he could not resist a few words of self-satisfaction. 'I do not know, as no one has written to tell me, how I am considered in France or how the public has reacted to my unprecedented advancement. In India, in Madras, above all in Îles de France and Bourbon I am infinitely more regarded than I deserve. If I call at Île de France they will go mad unless their enthusiasm is restrained.'[7] It was not, and the arrival of the hero of Cuddalore was a riot of flowers, sonnets, serenades and fireworks, sweetened by letters from Mme de Seillans, the first for six months, and soured by the decision to condemn the *Vengeur* as no longer seaworthy.

At the Cape there awaited him a tribute that penetrated his sceptical and embittered shell. As he sailed into Table Bay where Commodore Sir Richard King was already at anchor with ten of Hughes's squadron, the English ships, and some visiting Russians, were dressed overall and their officers came aboard to congratulate him upon his promotion. Suffren was deeply moved. But while the Dutch fêted him with an energy they might have better put to his support when the war was on, the celebrations were clouded by the condemnation of another brave ship. The *Exeter* had struck a rock on entering Table Bay and could not be refloated, despite the efforts of the *Illustre* and the *Hardi*. When Sir Richard came to thank him for their help, Suffren felt his disappointment keenly, for the *Exeter* and her sailors had proved a doughty foe. On 3 January 1784 he set off on the last lap of his journey for Toulon and the reception which his country, eager to welcome the one undisputed hero of the war, was preparing for him.

Sir Edward Hughes also left the Coromandel coast in October, taking the *Superb* and eight of his battle-scarred squadron round to Malabar to relieve Mangalore, still under siege by Tipu. On 9 November he, too, was dealt a sudden and unexpected blow when his flagship was struck by a gale in the roads of Tellicherry, dragged, fouled the *Sultan* and struck a sandbank. The ship's battered timbers disintegrated rapidly and, though only one man was missing, the admiral was stunned by the loss for some days and 'would have given all he was worth in the world to have had his ship safe and sound again'.[8] Sir Hyde Parker having gone down with the *Cato* on his way to relieve him, Hughes had to keep his station off Bombay until the end of 1784, and it was not until 16 May 1785 that he set foot once more on English soil.

He spoke his own epitaph when the House of Commons moved an address of gratitude for his services. 'Although I found it impracticable to ruin the French naval force in this country, every exertion in my power was made for that purpose consistent with the preservation of His Majesty's squadron on which the fate of the national possessions in this country greatly, if not wholly depend. I have, however, with the assistance of the brave men who served with me, been able effectually to disappoint and defeat all their designs of conquest in this part of the world.'[9] Duty, humanity, courage and dignity, if not genius, were his natural gifts. Having acquired 'a most princely fortune in India' estimated at over £40,000 per annum, he died an Admiral of the Blue in 1794, having distributed the greater part of it in unostentatious acts of charity, particularly to the families of the men who had served with him.

Suffren had paid his tribute earlier. 'It has been my fate,' he told William Hickey in Trincomali, 'to be opposed to him in three [at that point] different hard-contested battles, in every one of which Sir Edward Hughes in my humble opinion gave positive proofs that he possessed consummate skill and abilities equal to any man's I have ever had to deal with in my profession. His manner and general conduct, too, has uniformly been that of a brave and gallant officer, blended with the mild and benevolent disposition of a truly philanthropic citizen of the world ... a braver man does not exist.'[10] Mother Hughes deserves an honourable place in the annals of the Royal Navy, even though, for once, English beefsteaks had not proved quite equal to Provençal bouillabaisse.

On shore General Stuart's quarrels with Lord Macartney became more and more violent until the governor, recording that Stuart had once had a hand in the deposition of Governor Pigot, suspended him and shipped him home, where in 1786 the two men met in a duel. Macartney himself resigned in 1785 over the restoration of the Carnatic to Muhammed Ali, and when Hastings left he was offered, but declined, the office of governor-general. India was a challenge he did not care to prolong. As he told Charles James Fox in October 1783, 'my Russian embassy, Irish secretaryship and West Indian government did not all together require the exertion of my Madras Presidency, when I had to defend myself against a nest of hornets as well as against invading beasts'.[11] The Company presented him with a set of plate to celebrate his 'great pecuniary moderation'.

His subsequent career embraced an embassy to China where he successfully obtained an audience of his Celestial Majesty without performing the ritual kow-tow—probably his most refined diplomatic achievement—and later, his genial temper restored by milder air, he became unofficial ambassador to the Bourbons in exile, governor of the Cape, and died a martyr to gout, *aetatis*, 69, in 1806. Whatever his faults, public money never stuck to his fingers and, had he possessed firmer qualities of character, he might have made a worthy successor to Warren Hastings. But his temper had been another of Suffren's victims.

Tipu made his peace at Mangalore but remained implacable in his enmity to the British, unceasing in his resolve to destroy them or be destroyed. His fierce and hostile presence was one of the excuses for Napoleon's Egyptian campaign, and he was to fight the Company twice more until, on 6 May 1799, his savagely mutilated body was uncovered in the breach at Seringapatam. With him died a dynasty that had defied Britain for over 30 years. If Haidar and Tipu had proved staunch and ruthless enemies, they had proved more loyal allies than the French deserved, and the merchants of Philadelphia, when they named a privateer after the father, had been glad to welcome him as a friend and fellow fighter for freedom!

Suffren's welcome in France has already been described, and he endured the acclamation of Versailles with something approaching impatience. His friends were shocked when he declined an invitation to the royal *coucher* at which he was to receive his lieutenant-general's baton. He said he was ill, but if he was it did not keep him from dining with Castries the following day, when d'Estaing toasted 'the only real General among us'.[12] He was bored by the vapidity of the court, and all the honours that were showered on him could not compensate for the failure earlier to give him d'Albert de Rions, good officers, men and frigates when he wanted them. With these he might have had something to show for the two weary and fruitless years he had fought, unsupported, on the far side of the world. D'Estaing's toast, however, was a generous and gracious welcome from a senior officer. Four years before, Suffren had been just one of his captains. Now he was his equal, a rise not equalled even by d'Estaing himself.

Castries hoped that such promotion would act as an inspiration to more junior officers in the war with Britain that must surely be resumed before many years were out. 'It was Suffren's steadfastness alone that ensured the last success,' he wrote in a memorial to Louis XVI. 'It was to his example and courage that we must ascribe the vigour and obedience that decided the battle in our favour. It was his own enterprising and vigorous conduct which proved to the princes both of India and Europe that in another war the English can be defeated and their Empire be overthrown. He has proved that our nation does not lack men to lead it, and it is principally to him that we owe the recovery of that sense of superiority in our fleet which is recognized by all Europe.'[13] The king might need his services again. 'The most powerful argument for these rewards—and I consider it the decisive one—is His Majesty's resolve to have a vigorous navy and his determination to take action against all those officers who failed in their duty in the last war.'[14]

The king agreed. Suffren was admitted to the Orders of Saint-Esprit and Saint-Michel. The emblem of the first, being in France the supreme order of chivalry, to rival the Golden Fleece and the Garter, could share a chest with no other without royal permission. To a Knight of Malta no other Order could take precedence over the eight-pointed Cross. The king graciously gave permission for Suffren to wear both Orders together, and the Grand Master concurred. The sovereign also accorded him the privilege of entrée to the royal presence at any time. As the rules allowed for only four vice-admirals at any one time (a rank equivalent to a British admiral), Louis XVI created a fifth vice-admiral's post for the term of Suffren's natural life with a pension of 26,000 *livres*. He was Commander of Jalès and Saint-Christol in the Priory of St Gilles, worth over 12,000 *livres* a year, so that he was now a moderately rich man.

Yet the restless and ungracious temperament of the sailor looked for snubs. The rank he held now was shared by men who had shown more breeding than ability—d'Estaing, Saint-Aignan and the Prince de Montbazon—and if the king really wanted to show that the fleet was more than the preserve of jealous aristocrats, he should go further and make a sailor once more a marshal of France. Precedent, he reminded the king, was on his side. D'Estrée, Tourville and Châteaurenault had been marshals without his length of service and without fighting the enemy as often. Tourville, moreover, had been defeated at La Hogue, and Châteaurenault had allowed his squadron to be burned at Vigo. Victor-Marie d'Estrée, 1660–1737, had been the son of an admiral and grandson of a marshal of France; François-Louis de Châteaurenault, 1637–1716, both vice-admiral and marshal of France, had distinguished himself in the wars against the Barbary regencies, the Dutch and the English.

The navy was not the most popular service with the great families of France, not because it was hard but because it was thankless. The king had now an opportunity to show that glory was not the sole preserve of France's soldiers.[15] The king demurred, largely (it was said) because he really wanted to give the baton to d'Estaing, a much more assiduous courtier, and as long as he persisted in his refusal Suffren was convinced that his campaign had been in vain. Castries, himself a marshal of France, disguised the royal diffidence as well as he could, though he was popularly believed to have encouraged the king to deny Suffren the baton out of jealousy. Whatever the reason, his disappointment and disgust, together with boredom at the inactive life, drove the Bailli into voluntary retirement.

Stifled by Paris, where though covered with praise he felt more like a piece of furniture, surrounded by sculptors and gawping ladies, Suffren returned to Provence in July 1785. His *mocos* received him rapturously. His brother, Paul-Julien, at Marseilles with the galley-fleet of Malta of which he was now captain-general, hot from a cruise against Algiers, gave him a royal salute. At the theatre the *idole* playing the role of Racine's Iphigénie marched off the stage at the words 'Achille est couronné des mains de la victoire' and presented him with a crown of laurels. The Estates struck a medal in his honour. The local bards roughed together martial stanzas and the people of his home-town, Saint-Cannat, fêted him. It was laurels and verses all the way until at last the warrior and his widowed cousin were united at the wedding of her son, before an enormous *galantine à la suffren*, containing every spice he was known to relish.

30. The Last of a Crusader

What was he to do now? He was only 55, but that made him an old man in those days. He was immensely fat, and immoderate in his habits. Like so many active fat men, he was remarkably fit, but idleness does not suit such people and there was nothing that he chose to do. His mordant and depressive nature made him shrug off his country's ailments as being so ingrained in the system that they were beyond cure. He had tried to show how things could be done, but the powdered and bewigged generation that surrounded him seemed doomed. It was as if the shadow of the guillotine had already fallen upon his neck. He could have applied for release from his vows and married his cousin. 'I send you,' he wrote to her on 7 October 1784, 'a medal. Then I shall send you my bust and my portrait and you will have me in every form but that in which you ought to have me.'[1]

What did he mean? That these representations, the medal and the bust by Jean-Joseph Foucou, commissioned by the Estates of Provence, or the bust by Jean-Antoine Houdon, commissioned by the Estates-General of the United Provinces, which stands today in the Mauritshuis in The Hague, were all that a widowed lady could expect from a celibate Knight of Malta? That she deserved a second husband for the companionship of old age but it could not be he? Or simply that he was too busy or idle to call on her? The dispensation that he might easily have obtained, he never sought. Instead he accepted the Prince de Rohan's appointment as Malta's ambassador in Paris.

The Order of St John of Jerusalem, Rhodes and Malta was a

sovereign state and its ambassadors at the courts of all Catholic monarchs were appointed to look after the Order's financial interests. The Knights still held enormous estates across Europe, from which the tithe that went to Malta supported the sovereign state vowed to perpetual war against the spread of Islam in the Mediterranean. From time to time Catholic courts, hard pressed for money, invited the Church and the religious orders to make a voluntary donative in lieu of taxation. The ambassador's prime duty was to resist such requests as vigorously as possible, to argue that the Order's sacred duty of protecting Christian shipping from Islamic piracy would be impossible to discharge, and that the tiny revenue from the donative would soon be lost in the immense task of providing such protection from a national treasury.

This argument, used so often in the eighteenth century, was wearing thin as the threat from Islam declined and France in particular had forced diplomatic and commercial treaties upon the Barbary pirates. As a result the young French knights found the requirement to serve their caravans in Malta a tiresome duty since its navy had become so small and ineffectual, and though they were happy to wear the Cross and enjoy the privileges of knighthood, they resented its medieval disciplines. De Rohan hoped that a man so highly honoured by the king might be a more effective advocate than his predecessors and take a more personal interest in the island's affairs. The same insolence of rank which had plagued Suffren throughout his career had now crept into Malta, where his old friend, Grand Master de Rohan, was trying to tighten up a discipline that had been allowed to rot. A willing player, but not as it happened on his side, was the Papal representative in the island, who enjoyed the title of Inquisitor. For a century now the Inquisitors had tried to limit what they believed was the Grand Master's spiritual authority over an Order which still called itself The Religion. Matters of conscience were the province of the Church.

When a French novice chose to ignore the Grand Master's order confining him to his house after a fracas at the theatre, de Rohan offered him the reasonable alternatives of going home to France in disgrace or being shut up for a spell in Fort Manoel. The novice appealed to the Inquisitor as one might to Caesar, and it was a year before the Papal court upheld the Grand Master's decision to return him to his parents. By that time another novice had appealed to Rome. 'Every pettifogging tiff, forgotten here,' de Rohan wrote to Suffren, 'is published the next day in Rome where it is puffed out to all Europe as an affair of the greatest importance ... I can see no means of reconciliation other than to resign the rights of sovereignty to the claws of the Monsignori ... One letter from Vergennes would put at end to all these dissensions.' The Bailli conscientiously represented his chief's troubles to the Comte de Vergennes, but like his superior he found them trivial and distasteful.[2]

There were other, more serious, issues at stake: a bitter dispute between two professed Knights over promotion, which also involved an appeal to Rome; disputes, mainly of a personal nature, between members of the French Tongues; and most important a growing ground-swell of support for a Chapter-General, which the Grand Master was unwilling to convene as he saw it as a device of the malcontents to reduce his own authority, weak enough as it already was.

'You cannot imagine,' Suffren told Mme de Seillans after a year, 'how this Embassy tires me by the petty and boring detail its work involves. For there is nothing to do that is either serious or essential.'[3] In this he did less than justice to the Grand Master trying to keep the fabric of the Order from being torn asunder. But to a man who had fought a great campaign, the irritating complaints against recalcitrant novices, rude and rebellious knights, intriguing and captious Baillis reminded him of the rat-trap intrigues of Le Grand Corps. Why could not de Rohan break his subordinates as Suffren had broken Cillart, Maurville and Forbin?

He never visited Malta again but he had not neglected it. Even before leaving India he signed on some 50 Tamil cotton-spinners, both men and women, to help improve the island's cotton industry. As soon as the *Héros* reached Marseilles they were sent off to Malta. De Rohan was genuinely touched by the gesture and took the gentle Indians under his personal protection. The Irish history painter Henry Tresham drew them at work in Malta and exhibited the picture at the Royal Academy in 1789. They did not stay long in Malta. Suffren had also advised Calonne, then comptroller-general, to use Indians to assist in the manufacture of muslin in France. and the colony, or part of it, seems to have moved to Paris in 1784, being noted for their exotic appearance as they passed through Lyons by the city *Journal* on 28 September. Nor did they stay long in France, leaving after a couple of years because of the climate.[4] Suffren also brought back some mandarin orange trees which were also sent to Malta, famous for its fine, pithless oranges, shortly to be reintroduced by the British to India where they are known as 'maltas'.

The Maltese embassy was housed in the Hotel Montmorency, 1 rue de la Chaussée d'Antin, an ornate neo-Palladian building with colonnades and statuary, afterwards the site, first, of the Vaudeville theatre then of a cinema. Round the corner from the Opéra, and next door to the house later to be occupied by another hero, Gioacchino Rossini, it was in a moderately smart area, made easier to live in by the Grand Master's decree of 30 May 1786, conferring on Suffren the commandery of Troyes, worth 46,000 *livres* in rents. Here he sat to sketches for Pompeo Batoni to work up in Rome into the strange portrait that shows him sitting, as after a good alfresco meal in the old port of Naples, with which he had no connection, wearing the cordon of the Saint-Esprit in the shade of a palm tree and the old lighthouse.

He might as well have moved to live in Parthenopean isolation. He did not pay court at Versailles and, though he kept a watchful eye on navy matters, he had no time for committees and contempt for the men who sat on them. On the great *Ordonnances* of 1786 he was not consulted, but they met enough of his well-known criticisms of the old system for men to congratulate him on their excellence. With the international crisis of the early summer of 1787 there seemed a chance that he might emerge from his chosen obscurity. Rumours of war were thick in the air, the United Provinces were in turmoil and France and Prussia irreconcilably opposed. In the House of Commons, Charles James Fox denounced Pitt's commercial treaty with France and warned the nation against the malevolence of her ancient enemy. On the death of Vergennes the appointment of Montmorin seemed to give power to a war party of which Castries was a prominent member.

But rivalry between the new foreign and finance ministers paralysed the centre of action. When, in June 1786, the king visited the new fortifications at Cherbourg, so patently constructed to protect an invasion fleet, Suffren was omitted from his party so as to disarm the suspicions of the English. 'I am annoyed in one way, pleased in another,' he wrote to his cousin. 'The King has refused everybody and I have no wish to increase the number.

He has taken only four people with him, none of them courtiers, and I am delighted for my friend d'Albert who will receive him on board.'[5] In July, however, came the order he had hoped for but never expected, to proceed to Brest at once, to take over the armament there and select his own officers. He went to Cherbourg after all and provoked enough speculation to flatter him 'that I can still be a cause of some sensation in the world'.[6]

But it was soon clear that France could afford no military adventures, and in October the government signed a convention which abandoned its stand in the United Provinces. Suffren was suitably disgusted. 'See the peace assured by the most cowardly desertion of our Dutch allies who will now be our most terrible enemies. One is less sensible of our shame than of our lack of money ... Joy is universal.'[7] His command evaporated and he returned to the Hotel Montmorency.

'See me here,' he wrote to Mme de Seillans, 'an important person whom all Europe once came to visit, fallen into the humble estate of a Parisian bourgeois. At least it is better for my health and peace of mind.'[8] The year was saddened by the death of his other Pierrevert nephew, drowned off the North American coast looking for La Pérouse, and when the new year of 1788 dawned his withdrawal from public life was almost complete. He professed little faith in the arrêts de conseil, the édits, the lettres patentes which preluded the summoning of the Estates-General like a rash. So much paper, so much talk!

The society in which he believed and which had lost its nerve and the society which was emerging both failed to engage his sympathy. The French ambassador insulted the Dutch government, driving it further into the Triple Alliance with Prussia and Britain, while the political and sentimental alignment with Russia seemed to be aimed at the safety of France's two traditional allies, Sweden and Turkey. 'The storm gathers, the thunder grows, but no one thinks of anything but Parlements.'[9] He was afraid the British, 'who are armed while we are not', would intervene in the Baltic war. 'There is war at sea, battles have been fought in the Baltic and Black Seas, everywhere men are acquiring glory while I vegetate here, expecting to hear every day of some folly.'[10]

The only thing to cheer him up that summer was a visit from Tipu's ambassadors. The French still believed that Suffren's campaign had kept alive their chances to contest the empire of India with their ancient enemy, and Tipu's alliance was important enough for the Bailli to be wheeled out to look after them. He entertained them to a party with 'thirty pretty ladies, illuminations, martial music and a concert', and they took back with them one of the last letters he wrote.[11] 'If war breaks out again,' he told the nawab, 'and your power is in alliance with ours, with the knowledge that we have acquired in India I have no doubt the English must be thrown out, and I should assume with pleasure the command of the naval forces . . . It would be the summit of my desires to find myself able, in unity with you, to resume the liberation of the people of India from the rule of the English.' Behind the stirring phrase, the pin-prick of conscience. 'I must now write to you about those who are still detained in your estates . . .' He had more than once asked Tipu to release all those whom he had consigned to Mysore under the infamous arrangement of 30 June 1782, but they had still 11 years to endure in captivity.[12]

Apart from de Rohan, whose letters came in by every post with instructions to the three French Tongues of the Order on how to behave when the Estates-General met, everyone allowed him to stay on the touch-line of events. The strains of his active life and the penalties of an overindulged system had already ruined his digestion. His health declined and he was easily tired. Though worried about the growth of popular resentment against the Crown, he took no one's part, merely lamenting that while the Cardinal de Brienne was burned in effigy and the *garde de Paris* went about its business with unnecessary ferocity, not a man had been added to the armed services. He held no brief for the cardinal who was ignorant, presumptuous and despotic, but felt vaguely that his too-close association with the king menaced the security of the throne. Beyond this expression of political opinion he never strayed.

Suddenly, on 7 December 1788, while at dinner with Louis XVI's formidable aunt, Madame Victoire, the Bailli collapsed. Her physician at Versailles opened a vein in his arm, and when he had sufficiently recovered he was taken in his carriage back to the embassy in Paris. There a specialist in gout was called in and, since he had a theory that it was fatal folly to bleed a gouty person from the arm, he opened another vein in his leg. With these combined attentions the apoplexy was fatal. The indomitable heart, 59 years and four months old, could not withstand two doctors. and on the 8th the Bailli de Suffren was dead.

Two days later he was buried in the Hospitallers' church of St Mary in the Temple, sung to his rest by the Vicar-General of Aix, Monseigneur de Pierrevert, in the presence of his nephew, the governor of Saint-Tropez, and of the Bailli d'Havrincourt and the Commander d'Hauteville, representing respectively the King and the Grand Prior of France, the Duc d'Angoulême, the little boy who had made such a pretty speech about Plutarch five years earlier. The weather was foul and the ceremony brief.

In 1792 the bones of France's greatest sailor were torn from his tomb and scattered about the streets. The body which had enjoyed little repose in life was given little in death. Indeed the blood in the carriage, his known enmities, and his unquiescent spirit soon fed rumours of violence.

It would have been too tame for the victor of Cuddalore to die in his bed. Soon, it was said that the cashiered Captain Cillart, maddened by his disgrace, had set on him with a knife in the gardens of Versailles. Then it was confidently asserted that the Prince de Mirepoix had come to the ambassador to intercede for two of his nephews, broken on the India campaign. When the irascible and unrelenting sailor replied that he would not employ his credit for two such *jean-foutres*, the insult could be expunged only in blood. Suffren fell, mortally wounded, in a duel behind Bernini's equestrian statue of Louis XIV in the Bassin des Suisses at Versailles.

Alas for the stories. Cillart never returned to France. No Prince de Mirepoix had nephews who served with Suffren in India. But those who cannot accept that a man with so violent a temper should not have died a violent death have discovered a prince, de Salins, who had two relatives in the squadron of India, Bernard de Tromelin and Jacques de Lanuguy-Tromelin, the first the leader of the Île de France faction, the second the lieutenant in command of the *Pulvériseur* who had 'smirched his flag' by failing to attack five East Indiamen bound for China while the squadron was at Achin. To Suffren, both Tromelins deserved the title *jean-foutres*. Maddened by the insult, the disgraced *capitaine de vaisseau* stalked his prey after that dinner with Mme Victoire and engineered a fatal duel. So much blood in the carriage on return to the embassy seemed suspicious to Suffren's *maître d'hotel*.

But a large man plentifully bled in the arm for an apoplexy might continue to ooze blood during a long carriage journey home.

254 ADMIRAL SATAN

And Bernard de Tromelin was in the process of supplicating His Majesty for reintegration into Le Grand Corps. The murder of a vice-admiral of France would not *prima facie* have been a sensible way of supporting his case. In fact he was successful, but only after the king was dead. Tromelin took the revolutionary oath and was reinstated with the rank of vice-admiral by a desperate Convention in 1793. The sad and most probable truth is that the Bailli's end had been carefully prepared over many years by his intemperate appetite.[13]

Epilogue

Suffren's epitaph concluded with the distich:

> Qui Troiae rueret muros unus erat Achilleus
> Unus erat Suffren classes qui frangeret Angli

or, in English, 'Only Achilles could destroy the walls of Troy, only Suffren could break the battle fleets of England.' The medal struck by the Estates of Provence bore the legend:

> Le Cap protégé
> Trinquemalay pris
> Goudelour delivré
> L'Inde defendue
> Six combats glorieux.

Between them they epigrammatized the achievements of his life. The France he served was soon to be convulsed by revolution, and the saga of the Coromandel coast dimmed by the prodigious actions of the consulate and empire. The republic named a ship of the line after him, but it was at the restoration, when the Bourbons were anxious to show that even the *ancien régime* had heroes of its own to compare in virility and *terribiltà* with the formidable marshals of Napoleon, that Suffren came into his own. When Trublet de Villejégu, the hero of the *Flamand* at Cuddalore, felt impelled by the proclamation of the republic to leave the service he had adorned so conspicuously, he retired to write the history of the campaign in India. His work was followed in 1824 by a *Historical Essay on the Life and Campaigns of the Bailli de Suffren* by J.F.G. Hennequin. The definitive biography, however, did not appear in the reigns of either Louis XVIII or Charles X. The Chevalier Cunat set off from Brest to pursue his subject to Île de France, Ceylon and India and collected anecdotes from survivors. But his *History of the Bailli de Suffren* appeared only in 1852.

By that time it was clear that Suffren's remarkable career had had very little effect on France's navy. His campaign had neither influenced the course of the war of 1778–82 nor set an example for others to imitate. None of France's revolutionary officers showed the Suffren readiness for battle but Villaret-Joyeuse during the brief and tantalizing prelude to his encounter with Admiral Howe on the Glorious First of June 1794.

When Napoleon sent de Linois to Île de France in 1803, hoping to find in him a second Suffren, the hope was an illusion. Linois had served as a junior officer during the Coromandel campaign. Though he had with three ships inflicted a sharp reverse on Sir James Saumarez with six off Algeciras in 1801, he was beaten off the China convoy at the entrance to the Malacca Straits by East Indiamen only and, in Napoleon's words, 'made the French flag the laughing stock of the Universe'.[1] Saint-Félix was, by 1793, a prisoner of war in Île de France, now irrevocably in English hands. Cuverville had joined the émigré army of Condé. Trublet de Villejégu had retired. Bruyères was another émigré and Peynier, after a short spell as governor of the Leeward Islands, was an exile. If the sailors of the revolutionary fleet smoked cheroots and wore their breeches unbuttoned à la Suffren, the brilliance, flair and energy of the great commander were the inheritance of their enemies.

Before Nelson, on the eve of Trafalgar, read John Clerk's description of the battle of Sadras, he may not have known that it was the first occasion in the eighteenth century on which a French squadron had taken the initiative in attacking from the windward. The preferred French position was to receive an attack from the windward with their line well locked up so that, however it was approached whether in parallel or at right angles, it could do immense damage to the first vessels to come within range. At Sadras, 'Monsieur Suffrein has given us something new,' Clerk wrote, 'but only by having in his masterly seamanship, attempted a change and put in practice a new mode of attack from the windward.'² Sir Edward Hughes was thus induced to abide an engagement which he was otherwise inclined to have avoided . . . [and] . . nothing but a consciousness of inferiority somehow in his seamen can excuse Monsieur Suffrein or account for the retreat he made or why he drew off his superior number of ships after once having had the merit of bringing up all his squadrons to so masterly and advantageous an attack'.³

At Provedien, too, Hughes was on the defensive. Suffren attacked from the windward in a manoeuvre which proved him 'to be an officer of genius and great enterprise. If Monsieur Suffrein had wind enough first to bring down upon the van of his fleet to the attack of the British, and afterwards to bring up the rear division to support it, even within pistol shot of the British centre; and if the British rear could not in time get up to annoy a crippled enemy, this the more particularly illustrates the propriety and practicability of bringing up and directing the whole or any part of a force against a smaller part of the force of an enemy; and that the effect ought to have important consequences in battles at sea.'⁴

The most important consequences, Clerk claimed, were the Glorious First of June when Lord Howe, who had first received Clerk's thesis with reserve, broke the French line in two. Then in 1797, at Cape St Vincent, Jervis cut off and isolated a whole division of the Spanish fleet, and at Camperdown Duncan cut the Dutch line and concentrated his attack on the centre and rear. Nelson, too, had first doubled on and destroyed an inferior portion of Brueys's fleet at the Battle of the Nile. The new *Fighting Instructions* of 1799 included signals for breaking the enemy line so that once again a decisive battle at sea became a practical possibility. Now, in his last and most glorious battle, Nelson devised a tactic which used the 27 ships at his disposal to devastating effect and buried the concept of the line battle for ever.

Whatever Clerk inferred, it is not likely that Nelson owed much to Suffren in devising that tactic. He may have recognized in the French admiral's command of ships as instruments of aggressive, destructive war a fellowship of intent, but Suffren had not invented a new tactic; the concept of doubling and concentration had been bandied about the Royal Navy for a century. But he was unique in the French navy in using his squadron as part of a combined operation, the activities of which were dictated by the exigencies of the moment, not the distant imperatives of planning in Versailles or the rather limp tradition of Le Grand Corps that, somehow, did not expect to beat the English at their own game.

Admiral Mahan presented Suffren as the only French admiral to grasp the Nelsonian principle that the prime task of a naval force was to destroy that of the enemy. As a tactician, 'a driller of ships, he seems to have been deficient'.[5] Mahan thought that Suffren probably considered tactics a veil for timidity, and the evidence certainly suggests it. The concentration he aimed at eluded him on every occasion because he failed to ensure that his captains knew what was expected of them. At Porto Praya he confronted them with a situation quite outside their experience and they bungled it. At Sadras they assumed that the *Héros* stood away from the *Superb* because the rest of the line was not intended to close, despite the signal flying from her masthead. At Provedien, following the manoeuvres of the van, the whole line except the *Héros* and *Orient* luffed in order to keep their order and held off. At Negapatam they muffed the daring manoeuvre that would have given them the wind. At Trincomali the mystique of the terrible line caused them to expose the *Héros*, *Ajax* and *Illustre* to crucifixion. By the time Suffren came to fight his last battle he had learnt that only time-honoured tactics would do for sailors such as he commanded, and the whole squadron rose as one man to the occasion.

Since he believed that this catalogue of failure was due not only to inexperience but also to something worse, he dispensed with the services of six of his captains and broke three. He lost four in action. Hughes, in his turn, lost six in battle but reprimanded none. Suffren expected too much—'he had the right to expect more than he got,' concluded Mahan, 'but not that ready perception of the situation and that firmness of nerve which except to a few favourites of nature are the result only of practice and experience'.[6]

The truth was that Suffren was a bully. Though he could be tender to the Compagnie veteran Bouvet after his dismal showing at Sadras, and magnanimous to Villaret-Joyeuse when sending him on a dangerous mission before Cuddalore, and concerned about his sick and wounded, his habitual *mépris* for his colleagues resulted in threats and menaces. An anecdote told of him by his *moco* almoner, Delfini, is only too typical. While restlessly locking up his line before the battle of Cuddalore from the deck of the

Cléopâtre frigate, he noticed that one vessel was slow to find her position. 'Get into place,' he bellowed through his speaking trumpet. 'If you are afraid of English bullets, then you will feel some French ones.'[7]

Though he clearly did not like him, the minister, Castries, did what he could to see that some of the Suffren spirit survived the conservatism of Le Grand Corps. Though the navy had no incorruptible machinery for disciplining refractory officers, the minister endorsed all Suffren's recommendations to give the force of example. Cillart, Pallière and Maurville were cashiered. Landelle, Forbin and Tromelin were ordered to resign their commissions, and the king remained implacable to the end about the last. Tréhouret, who wrecked the *Bizarre*, and Boissière, second in command in the *Artésien* at Porto Praya, were retired early.

But old traditions die hard, and the few officers who had realized that the Bailli's success had been due to his inexhaustible appetite for attack and improvisation were either in disgrace or flight after 1793. The *Ordonnances* of 1786, which replaced the *gardes-marines* by *élèves de la marine* and opened a career in the navy to the *officiers-bleus*, were inspired by views he had expressed at various times with considerable force. But the old aristocratic monopoly on promotion was not broken, nor did the age of senior officers become younger. The *élèves*, though they were subjected to a six-year training under a discipline hitherto alien to the service, still had to submit proofs of noble birth. The explorer La Pérouse, from Kamchatka Bay in the Bering Straits, swore to Suffren that he found the *Ordonnances* perfect, but wished that 'like the ark of the covenant they could be defended by law from change for at least two centuries'.[8] By 1792, Revolution had changed everything.

Despite Suffren's grand hopes when he left Brest for the Cape and Île de France, there had never been any doubt that his campaign was to be merely a diversionary effort, while the great issue was fought out in the Atlantic. Castries undoubtedly hoped that Suffren's record would justify sending a squadron east to harass the English in India, to keep valuable ships tied up in a distant theatre of war, and perhaps to prompt the English to send reinforcements they could not spare from North American and Caribbean waters. What he could not have expected was that Suffren would keep his station off India and would put such spine into the Mysorean

army that it succeeded in posing a real threat to the survival of
Madras.

In the last analysis that was perhaps Suffren's greatest achievement. He had no permanent base from which to recruit fit seamen
and stores, and he had no special secret about the conservation
of manpower, no theory about health except that fresh air and
sea water were the only specifics against the fevers and other
maladies that affected seamen in the tropics. He just showed
an unbeatable gift for improvisation and opportunism, robbing
spars from prizes and wrecks, patching up his damaged vessels,
impressing any man no matter of what race as long as he could sail
a ship. He carried out careening at sea or in the uncertain offshore
waters of Sumatra, and lived off plunder. He was a true disciple of
his hero, Michael de Ruyter. One modern French naval historian
believes that no campaign like his was fought again until the battle
for the Falkland Islands in 1982.[9] The spirit of Suffren pervaded
the improvisation and opportunism of that campaign fought to a
successful conclusion so far from base.

Otherwise the most significant characteristic of Suffren's short
and climactic period of command was its Englishness. In fact there
is very little to justify the praise of Suffren's tactical sense in what
Creswell has called the 'fanciful ideas' of Clerk of Eldin, in Mahan's
great eulogy which was written to encourage the American navy
to behave as Mahan thought the British did, or in Lacour-Gayet's
history that wished to prove that the eighteenth-century failures of
the French navy were due to devotion to the wrong tactics. Suffren's
mentors at Sadras and Provedien had been Hawke at Toulon and
Finisterre, and Boscawen at Lagos Bay. There he had witnessed
the practical demonstration of initiative, of individual decision
in defiance, on occasions, of the prevailing signals (and even, at
Toulon, of a superior officer), of speed and opportunism.

Like his hero, Michael de Ruyter, who had himself taught him
these qualities, he believed that his purpose was to destroy the
enemy. No diversionary expedition could be justified unless it had
this end in view. He had fought Porto Praya to save the Cape. He
fought five battles to preserve the French expeditionary force and
keep Haidar Ali in the war. Had he been content with a secondary
role to Bussy's higher strategy, there would have been no campaign
for Bussy to fight. His pursuit of Hughes was ceaseless as well
as pitiless, and four of the battles had only one objective: his

destruction. No superior orders, like Souillac's to return to Île de France, or Bussy's to sail at once to Cuddalore, could be obeyed if they rendered this objective less likely.

His philosophy of the fleet-in-being, powerful in repose, relentless in action, overwhelming in attack, was not the philosophy of d'Estaing, de Guichen or de Grasse. Given fine ships and good training, given the vagaries of the wind and the possibilities of human error, admirals on both sides in the age of sail believed that a battle between nearly equal giants must be fought in single close-hauled line of battle. Victory would go to the side which fought better. It is possible that the relatively poor showing of the French navy throughout the eighteenth century stemmed from the fact that its squadrons were so many times on the defensive, so that morale generally was lower than that of a fleet used to attack. Suffren behaved as if he were a commander with captains and crews like Nelson's, which they were not. Attack was also the guiding principle of Horatio Nelson, but Nelson's instruments were superb.

The old salt had his own words for it in the poem *Mireio* by the Provençal poet, Mistral:

> The Bailli de Suffren who commands at sea
>   In Toulon harbour has given the signal—
> From Toulon harbour sail 500 men of Provence
>   Their great desire to fight the English,
>   Their vow never to return to hearth or home
>   Until the English they have put to rout.

They are in Indian waters in three verses, when

> The enemy a few short yards away from us,
>   The Bailli de Suffren, pale and intrepid,
> Stands motionless upon the deck and cries:
>   'Hold your fire, my children, let us grease
>   These English with our special oil of Aix.'

Then come the terrible battle of Trincomali and the sacrifice of the *Héros*:

> What broadsides! What a massacre!
>   With what a dreadful crash the mainmast broke,
> Shattering the deck with all its mariners.

But many an Englishman fell too and drowned,
Many a man of Provence seized his enemy,
Grappled him to his breast and dragged him down.

The battle over, Suffren thanks his men for their staunchness and courage. He will tell the king. But they know enough of the indifference of the high and mighty and give him no thanks for that. But:

'If you go up to Paris, bear in mind,
When they bow before you on your way
That none loves you like your sailors.
Know, good Suffren, if we had the power,
Before returning to our villages,
We'd carry you as king upon our finger-tips.'

The Bailli de Suffren left for Paris, ends Mistral's ancient mariner sadly:

They say the great men of that country
Were jealous of his great renown,
And his old sailors never saw him more.[10]

Appendix The battle squadrons of the Bailli de Suffren and Admiral Hughes

FRENCH:

	PORTO PRAYA	SADRAS	PROVEDIEN	NEGAPATAM	TRINCOMALI	CUDDALORE
Ajax (64)	—	Bouvet	Bouvet	Bouvet	Bouvet[1]	Dupas (Lieut.)
Annibal (74)	Trémigon[2]	Tromelin	Tromelin	Tromelin	Tromelin[3]	D'Aymar
Argonaute (74)	—	—	—	—	—	Clavières
Artésien (64)	Cardaillac[4]	Maurville	Maurville	Maurville[5]	Saint-Félix[6]	Vignes (Lieut.)
Bizarre (64)	—	Landelle	Landelle	Landelle	Landelle[7]	—
Brillant (64)	—	Saint-Félix	Saint-Félix	Saint-Félix	Kersauson	Kersauson (Lieut.)
Fendant (74)	—	—	—	—	—	Peynier
Flamand (50)	—	Cuverville	Cuverville	Cuverville[8]	P de Salvert	Salvert[9]
Hannibal (50)	—	Galles	Galles	Galles	Galles[10]	Beaulieu
Héros (74)	Suffren Moissac	Suffren Moissac	Suffren Moissac	Suffren Moissac	Suffren Moissac	Moissac —

Hardi (64)	—	—	—	—	—	Kerhué (Lieut.)
Illustre (74)	—	Pallière	—	—	Bruyères	Bruyères
Orient (74)	Pallière	Pallière	Pallière	Pallière	Pallière[11]	—
Saint-Michel (60)	—	—	—	—	d'Aymar	Beaumont
Sévère (64)	Cillart	Cillart	Cillart	Cillart[12]	Langle[13]	Langle (Lieut.)
Sphinx (64)	du Chilleau	du Chilleau	du Chilleau	du Chilleau	du Chilleau	du Chilleau
Vengeur (64)	Forbin	Forbin	Forbin	Forbin[14]	Cuverville	Cuverville
BRITISH:						
Africa (64)*	—	—	—	—	—	Macdonald
Bristol (50)*	—	—	—	—	—	Burney
Burford (70)	Rainier	Rainier	Rainier	Rainier	Rainier	Rainier
Cumberland (74)*	—	—	—	—	—	Allen
Defence (74)*	—	—	—	—	—	Newnham

Ship						
Eagle (74)	—	Reddal	Reddal	Reddal	Reddal	Clark
Exeter (64)	—	King	King	King	King	Smith
Gibraltar (80)*	—	—	—	—	—	Bickerton
Hero (74)	Hawker	Hawker	Hawker	Hawker	Hawker	King
Inflexible (64)*	—	—	—	—	—	Chetwynd
Isis (50)	Sutton	Lumley	Lumley	Lumley	Lumley[15]	Halliday
Magnanime (64)	—	Wolseley	Wolseley	Wolseley	Wolseley	Mackenzie
Monarca (70)	—	Gell	Gell	Gell	Gell	Gell
Monmouth (64)	Alms	Alms	Alms	Alms	Alms	Alms
Sceptre (64)	—	—	—	—	Graves	Graves
Sultan (74)	—	—	Watt	Watt	Watt[16]	Michel
Superb (74)	Hughes	Hughes	Hughes	Hughes	Hughes	Hughes
Worcester (64)	Wood	Wood	Wood	Wood	Wood[17]	J. Hughes

Ships marked * constituted the squadron of Commodore Sir Richard Bickerton

Notes

1. Bouvet de Précourt resigned his command after Trincomali on grounds of ill-health and died of scurvy in Île de France.
2. Trémigon died of his wounds at Porto Praya.
3. Tromelin also pleaded ill-health after Trincomali and returned to Île de France, where he resigned from the service. He spent years lobbying Castries to rehabilitate him, as he felt he had been treated most unjustly by Suffren, but the minister refused to act.
4. Cardaillac was killed in action at Porto Praya.
5. Bidé de Maurville was suspended after Negapatam and sent to Île de France, where he was arrested. On his return to France, he was imprisoned in the Île de Ré, cashiered and dismissed the service.
6. Saint-Félix resigned his command after Trincomali, like Bouvet and Tromelin on health grounds, but he returned to fight at Cuddalore. He was created chevalier and granted a pension.
7. Landelle was suspended following the wreck of the *Bizarre* at Cuddalore on 4 October 1782 and returned to Île de France, where he resigned the service.
8. Cuverville was made a chevalier of St Louis by Suffren immediately after Negapatam and recommended for a pension. He rose to be a *contre-amiral* in the restoration navy.
9. Perrier de Salvert was killed in action at Cuddalore.
10. Morard de Galles also resigned after Trincomali on health grounds.
11. Pallière was suspended after the wrecking of the *Orient* at Trincomali in February 1783 and was cashiered.
12. Cillart was suspended after Negapatam and sent back to Île de France. There he jumped ship and disappeared. Rumour was to connect his name with Suffren's death.
13. Bidé de Maurville de Langle was a relation of the captain of the *Artésien* suspended after Negapatam.
14. Forbin, Suffren's cousin, was suspended after Negapatam and sent back to Île de France, where he was cashiered and imprisoned in the Château du Pont St Esprit. He was later allowed to resign his commission.
15. Lumley was killed in action at Trincomali.
16. James Watt died of his wounds after Trincomali.
17. Wood was killed in action at Trincomali.

Glossary

Aback	a ship is taken aback when the wind strikes sails on its forward side, forcing them against the mast
Back	to manoeuvre the sails so that the ship is taken aback. Wind backs when it changes direction in an anti-clockwise direction (see *veering*)
Backstays	additional ropes to support a mast carrying sail in a fresh wind
Bear	to follow a certain compass bearing, in battle usually that of the ship it is intended to engage
Bear up	to put helm down and turn away from the wind; *bear down*: to turn into the wind, also to move towards the enemy even if the ship to do so has to bear up!
Bending	making fast with bends, knots, either sails or anchors
Beat, beat up	to tack to and fro to gain distance against the wind
Bower anchors	the main anchors of the ship to port and starboard of the bows
Braces	ropes used to turn the yard (*q.v.*) according to the direction of the wind
Bring to	check motion of a ship, often by turning into the wind
Cable	a measure of 100 fathoms, a cable's distance about 200 yards

Careen	to lay a ship on her side to repair or clean her hull
Close-hauled	(to the wind): sailing as nearly as possible towards the direction from which the wind is blowing
Cordage	the rigging
Escadres d'evolution	squadrons in manoeuvres, the name given to special cruises of French battle fleets, to test new signals and the manoeuvrability of newly built ships, before the American War of Independence
Fishes	splints to strengthen weak yards
Go about	to go from one tack (*q.v.*) to another. Opposite of wear (*q.v.*)
Halliards	ropes or tackle used for hoisting
Haul head round, haul off	to turn a ship's course using the wind away from its object
Haul the wind	when sailing before the wind, to alter course so as to steer as near as possible to the direction from which the wind is blowing
Heave-to	to bring a ship to a standstill by putting some sails aback (*q.v.*)
Jury (mast)	a temporary mast replacing one broken or lost
Lakh	one hundred thousand rupees
Larboard	the left side of the ship as seen from the stern; *larboard quarter*: some six points of the compass left of the present direction
Lee	the quarter to which the wind blows; *lee berth*: a position sheltered from the wind; *lee-shore*: the shore facing the lee-side of a ship; *lee-side*: the side of the ship away from the wind
Leeward	the direction towards which the wind is blowing; *to fall to leeward*: a common lapse in battle-line formation was to allow your vessel to be borne out of line by the wind
Leeway	the distance a vessel falls to leeward
Lie to	to turn the ship's head into the wind so that she remains nearly stationary
Luff	to turn a ship towards the wind, or to sail close to the wind

Mainmast	principal sail-bearing mast, usually the centre of three
Masts	have four members: mast, topmast, topgallant mast and royal, each of which can be struck or lowered in case of need
Mizzenmast	the rearmost mast of a three-masted vessel
Pay off	to fall away from the wind to leeward
Pistol-shot range	close quarters, about 50–100 yards
Quarter-deck	that part of the deck between the stern and mizzen or mainmast elevated to give a good vantage point for the commanding officer
Quartering	when sailing into the eye of the wind, a vessel made a zig-zag process to catch the wind in its mizzen sails which would be diverted to the fore and mainmast sails. Likewise, sailing before the wind, a ship could by quartering prevent the sternmost sails catching all the wind. Beating to quarters, the timing of the manoeuvre is controlled by drumbeat
Sails	take their name from the mast, viz. main, foresail, main topsail, main topgallant sail, main royal, mizzen sail, spanker, mizzen topgallant sail and mizzen royal
Ship of the line, line-of-battle ship	usually square-rigged, being rated first, second, third and fourth according to their size and number of guns. At the beginning of the eighteenth century fourth-raters were 50- and 60-gun ships, but towards the end of the century with ships carrying more than 100 guns, 74s were fourth-raters
Shrouds	ropes from the various points of the mast to the sides of the ship to keep the mast in place
Spring	a hawser attached to a ship's cable when at anchor and brought abroad at the stern, so that by hauling on it a ship could be slewed round to bring her guns to bear on the enemy on the cable
Standing rigging	the fixed ropes of a ship
Starboard tack	the right hand of the ship seen from the stern
Stays	strong ropes supporting masts

Studdingsails	narrow sails set temporarily at the outer edges of a square sail when the wind is light, run out on their own booms beyond the ends of the yards
Tack	the course of a ship; *change tack*: to alter the course by shifting the position of the sails; *to tack*: to sail zig-zag into the wind
Topgallantmast, yard, sail	next above the topmast and topsail and below the royal mast, the fourth and highest part of the mast, often of one piece with the topgallantmast
Topmast, topsail	the second mast or sail, immediately above the lower mast/sail
Veering	wind veers when it changes direction in a clockwise direction (opposite to *backing*)
Warp	to move a ship by hauling on ropes or warps, usually attached to posts on a wharf or to an anchor or to another ship
Wear	to change course with the wind astern
Weather-gauge	the fleet to the windward had the weather-gauge
Windward	having the wind behind, propelling forward
Yard	the horizontal beam for spreading square sails; *yardarm*: half a ship's yard, usually measured from the mast centre to the end

Notes

Prologue

1. Clerk of Eldin's second edition of 1804 describes the battles of Sadra and Provedien on pp 274–5 and 285–7 respectively. For discussion of Clerk's thesis: *The Mariners' Mirror*, vol xx, no 4; Caste, ch 15; Creswell, pp 190–96 (who, among other disagreements with Clerk, also disputes the French practice of firing high and the English low, which seems to have happened as a deliberate act only at the battle of Ushant, pp 126–7); Tunstall, pp 157–61 (who examines the concept of breaking the line and concludes that the English, like the French, believed that victory in battle was gained by a well-formed line of battle and instant obedience to signals).
2. Las Cases, vol 4, pp 93–4.
3. Cunat, p 340.
4. Ibid, p 340. There is a colourful but almost wholly inaccurate account by Alexandre Dumas of the triumphal reception in the early chapters of *The Queen's Necklace*. One of Suffren's nephews, misnamed the Comte de Charny, is given a principal role in the story which is quite unhistorical.
5. Hickey, *Memoirs*, vol 3, p 51.
6. Ibid, p 51.
7. Las Cases, vol 4, p 94.
8. La Varende, p 282.

Chapter 1: Beginnings, 1729–47

1. Clement XII's letters of 2 and 3 September 1737 dispensing both Pierre-André and his younger brother Paul-Julien from one quarter of nobility are in the Archives of the Order of St John in Malta, (AOM), 541: *Liber Bullarum, 1737* f 249 a.t., and the Grand Master's Bull of 23 September, ibid, ff 292–4.

2. The Suffren family origins: Roux, pp 275–6. Pierre-André's relations: *La Dictionnaire de la Noblesse* by Aubert de la Chenaye-Desbois et Badier, vol 18, pp 716–17. His direct forebears: *Le Bulletin des Amis du Vieux Saint-Cannat*, no 13, 1960; *Bibliothèque Nationale: Nouvelles Acquisitions Françaises* (BN, NAF), 9431, ff 4–21.
3. Suffren's admission as a Knight Hospitaller *de minorité*: AOM 3629: *Registro delle bolle di Cancelleria dell'Ordine Gerosolomitano: Dossiers Pierre-André et Paul-Julien de Suffren.*
4. Suffren's childhood: La Varende, p 17; Figarella, pp 14–20, most of it based on conjecture and hearsay.
5. The correspondence with Mme de Seillans was published in *Le Moniteur* of 1, 2 and 15 November 1859 and in *Le Petit Marseillais* of 22 February 1893. The despatches and private letters written to one of the commissioners of the Ministry of the Marine, by name Jean-Baptiste Antoine Blouin, *premier commis* in the French Admiralty, were edited by Régine Pernoud in 1941 (*Lettres Inédites*), who gave her kind permission to quote from them.
6. La Varende, Ch 8 *passim*, discusses Suffren's probable sexual proclivities but makes much out of very scanty evidence. There is as much to show he was attracted to pretty ladies as to pretty boys and very little evidence that he indulged either taste.
7. La Varende, p 41.
8. Pernoud, p 66, 26 March 1783.
9. Creswell, p 78.
10. Clerk, 1804 edition, p 117.
11. For the Battles of Toulon and Finisterre: Castex, pp. 214–224; Cunat, pp 5–10 and 12–17; Mahan, pp 233–7 and 240–14; Mackay (Finisterre), pp 69–83; Creswell, pp 62–91; Tunstall, pp 83–92.
12. Hickey, *Memoirs*, vol 3, p 53.

2: Malta, Minorca and Lagos Bay, 1747–60.

1. The obligations of a Knight of Malta are in Cavaliero, *The Last of the Crusaders*, pp 15–16, 224 and 231.
2. Pritchard, pp 64–6.
3. Recent biographers perpetuate two stories, the first of a duel Suffren fought in Malta with a Breton confrère who called him an olive merchant because of his *moco* complexion: La Varende, pp 24–5, repeated by Figarella, p 54. The rules against duelling were very strictly upheld on the island. The second, that in Malta Suffren sired a bastard, the composer Niccolò Isouard (Figarella, p 217), is almost certainly a canard. Figarella and Bertrand have a lot to say about his time in Malta, most of it impressionistic. Among the hard facts, Bertrand, pp 62–76, says he sailed first in a ceremonial galley cruise to show the flag of the Grand Master and went as far as Lisbon, and that he saw action on board a cruiser in a combined Franco-Maltese disciplinary action against Tripoli.

4. Mahan, p 253. For the Battle of Minorca: Castex, pp 229–33; Cunat, p 25; Creswell, pp 94–103.
5. La Galissonnière's recommendation to the minister of 3 August 1756: BN, NAF 9431, *Dossier Suffren*, f 150.
6. La Roncière, p. 157.
7. For the action in Lagos Bay: Mahan, pp 262–4; Castex, pp 233–5; Cunat, pp 26–8; Marcus, vol 1, pp 296–8; Creswell, pp 108–9.
8. Creswell, p 39.
9. The critique on French tactics by Bigot de Morogues, founder of the Académie de Marine, was contained in *Tactique navale ou Traité des Evolutions et des Signaux* 1763, designed to supersede the classic *L'Art des Armées Navales* of 1697, by Pierre l'Hoste. In 1765 Bourdé de Villehuet produced his *Le Manoeuvrier ou Essai sur la Théorie et la Pratique des Mouvements du Navire et des Evolutions Navales*. These became the two most influential tactical textbooks. For an analysis of the naval actions fought between Barfleur and the Battle of the Saints see Christopher Lloyd, *Armed Forces and the Art of War*, Cambridge New Modern History, vol 8, p 175, and Creswell, *passim*.
10. Castex, p 63, 1 July 1777.
11. Ibid, pp 260–83, for an exhaustive analysis of de Ruyter's influence on Suffren's tactical thinking.
12. Pritchard, p 66.
13. Ibid, pp 64–6.
14. La Roncière, p 185, quoting one of d'Estaing's captains.

3: War in the Mediterranean, 1760–78

1. The *Santissimo Salvatore* incident: Cavaliero, *Crusaders*, pp 142–3.
2. BN, NAF 9431, f 212 for the incident of the *Pléiade*, 16 July 1763; ff 225–7 for Suffren's *Mémoire sur la façon de réprimer les corsairs d'Alger* of 16 October 1763.
3. Ibid, ff 261–74.
4. Ibid, f 334, Choiseul to Suffren, 29 March 1767; f 287 for the accounts by the Chevalier de Framond of the *Caméléon* frigate; ff 289–90 for Maurville's narrative of the assault on El Arraich (Larache) (see also Bertrand, pp. 102–8); ff 307–8 for the minister's instructions to du Chaffault on 1 October 1765 to reward Suffren with his 'gratification'; f 320 for Suffren's request to Choiseul on 30 January 1766 to accompany the de Breugnon mission to Fez; ff 320–21 for his proposals for peace with Morocco.
5. *Mémoires du Duc des Cars* (Paris, 1980), vol 1, p 51.
6. Berchoux's *Gastronomie* (Paris, 1803), pp 165–6.
7. But, added William Hickey, *Memoirs*, vol 3, p 62, he had 'often with a very keen appetite been reduced to a musty biscuit, full of vermin with a small bit of stinking pork as my only sustenance during the 24 hours', and made the best of it.

8. *Memoirs*, vol 3, p 62.
9. E. Davin in *Bulletin des Amis de Vieux Saint-Cannat*, 1961, p 7.
10. Paul-Julien's promotion on 11 October 1768 to second officer of a galley: AOM 156 *Liber Conciliorum Status* (LCS), f 182. He became captain of the ship of the line *San Giovanni Battista* on 14 February 1776: AOM 158 f 419, and captain-general of the Maltese galley fleet in 1782.
11. AOM 156, Liber Conciliorum Status (LCS), f 344 a.t., 11 January 1770.
12. Orders to Bailli de Flachslanden, captain-general of the galleys, for the Bizerta expedition, 2 June 1770: AOM 272, LCS, f 199; his report of 21 June: ibid, f 206.
13. BN, NAF 9431, ff 357 and 359, de Boynes to Chevalier de Pennes, Maltese ambassador to Paris, 12 August 1772, supporting Suffren's request for a richer commandery in Malta.
14. Lacour-Gayet, p 457.
15. BN, NAF 9431, f 404, Suffren raised the possibility of being appointed next captain-general of the Malta galleys in a letter to de Boynes, while cruising in the *Mignonne* off Tunis, 2 May 1773.
16. Lacour-Gayet, p 460, Suffren to Sartine, 24 June 1773.
17. BN, NAF 9431, ff 449–59, Suffren's memorandum on water-softening and the use of the Greek acorn, and its reception in the Ministry.

4: Rhode Island and St Lucia, 1778

1. Lacour-Gayet, p 143.
2. Castex, p 241, Suffren to d'Estaing, 5 August 1778.
3. PRO, Adm. 1/488, ff 314–17, Howe's despatch of 17 August 1778; f 332, Captain Rayner to Howe, 18 August. Also James, pp 104–6, and Lacour-Gayet, pp 166–8.
4. *Sandwich Papers*, vol 2, p 303, Gambier's despatch of 19 July 1778.
5. BN, NAF 9431, f 518, Suffren to d'Estaing, before 8 September 1778.
6. Ward, vol 2, p 593.
7. For the action in Le Grand Cul de Sac: *The Barrington Papers*, vol 2, pp 124–6, Barrington's Journal for 15 December 1778. Calmon-Maison, p 232, for d'Estaing's account.
8. BN, NAF 9431, f 523, Suffren's despatch to d'Estaing, 18 December.
9. Lacour-Gayet, p 190.

5: Grenada and Charleston, 1779

1. BN, NAF 9431, ff 502–3, Sartine to Suffren and to Grand Master de Rohan, 2 May 1779.
2. AOM 1242, *Lettres reçues en 1779*, Suffren to de Rohan, 3 January 1779 (entered in order of writing).

3. BN, NAF 9431, f 526, Suffren to Mme de Seillans, 5 January 1779.
4. *Barrington Papers*, vol 2, p 241, 21 January 1779.
5. Lacour-Gayet, p 465, Suffren to Mme de Seillans, 8 February 1779.
6. Castex, p 244, Suffren to Mme de Seillans, 2 April 1779.
7. Calmon-Maison, p 262, d'Estaing to Sartine, 29 June 1779.
8. *Sandwich Papers*, vol 3, p 123, Byron's 'raw head and bloody bones' were the words of his chaplain.
9. Castex, p 248, Suffren to Mme de Seillans, 10 July 1779.
10. For the Battle of Grenada: Lacour-Gayet, pp 200–5; Calmon-Maison, pp 270–71; James, pp 147–53; Mahan, pp 324–8; Creswell, pp 132–40 and Tunstall, pp 161–4, where on p 164 he opines that had d'Estaing beaton Byron there would have been no Battle of the Saints.
11. Lacour-Gayet, pp 206–8, Suffren to Mme de Seillans, 10 July 1779.
12. AOM 1242, *Lettres reçues*, Suffren to de Rohan, 10 July 1779.
13. Lacour-Gayet, p 211, d'Estaing to Sartine, 21 August 1779.
14. Ibid, p 212, d'Estaing to Vergennes, 21 August 1779.
15. Uhlendorff, p 167.
16. *American Heritage, The Revolution* (New York, 1958), pp 322–3. For the Charleston fiasco: Lacour-Gayet, pp 220–3; James, pp 160–61; Ward, vol 2, pp 690–2.
17. Dull, p 162.
18. Martelli, *Jemmy Twitcher: A Life of the 4th Earl of Sandwich* (London, 1962), pp 116–17. Also Marcus, vol 1, p 459.

6: Straining at the Leash, 1780–1

1. BN, NAF 9431, ff 553, d'Estaing to Louis XVI, 26 February, 1780.
2. Ibid, ff 553 a.t., response to d'Estaing's memorandum of 26 February 1780. The account by Etienne Taillemite on the promotion flow in Louis XVI's navy: *Dossier Suffren: Revue Historique des Armées*, no 153, pp 21–31.
3. Ibid, f 584; d'Estaing to Sartine, 1 March 1780.
4. Ibid, f 573, Suffren to Sartine, 23 April 1780.
5. Ibid, f 587, Sartine to Suffren, 3 June 1780, and to Vergennes and Suffren, 22 August 1780.
6. Lacour-Gayet, p. 540, Suffren to Castries, 23 March 1783. The costs of copper sheathing: 'Copper and Shipping in the 18th Century' by J. R. Harris in *Economic History Review*, vol 19, no 3, December 1966, p 555. Suffren's *Mémoire sur la nécessité de doubler en cuivre les vaisseaux du Roi*: Roux, pp. 280–83. See also Cunat, pp 43–4, for Suffren's letter to Sartine, 14 August 1780.
7. BN, NAF 9431, ff 555–7, for Suffren's memorandum to the Conseils de Marine, February 1780. Their response, Chevalier, pp 507–8.
8. Ibid, f 555; Lacour-Gayet, p 468, from the introductory paragraph to Suffren's memorandum.

9. Lacour-Gayet, p 474, Suffren to Mme de Seillans, 26 February 1781.
10. Ibid, p 474, Suffren to Mme de Seillans, 18 March 1781.

7: Stormclouds in India

1. Sinha, p 93.
2. Forrest, vol 2, p 746: Coote to Hastings 10 November, 1779.
3. What a bullock carried and consumed: Dodwell, 'Transport and the Second Mysore War', *Journal of the Society of Army Historical Research*, October 1924, vol 3, pp 266–7.
4. Shepherd, p 128.
5. Forrest, vol 3, p 762: Coote to Hastings, 1 March 1781.
6. Chevalier, p 380.
7. Forrest, vol 3, p 76: Coote to Hastings 1 March 1781.
8. Roux, p 55.
9. Bancenel, p 419.

8: Porto Praya, 16 April 1781

1. Johnstone's objectives: Rutherford, 'Sidelights on Commodore Johnstone's Expedition to the Cape', *Mariners' Mirror*, vol 28, pp 201–3. Also Pasley, p 296; Richmond, p 133.
2. The preparation of Suffren's squadron in Brest, Martine Acerra, in *Dossier Suffren, Revue Historique des Armées*, no 153, pp 67–8.
3. Rutherford, p 220.
4. Blake, pp 28–32, Johnstone's despatch to the Earl of Hillsborough, 30 April 1781.
5. Blake, p 30.
6. Pasley, p 138.
7. Blake, p 30.
8. Blake, p 32. For the Battle of Porto Praya: Castex, *La Manoeuvre de la Praya passim*; Cunat, pp 50–60; Lacour-Gayet, pp 482–90; Moris, *Journal de Bord*, pp 274–7. Suffren also described the battle to William Hickey: *Memoirs*, vol 3, pp 56–8. Suffren's autograph account of 12 August: Pernoud, pp 38–9, 12 August 1781. For Johnstone's actions after the battle: Pasley, pp 136–40; Rutherford, 'Sidelights', pp 295–6.

9: Race to the Cape

1. Captain Sutton's court-martial, Johnstone to Sutton, 22 April 1781: *Letters which passed between Comm. Johnstone and Capt. Evelyn Sutton with respect to the bringing Capt. Sutton to trial* (London, 1787).
2. Blake, p 34, Johnstone to Hillsborough, 30 April 1781.
3. Chevalier, p 374, Suffren to Castries, 10 August 1781.

4. Cavaliero, 'John Dodsworth, A Consul in Malta,' *Mariners' Mirror* vol 43, iv, p 315. Also AOM 271, LCS, 21 July 1758.
5. Chevalier, p 374.
6. Lacour-Gayet, p 489, Castries to Suffren, 30 March 1782.
7. Ibid, p 487, Suffren to Mme de Seillans, 5 December 1781.
8. Lacour-Gayet, p 486.
9. Hickey, *Memoirs*, vol 3, p 57.
10. Ibid, p 57.
11. Ibid, p 58.
12. Lacour-Gayet, pp 488–9.
13. O. Warner, *A Portrait of Lord Nelson* (London, 1953), p 129.
14. Lacour-Gayet, p 492, Suffren to Castries, 10 August 1781.
15. Pernoud, p 39, 12 August 1781.
16. Pasley, p 174.
17. Castex, p 383, Percheron to Suffren, 24 July 1781.
18. Hickey, *Memoirs*, vol 2, pp 378 and 381.

10: Onward to India

1. Bernardin de Saint-Pierre, *Voyage à L'Île de France, 1773* (Paris, 1984), Letter XI, p 272.
2. Île de France as a naval base: Jean Meyer in the *Dossier Suffren: Revue Historique des Armées*, no 153, pp 8–9.
3. Pernoud, p 43, 23 September 1781.
4. D'Unienville, p 60.
5. Pernoud, p 46, 4 December 1781.
6. Ibid, p 44, 23 September 1781.
7. Castex, p 413, d'Orves to Castries, 28 November 1781.
8. Mautort, pp 182–3.
9. The new route to India: Moris, *Journal de Bord*, p 388. On 18 January 1782, the squadron turned north at longitude 88.15, latitude 2.40; on the 29th the route was set for the Coromandel coast at longitude 86.2, latitude 8.41.
10. Mautort, p 189.
11. A report of what he told Erasmus Gower, captain of the *Medea* frigate, in a letter to Philip Carteret, 18 or 25 January 1784 in Dixson Library, Sydney, Australia, Add MSS 387.
12. Cunat, p 101. Also *Journal de Bord*, p 346, 4 February 1782.

11: Admiral Hughes

1. Richmond, p 88. His earlier career: Charnock, vol 6, pp 65–73; Beatson, vol 5, pp 561 et seq; Laughton, pp 110 et seq; Richmond pp 88–116.
2. Mautort, pp 249–50.
3. Richmond, pp 90–91.
4. Hickey, *Memoirs*, vol 3, p 116.

5. Ibid, p 116.
6. Sinha, p 93.
7. Wylly, p 257.
8. *Private Correspondence of Lord Macartney (PCLM)*, p 160: Coote to Macartney, Porto Novo, 4 July 1781.
9. Wylly, p 254: Coote to Supreme Council, 29 November 1781.
10. Richmond, p 162: Macartney to India House, 29 October 1781.
11. British Library (BL) Add. MSS. 22453, f 79 a.t.: Hughes to Macartney 1 January 1782.

12: The Battle of Sadras, 17 February 1782 (1)

1. La Varende, p 188. For the preliminaries to the Battle of Sadras: PRO, Adm. 1/164, Hughes's despatches of 17 January and 4 April 1782; *Journal de Bord*, pp 352–5; Richmond, pp 191–3; Cunat, pp 103–10.
2. Pernoud, p 47, 5 April, 1782.
3. Ibid, p 47.
4. Castex, p 306.

13: The Battle of Sadras (2)

1. Ralfe, *Naval Biography*, vol 1, p 229.
2. Mautort, p 200.
3. Lacour-Gayet, p 504, Suffren to Castries, 12 March 1782.
4. Ibid, p 501.
5. Sandwich Papers, vol 3, p 215: Rodney's despatch of 31 May 1780.
6. Mautort, p 201.
7. Pernoud, p 51, 5 April 1782.
8. Cunat, p 113. Bouvet's attempted manoeuvre is not recalled in the *Journal de Bord* and is denied by Chevalier, p 396.
9. Forrest, vol 3, p 854, Hastings to Hughes, 4 April 1782. For the battle: PRO, Adm. 1/164, Hughes's despatch of 4 April. Also *Journal de Bord*, pp 355–7; Mahan, pp 380–86; Richmond, pp 193–201; Chevalier, pp 391–6; Cunat, pp 110–16.

14: Haggling with Haidar Ali

1. *PCLM*, p 18, Macartney to John Macpherson, 11 January 1782.
2. Ibid, p 26, 3 February 1782.
3. *Archives Nationales Colonies*, C2 vol 155, ff 36–40, 'Conditions du Traité à conclure avec le Nabab Ayder Aly Khan'.
4. Ibid, f 118, Piveron de Morlat to Souillac, 11 March 1782.
5. *Journal de Bussy*, p 36.
6. Sen, p 280.
7. PRO, Adm. 1/164, Hughes to Lord Weymouth, 10 May 1782.
8. Ibid, 10 May 1782.
9. Lacour-Gayet, p 508, Suffren to Mme de Seillans, 1 April 1782.

15: The Battle of Provedien, 12 April 1782

1. Charnock, vol 6, p 550n.
2. PRO, Adm. 1/164, Hughes's despatch of 10 May 1782. For the Battle of Provedien: Chevalier, pp 399–408; Cunat, pp 127–39; Richmond, pp 210–22; Mahan, pp 388–94; Lacour-Gayet, pp 509–12. For Suffren's accounts: Chevalier, p 408, Lacour-Gayet, pp 513–14, 16 April 1782; Pernoud, p 55, 23 April 1782.
3. Richmond, p 222, Hughes's diary entry 12 April 1782.
4. PRO, Adm. 1/164, Hughes's despatch, 10 May 1782.
5. Lacour-Gayet, p 513, Suffren to Castries, 16 April 1782.
6. Chevalier, p 408.
7. Lacour-Gayet, p 413.

16: The Marquis de Bussy

1. BN, NAF 9433, f 64: *Mémoire du Roi*, 11 November 1781. See also Sen, pp 295–306; *Journal de Bussy: Explication . . . sur l'Expédition de l'Inde*, pp 1–9 and *Réflection sur l'Etat des Affaires dans l'Inde*, pp 152–72.
2. Ibid, f 65, *Mémoire du Roi*.
3. Pernoud, p 59, 29 September 1782.
4. Richmond, *Mariners' Mirror*, vol 13, 1927, pp 406–9.
5. Cunat, p 148.
6. Castex, p 316; Lacour-Gayet, p 518, Suffren to Souillac, 1 May 1782.
7. Roux, p 109; Cunat, p 147, Souillac to Castries, 18 June 1782.
8. *Journal de Bussy*, entries 10–28 March 1782, pp 15–23.
9. Richmond, *Navy in India*, p 305, Bickerton's instructions, 22 January 1782.

17: Keeping the Coast

1. PRO, Adm. 1/165, Bickerton's despatch, 29 April 1782.
2. Cunat, p 143, Roux, p 108, Suffren to Souillac, 24 April 1782.
3. Forrest, vol 3, p 865, Hughes to Macartney, 1 May 1782.
4. Ibid, 1 May 1782.
5. Cunat, p 157; Chevalier, p 413 (who mistakenly puts Forbin in command of the *Artésien*).
6. PCLM, p 196, Macartney to Sulivan, 26 April 1782.
7. Ibid, p 44, Macartney to Macpherson, 12 May 1782.
8. Wilks, vol 2, p 373.
9. Mautort, p 233.
10. Mautort, pp 233–5; BN, *Archives Nationales, Colonies*, C2, vol 155, ff 130–35, Piveron de Morlat to Souillac, 31 July 1782; Sheik Ali, p 280, Bancenel, p 630, and *Journal de Bussy*, pp 122–3: 'Mémoire de Canaple', 16 September 1782.
11. Forrest, vol 3, p 873, Coote to Select Committee, 11 June 1782.

12. *PCLM*, p 47, Macartney to Macpherson, 12 June 1782.
13. BN, *Archives Nationales, Colonies*, C2, vol 155, ff 137–8, Piveron to Souillac, 31 July 1782. *Journal de Bussy*, p 390, 21 June 1782.
14. Richmond, p 235, Hughes to Macartney, 25 June 1782.

18: Suffren's Shame

1. Hickey, vol 3, pp 59–61.
2. Lacour-Gayet, p 520, Suffren to Souillac, 2 July 1782.
3. Ibid, Suffren to Castries, 2 July 1782.
4. BL, Add. MSS. 22453, f 149, Macartney to Hughes, 15 October 1782, enclosing his draft cartel to du Chilleau.
5. Wilks, vol 2, p 402.
6. Dodwell, p 141, Hastings to Macpherson, ? July 1782.
7. *Journal de Bussy*, p 322, 12 March 1782; *Journal de Bord*, p 400, 30 June 1782.
8. Roux, p 118, Cunat, p 163, Suffren to Souillac, 2 July 1782.
9. Mahan, p 398.
10. Richmond, p 237. For this incident *Journal de Bord*, p 402.

19: The Battle of Negapatam, 6 July 1782

1. PRO, Adm. 1/164, Hughes's despatch of 15 July. For the battle: Richmond, pp 239–45; *Journal de Bord*, pp 404–5; Chevalier, pp 418–26; Mahan, pp 398–400; Cunat, pp 168–76; Lacour-Gayet, pp 521–3.
2. PRO, Adm. 1/164, Hughes's despatch of 8 July, annexure to Suffren, 7 July, and Suffren to Hughes, 8 July, constitute the claims and counter-claims to the *Sévère*. For what went on on board, *Journal de Bord* p 406; Cunat, pp 177–8 and Chevalier, p 422.

20: Suffren Meets Haidar Ali

1. Lacour-Gayet, p 524, Suffren to Castries, 22 July 1782.
2. Ibid, p 525.
3. Ibid, p 525.
4. Ibid, 524; Cunat, p 166.
5. PRO, Adm., 1/164, Hughes's despatch of 12 August 1782.
6. BL Add. MSS. 22453, ff 135–8, Hughes to Macartney, 15 July 1782.
7. *PCLM*, p 55, Macartney to Macpherson, 26 July 1782.
8. Cunat, p 152.
9. BN, *Archives Nationales, Colonies* C2, vol 155, ff 143, Piveron to Souillac, 31 July 1782.
10. Suffren's elevation to Bailli Grand Cross of the Order of St John of Jerusalem: AOM, *Liber Bullarum*, 1780, ff 405 a.t. – 406. (The year ran from 1 April 1780 to 31 March 1781.).

11. Mautort, pp 242–3.
12. Bancenel, p 632.
13. Cunat, p 191. Mautort, pp 242–3, for the meeting with Haidar; p 305, for the elephant going mad: Bertrand, pp 266–8.
14. BN, *Archives Nationales Colonies*, C2, vol 155, f 146, Piveron to Souillac, 31 July 1782.
15. Chevalier, 429.
16. *Journal de Bussy*, pp 100–2.
17. *PCLM*, p 56, Macartney to Macpherson, 26 July 1782.

21: Trincomali Taken

1. BL, Add. MSS., 22453 f 140 a.t., Hughes to select committee of Madras, 15 July 1782.
2. PRO, Adm. 164/1: Hughes's despatch, 20 October 1782 with annexures, was a defence of his actions before and after the loss of Trincomali.
3. Ibid, 20 October 1782.
4. Ibid, 20 October 1782, annexure 10: Hughes to select committee, 9 August 1782.
5. Ibid, annexure 11: Hughes to select committee, 10 August 1782.
6. Cunat, p 200.
7. Pernoud, p 61, 29 September 1782.
8. The capture of Trincomali: *Journal de Bord*, pp 421–4; Pernoud, p 61, 29 September 1782, Cunat, pp 208–11.
9. *Annual Register*, 1783, p 72.
10. Cunat, p 215.
11. Preliminaries to battle: Richmond, pp 271–4; Cunat, pp 213–16.

22: The Battle of Trincomali, 3 September 1782

1. PRO, Adm. 1/164, Hughes's despatch, 30 September 1782. For the battle also: Richmond, pp 274–81; Chevalier, pp 432–6; Lacour-Gayet, pp 521–3; Cunat, pp 216–26; Mahan, pp 404–8.
2. *Journal de Bord*, p 430, 3 September 1782.
3. Bancenel, p 635.
4. Ibid, p 636.
5. Cunat, p 223.
6. *Memoirs*, vol 3, p 109.
7. PRO, Adm. 1/164, 30 September 1782.
8. Pernoud, p 61, 29 September 1782.
9. Chevalier, p 440, Suffren to Castries, 29 September 1782.
10. *Annual Register*, 1783, p 75.
11. Castex, p 311, Suffren to Castries, 29 September 1782.
12. Lacour-Gayet, p 533.
13. Pernoud, p 61.
14. Chevalier, p 437.

15. Mahan, p 407.
16. Lacour-Gayet, p 531.
17. Bancenel, p 636. *Journal de Bussy*, pp 203–10: Tromelin to Souillac, 29 October, to Bussy, 3 November; Souillac to Tromelin, 29 October and Tromelin to Souillac, 30 October 1782. D'Unienville, p 125, disputes the words used by Suffren, who hearing what Tromelin had to say contented himself with the words: 'I know. None needs reproach himself if he has done all he can.'
18. *Journal de Bussy*, pp 214–15, 8–18 September 1782.
19. *Memoirs*, vol 3, pp 66–7.
20. Lacour-Gayet, p 533, Suffren to Castries, 29 September 1782.
21. Bancenel, p 636.

23: Waiting for Bussy

1. Pernoud, p 62, 29 September 1782.
2. Castex, p 210, Suffren to Souillac, 14 September 1782.
3. *Journal de Bussy*, p 143, Launay to Bussy, 2 August 1782.
4. Ibid, p 147.
5. Roux, p 290, Suffren to Bolle, the intendant of the squadron, 23 April 1783.
6. D'Unienville, p 104.
7. Bancenel, pp 633–5.
8. *Journal de Bussy*, pp 288–9.
9. Cunat, p 363, Piveron to Suffren, 3 October 1782. Piveron's correspondence with Suffren is in *Archives Nationales, Colonies*, C2, vol 155, ff 177–83.
10. Cunat, p 366, Suffren to Haidar, 6 October 1782.
11. Ibid, p 367, Suffren to Piveron, 6 October 1782.
12. Ibid, p 369, Piveron to Suffren, 12 October 1782.
13. Ibid, pp 374–5, Piveron to Suffren, 17 October 1782.

24: Winter, 1782–3

1. PRO, Adm. 1/164, Hughes's despatch of 20 October 1782, annexure 16: Hughes to select committee, 8 September 1782.
2. Ibid, Hughes's despatch of 20 October, 1782.
3. Ibid, Hughes's despatch, annexure 22: Hughes to Coote, 21 September 1782.
4. Ibid, Hughes's despatch, annexure 24: Hughes to Coote, 25 September 1782.
5. Ibid, Hughes's despatch, annexure 27: Hughes to select committee, 7 October 1782.
6. Ibid, Hughes to select committee, 7 October 1782.
7. Ibid, Hughes to select committee, 7 October 1782.
8. Ibid, Hughes's despatch of 20 October 1782, annexure 28: Hughes to select committee, 8 October 1782.

9. Ibid, Hughes's despatch of 20 October 1782.
10. Ibid, Hughes's despatch, annexure 41: Stuart to Hughes, 11 October 1782.
11. Dodwell, p 171.
12. Ibid, p 171.
13. *PCLM*, p 200, Macartney to Sulivan, 29 August 1782.
14. Ibid, p 98, Macpherson to Macartney, 3 October 1782.
15. Cunat, pp 248–50; *Journal de Bord*, pp 445–58.
16. Cunat, p 248.
17. Pernoud, pp 63–4, undated, probably 15 October 1782.
18. Roux, p 167, Suffren to Mme de Seillans, 30 November 1782.
19. Chevalier, p 450, Suffren to Bussy, 26 November 1782.

25: Bussy in India

1. BL, Add. MSS. 22453, ff 153–5, 166, Macartney to Hughes, 6 January 1783, and Hughes to Macartney, 12 January, enclosing Captain MacDowell's report from Trincomali.
2. PRO, Adm. 1/166, Hughes's despatches of 15 January and 8 February 1783, Annexure: 31 December 1782.
3. *Journal de Bord*, pp 470–71, 11 January 1783.
4. Cunat, p 261.
5. *Neshani Hyduri*, p 3. BN, *Archives Nationales, Colonies*, C2, vol 155, ff 206–12: Piveron's account of the precautions to ensure secrecy to Souillac of 16 February 1783.
6. Roux, pp 168–9, Piveron to Suffren, 9 February 1783.
7. *Journal de Bussy*, p 317, d'Hoffelize to Launay, 23 February 1783.
8. Cunat, pp. 375–6, Suffren to Piveron de Morlat, 6 February 1783.
9. Pernoud, p 66, 26 March 1783.
10. Hickey, vol 3, p 39.
11. Ibid, p 62, 21 January 1783.
12. Ibid, p 63.
13. Ibid, p 64.
14. Ibid, p 76.
15. Chevalier, p 480.

26: The Siege of Cuddalore

1. Hickey, *Memoirs*, vol 3, pp 87–8.
2. Forrest, vol 3, pp 899–90, Hastings to Macartney, 13 October 1782.
3. Ibid, p 903, Select Committee of Fort William to Coote, 18 November 1782.
4. Wylly, p 341, Hastings to Shelburne, 12 December 1782.
5. Lacour-Gayet, p 541, Suffren to Castries, 23 March 1783.
6. Roux, pp 180–81.
7. Cunat, pp 276–7.

8. Hickey, *Memoirs*, vol 3, p 101. See also BL, Add. MSS. 22453, f 160 a.t. Macartney to Hughes, 13 April 1783.
9. Forrest, vol 3, pp 944–5, select committee to Coote, 24 April 1783. See also Hickey, *Memoirs*, vol 3, pp 103–7; Wylly, pp 346–50.
10. *Journal de Bussy*, pp 323–4, entry for 12 March 1783.
11. Barras, *Mémoires*, vol 1, p 40. See also *Journal de Bord*, p 495; Sen, pp 333–42.
12. Cunat, p 412, Suffren to Castries, 26 April 1783.
13. Sen, p 361, Bussy to Suffren, 6 May 1783. See also Pernoud, pp 69–70, 4 or 5 June 1783.

27: The Fleet to the Rescue

1. *Annual Register*, 1783, pp 88–102; Wilks, vol 2, pp 460–2.
2. PRO, Adm. 1/166, Hughes's despatch of 25 July 1783.
3. Cunat, p 233, Suffren to Souillac, 28 May 1783.
4. La Varende, p 282.
5. BL, Add. MSS. 22453, f 174, select committee to Hughes, 21 May 1783.
6. *Journal de Bord*, p 512, 31 May 1783.
7. Pernoud, p 70, 4 or 5 June 1783.
8. BL, Add. MSS. 22453, f 180, Hughes to Macartney, 9 June 1783.
9. Ibid, f 183 a.t., Stuart to Hughes, 9 June 1783.
10. Ibid, f 184.
11. Pernoud, p 70, 4 or 5 June 1783.
12. Cunat, pp 295–6.
13. Lacour-Gayet, p 542, Suffren to Castries, 11 April 1783.
14. Cunat, p 296.
15. Bancenel, p 636.
16. Richmond, p 359.
17. Ibid, p 359.
18. Mautort, p 298.

28: The Battle of Cuddalore, 20 June 1783

1. Richmond, p 360, Hughes to Stuart, 15 June 1783.
2. PRO, Adm. 1/166, Hughes's despatch of 25 July 1783. For the preliminaries to the Battle of Cuddalore: Richmond, *Mariners' Mirror*, vol 13, pp 226–36; Richmond, *Navy in India*, pp 356–68; Cunat, pp 296–301; *Journal de Bord*, pp 517–27.
3. BL, Add. MSS. 22453, f 193 a.t., Hughes to Macartney, 23 June 1783.
4. Cunat, p 312.
5. Dixson Library, Sydney, Add. MSS. 387, Erasmus Gower to Philip Carteret, 18 or 25 January 1784.

29: The War Is Over

1. Pernoud, p 72, 23 July 1783.
2. Chevalier, p 480, Suffren to Castries, 23 July 1783.
3. Pernoud, p 74, undated, probably September 1783.
4. Glachant, p 299, Suffren to Vergennes, 15 October 1783.
5. Ibid, p 299.
6. Roux, p 178, Suffren to Mme de Seillans, 13 September 1783.
7. Cunat, p 557, Suffren to Mme de Seillans, 13 September 1783.
8. BL, Add. MSS. 22453, f 213 a.t., Cuthbert to Macartney, 15 January 1784.
9. Richmond, p 379.
10. Hickey, *Memoirs*, vol 3, p 56.
11. *PCLM*, p 224, Macartney to C. J. Fox, 13 October 1783.
12. Cunat, p 340.
13. Lacour-Gayet, p 555, Castries's memorial to Louis XVI, 2 April 1784.
14. Ibid, p 556.
15. Chevalier, p 505.

30: The Last of a Crusader

1. Roux, p 219, Suffren to Mme de Seillans, 7 October 1784.
2. Cavaliero, *The Last of the Crusaders*, pp 169–80.
3. Roux, p 220, Suffren to Mme de Seillans, 11 April 1786.
4. AOM, 1583, f 168, de Rohan to Suffren, 20 May 1784; Roux, p 215; R. Lacour-Gayet, *Calonne*, Paris, 1963, p 154n; Bertrand, pp 319–20.
5. Roux, p 224, Suffren to Mme de Seillans, ? July 1787.
6. Ibid, p 224, Suffren to Mme de Seillans, 17 July 1787.
7. Ibid, p 225, Suffren to Mme de Seillans, ? October 1787.
8. Ibid, p 225, Suffren to Mme de Seillans, ? October 1787.
9. Ibid, p 226, Suffren to Mme de Seillans, 27 June 1788.
10. Ibid, p 228, Suffren to Mme de Seillans, 8 August 1788.
11. Boutet de Monvel, p 230.
12. Roux, p 227, Suffren to Tipu Sultan, 27 September 1788. Five years earlier, Suffren had written to Hughes from Pondicherry, 'relative to those I confided to the charge of the Bahauder [sic], I have not waited for your demand to reclaim them. I have repeatedly done it and I hope he will pay attention to my request.' It had been an idle hope: Suffren to Hughes, 19 September 1783, enclosed in Hughes's despatch of 30 September: PRO, Adm. 1/166.
13. M.A. Jal, *Scènes de la Vie Maritime* (Paris, 1832), vol 3, p 161; Cunat, p 345; Roux, pp 293–4; La Varende, pp 316–20, Bertrand, pp. 323–7.

Epilogue

1. Parkinson, p 234.
2. Clerk, 2nd edition, p 274.
3. Ibid, p 275.
4. Ibid, p 287.
5. Mahan, p 415.
6. Ibid, p 416.
7. Bertrand, p 296.
8. Lacour-Gayet, p 571, La Pérouse to Suffren, 22 September 1787.
9. P. H. Masson, 'L'Affaire des Malouines' in *Dossier Suffren*, pp 13–9, *Revue historique des Armées*, 153, (Paris 4/1983).
10. *Mireio, pouemo provençau de Frederi Mistral*, Avignon, 1859, pp 17–28. Quotations from *Chant Premier*, stanzas i, vi, viii, xii and xiii, translated by the author.

Bibliography

Abbreviations:

Add. MSS.	Additional Manuscripts, British Library, London
Adm.	Admiralty Records, Public Records Office, London
AN	Archives Nationales, Paris
AOM	Archives of the Order of St John of Jerusalem, Valletta, Malta
NAF	Nouvelles Acquisitions Françaises
BN	Bibliothèque Nationale, Paris
PCLM	Private Correspondence of Lord Macartney (see Macartney in list of printed sources)

Manuscript Sources

Bibliothèque Nationale, Paris: Nouvelles Acquisitions Françaises

Dossier 9368	*Corréspondance de Piveron de Morlat avec M. de Suffren, 1782–3*
Dossier 9370	*Rélation de la Campagne Navale du Bailli de Suffren dans l'Inde, redigée par le chapelain du Vengeur, 1781–4*
Dossier 9371	Idem, *par de Froberville, Lieutenant d'une Compagnie embarqué sur l'Ajax*
Dossier 9372	*Corréspondance du Marquis de Bussy avec . . . Suffren . . . Castries . . . Falck . . . Macartney etc.*
Dossier 9401	*Campagne de Suffren avec l'Etenduère, 1747*
Dossier 9431	*Le Bailli de Suffren et la Marine de son temps: sa famille etc, jusqu'à 1780*
Dossier 9432	*La Campagne de Suffren dans l'Inde*
Dossier 9433	*Le Bailli de Suffren et le Marquis de Bussy, corréspondance etc.*

Bibliothèque de la Marine, Paris
Dossier 122   *La Campagne du Bailli de Suffrèn dans les Mers de l'Inde, 1780–4: Rélation des faits mémorables de M le Bailli de Suffren*

Archives Nationales, Paris
Colonies C.2.
Dossier 155   *Corréspondance de Piveron de Morlat avec le Vicomte de Souillac*

Royal Malta Library, Valletta

AOM 155   Liber Conciliorum, 1764–6
AOM 156   Liber Conciliorum, 1767–9
AOM 158   Liber Conciliorum, 1773–5
AOM 159   Liber Conciliorum, 1776–7
AOM 271   Liber Conciliorum Status, 1755–63
AOM 272   Liber Conciliorum Status, 1764–72
AOM 273   Liber Conciliorum Status, 1773–83
AOM 541   Liber Bullarum, 1737
AOM 1242   Lettres réçues par Grand-Maître de Rohan, 1779
AOM 1584   Régistre des Lettres de SAE le GM de Rohan, 1784
AOM 3545   Processi delle Prove dei Cavalieri Francesi: Louis Victoire de Suffren
AOM 3629   Idem, Pierre-André et Paul-Julien de Suffren

British Museum, London
Add. MSS. 22453   *Official copies of the Public Correspondence of Lord Macartney, vol. XV, with Sir Edward Hughes, 27 June 1781 to 30 November 1784*

Public Records Office, London
Admiralty Series
Adm. 1/310   Admiral Barrington and Commodore Hotham, 1776–81
Adm. 1/488   Admiral Howe, 1777–9
Adm. 1/164   Admiral Hughes, 1771–82
Adm. 1/165   Commodore Bickerton, 1782–5
Adm. 1/166   Admiral Hughes, 1782–5
Adm. 7/737   Admiral Hughes: Journal, 1778–80

Adm. 7/748	Idem. 1780–3
Adm. 7/739	Idem. 1783–5
Adm. 7/741	Log of HMS *Superb*, 1780–2
Adm. 7/742	Idem. Feb.-Nov. 1783
Adm. 7/747	Admiral Hughes: General Correspondence, 1778–80
Adm. 7/748	Idem. 1780–3
Adm. 7/749	Idem.: Correspondence with Secretary of State, 1779–82
Adm. 7/750	Idem. 1782–4
Adm. 7/751	Idem.: Correspondence with Admiralty, 1779–82
Adm. 7/752	Idem. 1782–85
Adm. 7/755	Idem.: Correspondence with Select Committee at Madras, 1781–2
Adm. 7/756	Idem. 1782–3
Adm. 51/947	Log of HMS *Superb*, 1770–82
Adm. 51/4360	Idem. 1780–2
Adm. 51/610	Log of HMS *Monmouth*, 1781–4
Adm. 51/4262	Log of HMS *Monarca*, 1780–4
Adm. 51/868	Log of HMS *Sceptre*, 1781–4
Adm. 51/945	Log of HMS *Sultan*, 1778–85
Adm. 51/453	Log of HMS *Hero*, 1764–84
Adm. 51/484	Log of HMS *Isis*, 1780–3
Adm. 51/315	Log of HMS *Exeter*, 1780–4
Adm. 51/395	Log of HMS *Gibraltar*, 1780–4

Printed Sources

Acerra, Martine,	'La mission des Arsenaux de Marine au Temps de Suffren', in *Dossier Suffren; Revue Historique des Armées*, 153 (Vincennes, 4/1993)
Annual Register,	vols 1779–83
Bancenel, F. X. de,	'Avec M de Suffren' in *La Revue de Paris*, Sept–Oct 1911
Barras, Paul de,	*Memoirs*, vol 1, trans. C.E. Roche (London, 1895)
Barrington Papers,	vol 2, ed. Bonner Smith in *Navy Records Society* (London, 1941)
Barrow, Sir John,	*Some Account of the Public Life of Lord Macartney* (London, 1807)

Beatson, Lt-Col. A., *A View of the Origin and Conduct of the War with Tippoo Sultan* (London, 1800)

Beatson, R., *Naval & Military Memoirs of Great Britain from the Year 1727 to 1783*, vol. v (London, 1804)

Bengal Past & Present, vol 43, pt 2, 'A note on Henri de Lallée'

——— vol 47 pt 1, 'A Brave but Unfortunate Officer: Lt-Col William Baillie' by A. Cassells

——— vol 49, pt 1, 'The Diary of Samuel Hickson, 1775–85,' ed. J.G. Brooker

Bertrand, Michel, *Suffren de Saint-Tropez aux Indes* (Paris, 1991)

Blake *Remarks on Commodore Johnstone's Account of His Engagement with a French Squadron* (London, 1782)

Boudriot, Jean, 'Les Navires de Combat de la Guerre de l'Indépendance Américaine', in *Dossier Suffren; Revue Historique des Armées*, 153 (Vincennes, 4/1983)

Boutet de Monvel, R., *La vie Martiale du Bailli de Suffren* (Paris, 1929)

Bowring, L. B., *Haidar Ali and Tipu Sultan and the Struggle with the Musalman Powers of the South* (Oxford, 1893)

Boyd, Hugh, *Miscellaneous Works . . . including his Journal of an Embassy to the King of Kandy* (London, 1800)

Busson, J. P., 'Suffren et Ses Amis', in *Dossier Suffren; Revue Historique des Armées*, 153 (Vincennes 4/1983)

Calendar of Persian Correspondence, vol v, 1776–80; vol vi, 1781–5, ed. A.F.M. Abdul Ali (Delhi)

Calmon Maison, J. J. R., *L'Amiral d'Estaing* (Paris, 1910)

Campbell, John, *Naval History of Great Britain, including the History and Lives of the British Admirals*, vol. 1 (London, 1818)

Carré, A., 'Aspects Médicaux de la Campagne de l'Inde', in *Dossier Suffren; Revue Historique des Armées*, 153 (Vincennes, 4/1983)

Castex, Raoul, *Les Idées Militaires de la Marine au 18ème siècle* (Paris, 1911)

——— *La Manoeuvre de la Praya* (Paris, 1912)

Cavaliero, Roderick, *The Last of the Crusaders* (London, 1960)
'Admiral Suffren in the Indies', *History Today*, (London, July 1970)

——— 'The Bailiff de Suffren', *Annales de l'Ordre Souverain Militaire de Malte* (Rome, XXème année, 1962), nos 3 and 4

——— See *Mariners' Mirror*

Charnock, John, *Biographia Navalis* vol vi (London, 1797)

Chevalier, E., *Histoire de la Marine Française pendant la Guerre de l'Indépendance Américaine* (Paris, 1877)

Clerk of Eldin, J., *An Essay on Naval Tactics, Systematic & Historical* 2nd edn (Edinburgh, 1804)

Clowes, W. L., *The Royal Navy; A History from the earliest Times to the Present*, vol iii (London, 1898)

Creswell, J., *British Admirals of the 18th Century: Tactics in Battle* (London, 1972)

Cunat, Le Chevalier, *Histoire du Bailli de Suffren* (Rennes, 1852)

Davin, E., *Suffren* (Aix en Provence, 1947)

Deherain, H., 'Une Escale du Bailli de Suffren dans les Dardanelles, 16–19 janvier, 1773', in *Bulletin de la Section de Géographie* (Paris, 1925)

Dodwell, H. H., *Warren Hastings's Letters to Sir John Macpherson* (London, 1927)

Dull, J. R., *The French Navy and American Independence* (Princeton, 1975)

Feiling, Keith, *Warren Hastings* (London, 1955)

Figarella, Jean, *Suffren ou les Caprices de la Gloire* (Aubanel, 1984)

Forrest, G. W., *Selections from the State Papers of the Governors-General of India: Warren Hastings*, 2 vols (Oxford, 1910)

—————   *Selections from the Letters, Despatches and Other State Papers preserved in the Foreign Department of the Government of India, 1782–5*, 3 vols (Calcutta, 1890)

Fortescue, J. W.,   *The History of the British Army*, vol 3 (London, 1902)

Fort-William – India House Correspondence, 1782–5, ed. B. A. Saletore (Delhi, 1959)

Glachant, R.,   *Histoire de l'Inde des Français* (Paris, 1965)

—————   *Suffren et le Temps de Vergennes* (Paris, 1976)

Gleig, G. R.,   *Memoirs of the Life of the Rt. Hon. Warren Hastings*, 3 vols (London, 1841)

Guérin, Léon,   *Histoire Maritime de France* (Paris, 1863)

Hasan Khan, M.,   *The History of Tipu Sultan* (Calcutta, 1951)

Hennequin, J. F. G.,   *Essai Historique sur la Vie et les Campagnes du Bailli de Suffren* (Paris, 1824)

Hickey, William,   *Memoirs*, ed. A. Spencer, vols ii–iii (London, 1923)

Hussain Ali Khan Firmani,   *The Neshani Hyduri, The History of Tipu Sultan*, trans. Colonel W. Miles, 1864 (Calcutta, 1958)

James, Sir W.,   *The British Navy in Adversity* (London, 1781)

Johnstone, George,   *Letters . . . between Commodore Johnstone & Captain Sutton* (London, 1781)

—————   *Considerations on the Question now in Litigation between Commodore Johnstone and Captain Sutton* (London, 1787)

Labat, G.,   *Le Bailli de Suffren. Documents inédits sur la Campagne de l'Inde, 1781–4* (Bordeaux, 1901)

Lacour-Gayet, G.,   *La Marine Militaire de la France sous le Règne de Louis XV* (Paris, 1902)

     La Marine Militaire de la France sous le Règne de Louis XVI (Paris, 1905)

Las Cases, E.,   *La Vie Privée et Les Conversations de Napoléon à St Hélène*, vol 4 (London, 1823)

Laughton, G. K.,   *Studies in Naval History* (London, 1887)

Lawrence, A. W.,   *Captives of Tipu* (London, 1929)

Lewis, C. L.,   *Admiral de Grasse and American Independence* (Annapolis, 1945)

Love, H. D.,   *Vestiges of Old Madras, 1640–1800*, vol ii (London, 1913)

Macartney, George,   *The Private Correspondence of Lord Macartney*, ed. C. C. Davies (London, 1950)

Mackey, R. F.,   *Edward Hawke* (London, 1965)

Mackesy, P.,   *The War for America* (London, 1964)

Mahan, A. T.,   *The Influence of Sea Power upon History, 1660–1783* (New York, 1957)

Malleson, G. B.,   *Final French Struggles in India on the Indian Seas* (London, 1878)

———   *History of the French in India from the Founding of Pondicherry in 1674 to the Capture of the Place in 1761* (London, 1893)

Marcus, G.,   *A Naval History of England*, vol 1 (London, 1961)

Mariners' Mirror   vol 13, 1927; Admiral G. A. Ballard, 'The First and Second Anglo-French Conflicts in the Indian Ocean'; 'The Last Battlefleet Struggle in the Bay of Bengal'; 'Hughes & Suffren'; Admiral Sir H. W. Richmond, 'The Hughes–Suffren Campaign'

———   vol 28, 1942: G. Rutherford, 'Sidelights on Commodore Johnstone's Expedition to the Cape'

———   vol 43, 1957: Roderick Cavaliero, 'John Dodsworth: A Consul in Malta'

Martineau, A., ed.,   *Journal de Bussy* (Pondicherry, 1932)
                        Bussy et l'Inde Française (Paris, 1935)

Mautort, Tillette de,   *Mémoires* (Paris, 1895)

Meyer, Jean,   'Operations, Géo-Stratégiques: La Campagne de Suffren', in *Dossier Suffren, Revue Historique des Armées*, 153, 6–10 (Vincennes 4/1983)

Moris, H., ed.,   'Journal de Bord du Bailli de Suffren dans son Expédition des Indes', reproduced in *Société des Lettres, Sciences et Arts des Alpes Maritimes; Annales etc.*, vol xi, 260–609 (Nice, 1887)

Munro, Innes, — *Narrative of the Military Operations on the Coromandel Coast, 1780–4* (London, 1789)

Ortolan, T., — *Lettres Inédites du Bailli de Suffren* (Paris, 1859)

Parkinson, C. N., — *War in the Eastern Seas, 1793–1815* (London, 1954)

Pasley, R. M. S. ed., — *Private Sea Journals, 1778–82*, kept by Sir Thomas Pasley (London, 1931)

Patterson, A. T., — *The Other Armada* (Manchester, 1960)

Pernoud, Régine, — *La Campagne des Indes: Lettres Inédites du Bailli de Suffren* (Nantes, 1941)

Pérusse, J.-F. de, — *Mémoires du Duc des Cars*, vol i (Paris, 1890)

Pritchard, J., — *Louis XV's Navy, 1748–1762: a Study of Organisation and Administration* (Kingston, Ontario, 1987)

Ralfe, J., — *Naval Biography in Great Britain*, vol. i (London, 1828)

Richmond, H. W., — *The Navy in India, 1773–83* (London, 1931)

Roncière, Bourel de la, — *Histoire de la Marine Française* (Paris, 1934)

Roux, J. S., — *La Bailli de Suffren dans l'Inde* (Marseilles, 1862)

Rutherford, G., — *see Mariners' Mirror*

Sandwich Papers, — *The Private Papers of John Montagu, Earl of Sandwich*, ed. Barnes & Owen, vols ii-iii (London, 1934–6)

Sen, S. P., — *The French in India* (Calcutta, 1958)

Sheik Ali, B., — *British Relations with Haidar Ali* (Mysore, 1963)

Shepherd, E. W., — *Coote Bahadur* (London, 1956)

Sinha, S. K., — *Haidar Ali* (Calcutta, 1949)

Taillemite, E., — 'La Marine et ses Chefs pendant la Guerre de l'Indépendance Américaine' in *Dossier Suffren; Revue Historique des Armées*, 153 (Vincennes, 4/1983)

Tantet, M. V., — *L'Ambassade de Tippou Sahib à Paris en 1778* (Paris, 1899)

Tessier, O., — *Lettres Inédites du Bailli de Suffren* (Paris, 1893)

Troude, O.,   *Batailles Navales de la France*, vol. ii (Paris, 1867)

Trublet de Villejégu,   *Histoire de la Campagne de l'Inde sous les Ordres de M le Bailli de Suffren* (Paris, 1802)

Tunstall, Brian,   *Naval Warfare in the Age of Sail: the Evolution of Fighting Tactics, 1650–1815* ed. Nicholas Tracy (London, 1990)

Uhlendorff, B. A. ed., *The Siege of Charleston* (Ann Arbor, 1938)

Unienville, R. d',   *Hier Suffren* (Mauritius, 1972)

Varende, J. B. M. M. de la,   *Suffren et ses Ennemis* (Paris, 1948)

Vergé-Franceschi, M.,   *Guerre et Commerce en Mediterranée, IXe-XXe siècles* (Veurier, 1991)

Villiers, P.,   *La Marine de Louis XVI*, vol 1: 'de Choiseul à Sartine' (Grenoble, 1985)

Ward, C.,   *The War of the Revolution*, vol ii (New York, 1952)

Wilks, Col. M.,   *Historical Sketches of South India in an Attempt to trace the History of Mysore*, vol ii (London, 1810–17)

Wylly, Colonel H. C.,   *The Life of Lt.-Gen. Sir Eyre Coote, KB* (Oxford, 1922)

Index

Ghats (or Ghauts), 55, 144
Ghulam Ali Khan, 166
Gibraltar, 7, 15, 30, 31, 46, 60, 137
Gingee (Carnatic), 143
Glorious First of June (1794), battle of, 256–7
Goa, 204, 227
Gorée, 46, 62–3
Gower, Captain Erasmus, 227, 238–9
Grand Corps de la Marine see Marine, Grand Corps de la; Navy, French
Grand Cul de Sac, Le (St Lucia), 35–6, 43, 65, 68, 104
Grand Master of the Knights of Malta see Malta; Despuig; Pinto; Rohan
Grand Mughal see Mughal
Grasse, François-Joseph-Paul, Comte de, xiii, 13, 23, 38, 47, 49, 61–3, 128, 151, 202, 208, 226, 240, 261
Graves, Captain Samuel, 165, 215; Admiral Thomas, xiv
Grenada, 39–41, 43, 60–1, 88, 96–7, 123, 148
Grenier, Comte de, 86
Grieux, Chevalier des, 24
Gros Ilot Bay (St Lucia), 36, 38
Grotius, Hugues van Groot, 74
Guadaloupe, 36, 41, 62
Guichen, Admiral Luc-Urban de, 135, 151, 159, 261

Hague, The, 247
Haidar Ali, xvi, 84–6, 198, 201, 205, 221, 243, 260; origins and career, 54; invades Carnatic, 55–9; campaign in Carnatic, 82, 86, 93–4; expects French expeditionary force, 88, 98–9, 101; rejects English overtures for peace, 97, 132; and the French expedition, 104, 113–8, 141–5; and Bussy, 130, 189–90, 192–6, 203; and Suffren, 134, 147–50, 165–70, and Coote, 188; death, 206–8; see also Mysore; Tipu Sultan
Haidarnagar, 208
Halifax, 33
Hastings, Warren, 53, 56, 58–9, 104, 113–4, 149, 199–200, 214, 243
Hauteville, Bailli d', 253
Havana, 25
Havrincourt, Bailli d', 253
Hawke, Captain Edward, xiii, 8–10, 14, 16, 18, 107, 260

Hawker, Captain, 68, 154
Hennequin, JFG, 256
Henry of Navarre, xviii
Hervey, Captain Augustus, 74
Hickey, William, 201; on Suffren's appearance, xvi–xvii; 6, 24–5; account of Porto Praya, 75; on Charlotte Dee, 79; on Hughes's appetite, 95; on Suffren's proposed exchange of prisoners, 147–8, 150; with Suffren at Trincomali, 6, 161, 209–14; Hughes's account of Suffren's gallantry, 182; Saint-Félix's interview with Suffren, 186–6
Hicky, William, 94
Hierro, island of (Canaries), 63
Hindustan, 58
Hinrichs, Captain, 42
Hoffelize, Colonel d', 144–5, 192, 194, 207, 218
Holland see United Provinces; Dutch
Holland House, 97
Hooghly, river, 198, 205
Hornby, Governor William, 172, 205
Hotham, Commodore, 34
Houdon, Jean-Antoine, 247
Hout Bay (Cape of Good Hope), 78–9
Hogue, La (English Channel), 245
Howe, Vice-Admiral Richard, Viscount, xiv, 31–4, 44, 256–7
Hughes, Vice-Admiral Sir Edward, appearance and nicknames, 94–5; career before 1782, 93, 95–6; and Eyre Coote, 96–7; takes Negapatam, 98; and Trincomali, 99–100; prelude to battle of Sadras, 101–8; battle of Sadras, 109–113, 115; and Macartney, 114; refits after battle, 114; feels lack of frigates, 118–9; frets about Trincomali, 119–20; battle of Provedien, 121–8; returns to Madras, 129, 132–6; back in Trincomali, 139–40; surprises Suffren off Cuddalore, 145; proposes exchange of prisoners, 147–50; sights Suffren's squadron, 151; prepares for combat, 152–3; battle of Negapatam, 154–60; claims Sévère, 160–1; welcomes first of Bickerton's squadron, 165–6; worries again about Trincomali, 170–1, 174–5; prelude to battle, 176–8; battle of Trincomali, 179–82; his squadron's wounds,